# Two Journeys: Undiminished and Unforgotten

LAURENCE SMITH

Copyright © 2024 Laurence Smith

All rights reserved.

ISBN: 979-887-640-0208

# DEDICATION

To my son Jeremy, his carers at Woodcock Dell and the Norwood family.

To my wife and family for their patience with me!

All royalties from the sale of this book will be donated to Norwood.

*"O the mind, mind has mountains, cliffs of fall frightful, sheer, no-man-fathomed. Hold them cheap may who ne'er hung there. Nor does long our small durance deal with that steep or deep. Here! Creep, wretch, under a comfort serves in a whirlwind: all life death does end and each day dies with sleep."*

"Mountains of the Mind," by Gerard Manley Hopkins (1844-89)

# CONTENTS

| | |
|---|---|
| Acknowledgments | i |
| Preface | 1 |
| Underweight and outnumbered | 3 |
| His head's too small | 5 |
| Under the toy gantry | 6 |
| The microcephaly club | 8 |
| Severe developmental problems | 10 |
| Rise of the anger-monster | 14 |
| Gone camping | 16 |
| The dustbin gang | 18 |
| No walking or talking | 20 |
| What's he staring at? | 24 |
| Fits and starts | 28 |
| Job | 33 |
| First birthday | 35 |
| Small signs | 37 |
| Bureaucracy | 39 |
| Norwood and the village people | 41 |
| Tough love | 43 |
| Positives and negatives | 45 |
| Another leap | 48 |
| JD | 49 |
| Puma Forest | 50 |
| Extension | 52 |
| Escape to France | 53 |
| (Star) trek to the museum | 55 |
| Lost at sea | 57 |
| All fine and beautiful | 61 |
| Feeding the carpet | 62 |
| Little sister | 65 |
| A ride in an ambulance | 67 |
| The paediatrician calls | 69 |
| The case of the missing wardrobe | 71 |
| Doubling up | 73 |

| | |
|---|---|
| New medicine | 75 |
| Who are you? | 77 |
| Is this yours? | 79 |
| Breaking down walls | 82 |
| A ride in the forest | 85 |
| Eating out | 88 |
| The quiet community | 90 |
| Sun, sea and kindness | 93 |
| Grandparents | 95 |
| Re-booting the gawpers | 98 |
| Therapy with horses | 100 |
| Bloody stairgate! | 102 |
| Crawling | 106 |
| The beautiful game | 107 |
| Back pain | 110 |
| Big blue ball | 113 |
| The lady in dark glasses | 115 |
| Vigil | 117 |
| Bike | 120 |
| Do the car wash | 122 |
| He communes with God | 124 |
| Las Ramblas | 126 |
| Incident at Waitrose | 130 |
| Bar Mitzvah | 133 |
| New bedroom | 136 |
| Can we pray for him? | 138 |
| Where's big sis? | 141 |
| Font Romeu | 143 |
| Wrestling with tents | 146 |
| A promise | 149 |
| The white nuns and the sacred mountain | 153 |
| The cackling lady | 156 |
| Walking to walk | 159 |
| Hailstorm at Fort Lagarde | 163 |
| Arrested by the Army | 165 |

| | |
|---|---|
| The Western Wall | 168 |
| The Dead Sea | 171 |
| Respite | 173 |
| Empire state of mind | 175 |
| Charlie the mutt | 186 |
| Buckets 'n' spades | 190 |
| A night out with the boys | 192 |
| Parents get lost | 193 |
| Changes | 195 |
| Woodcock Dell | 197 |
| Letting go | 199 |
| New home, new family | 202 |
| Last day in school | 203 |
| Leaving | 204 |
| They want to operate on him! | 207 |
| Sir Andrew will see the young man now | 211 |
| The promise | 215 |
| The big wheel of terror | 221 |
| Pants all the way down | 223 |
| A step nearer | 229 |
| Talking and doing | 231 |
| Birthright | 235 |
| Some manly shopping | 240 |
| Our friends in the foothills | 243 |
| Some vigorous exercies | 245 |
| Expedition to the Pyrenees | 247 |
| The mad dog of Bouriege | 250 |
| A full-on day | 252 |
| Food | 257 |
| More questions than answers | 260 |
| Closing window | 262 |
| When dad jokes go wrong | 263 |
| Nocturnal activities | 265 |
| Return to Norwood | 268 |
| The land down under | 270 |
| Bloody man! | 275 |

| | |
|---|---|
| Heat | 279 |
| Old bull ant | 283 |
| Bad manors | 285 |
| Long journeys | 291 |
| The best laid plans | 293 |
| Point of no return | 298 |
| Addicted | 301 |
| A card for Mister Wilson | 303 |
| International rescue | 305 |
| Tough training | 307 |
| Let's parlez | 308 |
| Don't forget the kibble! | 311 |
| A reminder | 314 |
| Grandparents and uncle | 316 |
| A watery trudge | 317 |
| The blue dot and the green line | 319 |
| The anomaly | 321 |
| Musings of a long-distance rambler | 323 |
| Human tortoise | 325 |
| Same but different | 327 |
| Le patou | 330 |
| What can possibly go right? | 332 |
| Lost in Surrey | 334 |
| If I were famous | 337 |
| Eight sisters | 339 |
| Training with the Army | 343 |
| A skirmish | 345 |
| Obsession | 347 |
| Driving around the bend | 349 |
| Poor me | 350 |
| Words from the heart | 354 |
| Pain in the neck | 358 |
| A tear-down | 359 |
| Man-flu | 364 |
| Pages | 366 |
| Last visit | 368 |

| | |
|---|---|
| Time dilation | 371 |
| Pre-flight checks | 373 |
| The first step is the hardest | 375 |
| EPILOGUE | 381 |

# ACKNOWLEDGMENTS

To Kevin James Hall for his immense patience and dedication to licking this book into shape - and how it was needed!

To my wife, Liz, for listening to readings of this book whilst grappling with the M25 traffic, on our way to visit Jeremy.

To all the people we met on Jeremy's journey, especially the wonderful warm NWSS community, the dedicated carers at Woodcock Dell and in other Norwood homes. You carried us.

To Ben Fletcher, for his outstanding artwork!

# PREFACE

I stood on a ledge, inches from a three-hundred-foot chasm, torn between two choices. Should I grab the cable hanging down the rock face, or turn around and flee? Was I strong enough to haul myself and fifty-pounds extra weight up a sheer cliff? One slip would mean certain death, and no one would know where I fell. My fear of heights kicked into gear - run! But fleeing would be tricky, with so little space on the narrow shelf to turn a bulky rucksack through a hundred-and-eighty degrees. And if I took the easier choice, the journey would be over, and I would forever regret abandoning my cause.

At every moment we make choices, most of which are so trivial that we forget them instantly. Butter or margarine? Blue or grey socks? But some are so monumental, life-changing and influence more than just ourselves, that they last in our memories forever, like the choice I had to make before that huge sun-bleached limestone crag.

Twenty-four years earlier, my baby son Jeremy was diagnosed with profound learning and physical disabilities.

My wife and I were told he would need one-to-one care all his life. He would never walk or talk, go to school, have a job, be independent, marry or have children. We had to make the same choice as I had on that narrow ledge. Either we take on a mountain and lift him over the obstacles he would face, or we could give in without a fight. Were we strong enough? What future would we, Jeremy, and his siblings have? If we let someone else take on the responsibility of caring for him, then we would fail as parents and live in regret.

This book is a tale of two journeys that seem unrelated – Jeremy's and mine. Yet the second, a five-hundred-and-forty-mile trek along the Pyrenees for my son's care home, exposed the first to a different light. Both had ups and downs. Darkness, fear and depression became light and joy in seconds. I want this story to offer hope to carers of loved ones who cannot survive on their own.

Nothing could prepare me for the physical and psychological challenge of that second journey. I was a sixty-one-year-old retired IT consultant who had never walked more than ten miles in a day and never attempted any long-distance trek before. I had a terrible fear of heights, a poor sense of direction and obsessed about the things that could go wrong. I hope that this book will inspire anyone wanting to take on a similar venture.

# UNDERWEIGHT AND OUTNUMBERED

March 30th 1992. As traffic queued, stations filled, and children set off for school, Jeremy David Terence slipped into a waking world fast asleep. A midwife cut the cord and deposited him on some weighing scales. He remained silent.

Through a blue mask, she announced, "his weight's low – just on five pounds."

"A few ounces lighter," she added, "he would've needed incubating."

She glanced across the delivery ward at a device resembling a fish tank.

Unlike his two sisters who took their time, Jeremy arrived quickly, in a hurry to start life. On the drive to the hospital, Liz cried, "it's happening!"

"Shall I pull into the school and find help?"

"No! Keep going! The baby will be out by the time you've found someone."

Probably a good decision. Kids peering through classroom windows while I wrestled with an umbilical cord in the back seat of the car. Unnecessarily dramatic. Apart from that, I am like most fathers – utterly helpless in the art of delivering babies.

We screeched into a parking spot outside the emergency entrance and a porter wheeled her to the Maternity Ward. Moments later, Jeremy popped on to the delivery bed. No anaesthetic, needles, cups of tea or tasty biscuits. His was the quietest arrival of our three children.

Jeremy and I belong to a predominantly female tribe.

My oldest sister has two daughters and a son, my second sister has three daughters, my younger brother has a son and a daughter, Liz's brother has three daughters, and we have two daughters aged five and three, and now, a son. He will be one of only two boys among nine girl cousins and two sisters. He is outnumbered.

Where will his journey in life take him? Will he be musical? Will we play football in the park together? Will we go out for a beer and curry? Will he sing in my choir? Who will he marry and what will his children be like? There are so many things to look forward to and wrong turns to avoid.

His sisters, Roxanne and Victoria, have a little brother to play with, to dress up and practice their make-up skills on. Little Jeremy does not appreciate the joys of life that lie ahead.

Victoria (aged three) and Roxanne (aged five) holding Jeremy in 1992

# HIS HEAD'S TOO SMALL

We were picnicking with friends, when Liz pointed out the difference in head size between their four-month-old Dom, and Jeremy.

"Yes, but Dom's a month older," I protested, "his head would be larger – there's plenty of time for Jeremy to catch up."

She fidgeted while her eyes flicked between Dom, playing with his feet and cooing a few yards away, and Jeremy, lying still and silent on the rug beside us.

"Well, I'm going to take him to the doctor for a check-up," she whispered, so as not to broadcast her concern beyond our little bubble of worry.

I tried to lighten her dark thoughts, "he's fine - you've seen how he responds to music – he will be a musician I reckon."

She looked down at Jeremy, then glanced at Dom again.

"There's something wrong, I feel it."

"Would you like me to see the doctor with you?"

She hesitated and looked down, "no, I suppose not."

Married for eight years, I knew her well enough to read her real answer – *yes, I would*. I *could* go to the doctors with her, but it would mean cancelling client meetings and killing off a chance to prove to my employer that my specialism in Artificial Intelligence (AI) is still in demand. Then there would be nothing on the horizon. My job would be on the line and that would be no good for anyone, no matter how small – or big – Jeremy's head is. If only AI could help me choose.

# UNDER THE TOY GANTRY

Never dismiss a mother's instincts. The doctor confirmed Liz's suspicions – Jeremy's head *is* too small, and he is not doing the things that a baby of his age should be. There could be a connection, surmised the doctor, which needs to be investigated urgently. Liz left the surgery in a worse state than before. I should have gone with her.

Despite the news, we remain at opposite ends of a spectrum of optimism. Liz thinks the worst while I stubbornly refuse to accept anything negative about my baby son. I lie beside him under his toy gantry and tickle his toes. Nothing. Clap my hands and he stares at the ceiling. Tinkle a bell suspended a few inches over his head. Silence. Deep down I fear for him, but I must not let Liz know. Instead, a light of hope flares and illuminates every tiny movement, eye flicker, head turn and finger twitch.

"There! Did you see that?"
"What?"
"He blinked, definitely, *and* he moved his head!"
"Did he? Well, maybe …"

For the first time in weeks, Liz smiled faintly. Every small positive warms the soul and strengthens my belief in him, that he is OK. The chance of him not being normal are remote.

The doctor thinks he could be partly deaf, which would certainly inhibit stimulation. But why does he respond to music? 'Una furtiva lagrima,' begins the aria from Donizetti's opera 'L'elisir d'amore', and his eyes dance.

Not looking at anything in particular, but they are wide open, and he is *thinking*.

But when there is no music, he stares into space, and looks through me. Come to think of it, I cannot recall if he has *ever* really looked at me or anything I have rattled or waved. He is so absent. He lives in his own world, and we are not there with him. Liz has given up breast-feeding because she does not how much milk he has taken. With no sleep pattern, he will cry for hours, doze, wake and cry again. We are *so* tired. The sleep deprivation makes us irritable and anxious. But we dare not show any outward sign, because Roxanne, Victoria and Jeremy will suffer, making us more anxious – like a spinning wheel that cannot be stopped.

Liz is taking him to the children's hospital for an X-ray and blood test next week. The X-ray will tell us if his skull plates have fused too early, which would explain his small head size. We can only hope that there is a healthy brain inside trying to grow. The blood test will see if he has an infection that is making him lethargic. A virus *must* be delaying his development. When they identify it, they will treat it, and Jeremy's and our lives will return to normal.

Wrestling with uncertainty and confusion, I try to be positive and think of our annual summer holiday in two weeks' time. Eighteen days of camping in Vannes in France, after a four-hundred-mile drive along the north coast with a car full of small people, luggage, toys and used nappies. The break will be an escape from all that has happened and, maybe, about to happen after Jeremy's next test.

# THE MICROCEPHALY CLUB

Another busy work week and even busier home week race past the chequered flag. Jeremy had an X-ray and blood test at the children's hospital. The nurse phoned afterwards to tell us that Liz and I *must* see the paediatrician on Wednesday for a preliminary prognosis. Her stress on "must" means the appointment is too important to miss. A shadow has been cast over our holiday, starting two days later. Grim news must be delivered in person. I did not give Liz's motherly instinct enough credence because I did not want to accept that there is anything wrong with my son. I did not go with her to his X-ray or blood test because I thought they would find a virus, and he would be cured. If they found anything treatable, then they would have told us at the time, or when the nurse called, rather than delay for a week. So, there is no choice, I *must* go. Family comes first, and work must wait.

My vocabulary has expanded by one word, 'microcephalic'. Jeremy is officially that, according to the nurse. It means 'has a small head', which is week-old news to us. He has been given a label that would not have been my first choice. I would have preferred 'genius' or 'gifted'. But maybe we should turn his label into a positive and crush those parents who fast-track their offspring into MENSA and like to brag about their precious little prodigies.

"MENSA? Is that all? Our Jeremy is in the Microcephaly Club," we would boast with false pride. Although the irony would probably not be lost on them.

Even though Jeremy belongs to an exclusive club, it may not be that serious. Having a small head might be just a physical thing that has no bearing on his mental capacity. We will see where the road to the children's hospital takes him. They might say, "well, Jeremy has a small head *and* he has a bug that's making him lethargic. He will be OK in a few months' time." I remain optimistic until next Wednesday when the truth will be revealed.

# SEVERE DEVELOPMENTAL PROBLEMS

Late July 1992.

Liz, Jeremy and I saw the paediatrician at the children's hospital today. I do not know how to break the news to my mum and dad. Liz does not know how to tell her parents either. There are so many people we must tell. We cannot even speak to each other because it hurts so much. Repetition is admitting the truth, and I am not ready for that. My son has been replaced by a rag doll. He is not the same beautiful baby boy who arrived in this world so full of promise only four months ago. I want to scream in pain, but that would frighten Roxanne and Victoria. We must maintain some semblance of normality for their sakes.

"Jeremy is microcephalic because he has a small brain," announced the paediatrician with brutal directness, "the X-ray confirms that his skull plates haven't fused."

Numbed by the news, she continued, "his blood test results confirm the presence of Cyto-Megalovirus, CMV, that may explain the reason."

"I must tell you that his limited brain capacity means that there will be severe developmental problems."

Severe developmental problems. Our hopes for Jeremy's bright future were extinguished by three words. I imagined his response to music. He will *never* play football with me. He will *never* sing in the choir with me. And we will *never* go for a beer and curry together. Never, never, never for now and ever. This is my come-down, a reality-check for being like so many proud parents are when they present their new-born to relatives and friends. The headline in tomorrow's 'Shit News' reads 'Smug dad humbled.' I was excited for the life he would lead, the home he would make and the career he would have. What will his future be now?

Liz and I sat in silence while the paediatrician dished up cold facts over her desk. Brain growth expands the skull and Jeremy's had not expanded, so his brain had not grown. Q.E.D.

"And the larger the brain, the more intelligent the person is likely to be," she continued, "the reverse is also true."

"Fewer neurones and synapses," I muttered, absently.

"Exactly," she beamed, "like having a smaller calculator."

"But I need to investigate the probable causes of Jeremy's condition. CMV is one, but there could be others."

Rummaging inside a drawer, she extracted a sewing tape and stood up, "he may have inherited a small head from one or both of you."

She wrapped the tape around my head, then Liz's, and announced her conclusion, "as suspected, your heads are larger than average. So, we can rule that out."

"Forgive me, but I must explore the possibility that you are related, as there could be a genetic reason for Jeremy's condition."

Too much. His brain is not growing, so why dig to find the cause, especially if it unearths the possibility that Liz and I are distant cousins? Could our long-forgotten antecedents have unknowingly interbred? *Really*? I protested, "but Liz's ancestors lived in Poland and Corfu, and mine were a thousand miles away, in Ireland and

England."

The doctor replied calmly, "but there could still be a connection."

"Definitely not," I spoke quickly, eager to bring the subject to a swift end, "Liz has long Jewish ancestral roots, whereas mine are a mix of Irish Catholic and English Baptist. Jews and Christians lived in separate communities, so there is no chance of us being related."

She sighed before answering, "I tend to agree, and I am sorry if this has been uncomfortable for you, but I had to understand why your son is microcephalic."

After an awkward silence, she declared, "CMV may have done damage, but I can't be sure, so I would like him to have a Computerised Tomography scan, or 'CT scan', to build a 3D image of his brain."

Severe developmental problems, possible interbreeding, and now brain damage. My head spun too quickly for me to form any words.

"I will book him in for a CT scan and when the results arrive, we will need to see each other again," she said.

She treated us to a second course of cold facts. CMV is a common virus - a third of women catch it, sometimes during pregnancy. In a few cases, the virus is passed on to the foetus, where it may inflict damage, such as mild hearing loss. I mentioned that Liz had had a prolonged cold-like illness in December last year, "a common symptom," the doctor said. The probability that CMV has inflicted severe brain damage was "about one in sixty thousand," she said.

Having dropped us into an abyss, she asked us if we had any questions. Liz did not answer. My brain could not think of an intelligent question. My head was empty, detached, as if watching a film.

*"Two parents with a small baby faced a doctor at her desk. The parents appeared nervous. They shook her hand politely and, without smiling, waited to receive the news they wanted to hear. That their son was fine, it was just a virus that could be treated easily, and there*

*were no long-term consequences. The sound in the film was muted. The doctor's lips moved and the colour in the parents' faces drained, whitening then greying and aging twenty years in as many seconds. Then they got up and left.*

*Fin."*

We left in a trance, lost in our thoughts. I put my rag-doll-son into the car-seat and drove in silence the few miles home. "Severe developmental problems," what does that mean? What kind of developmental problems? Twenty minutes after the paediatrician asked, "any questions?" a thousand popped into my head. No one can offer us help or advice. Who can we turn to? Perhaps my sister, Lorraine and brother-in-law, John? They had lost a baby to an unexplained cot-death. We had lost a child too, except, we had not. He was still with us and must make the most of life wearing his microcephaly badge and crippled with severe developmental problems.

Liz and I wept as Jeremy slept in blissful ignorance of the life sentence handed to him. We did not need to look or speak – ours was a telepathic grief. A tiny virus, no more than eight millionths of an inch in size, had destroyed our son. I felt a sudden and intense hatred for something so small, yet so destructive and *evil*. But I am determined to keep us together and fight this monster.

Julie, our child-minder, was the first to hear Jeremy's prognosis. She read the results written on our faces as she brought Roxanne and Victoria home. We cannot tell our daughters about Jeremy. What could we say? Roxanne is five years old and Victoria only three. How could we explain it to them? We must carry on as if nothing has happened, and all must be rosy. Tomorrow, we will pack for our trip to France on Sunday. There is so much baggage to take, but we will leave the emotional stuff behind.

# RISE OF THE ANGER-MONSTER

Is it normal to feel so angry? Especially when I cannot direct my anger at anything. Is this what it feels like to lose a child? Shock, then grief, now anger. A burning all-consuming anger. Why was the paediatrician so callous? I hate her for it. Why was Jeremy, our four-month-old son, selected by this virus? I hate that too. But I can do nothing about a virus, the paediatrician explained that it is even more complex than the AIDS virus. There is no magic cure that will bring our son back to us.

The paediatrician cast us into a pit of despair and left us to climb out without a rope. The nurse was sympathetic, even apologetic, and gave us the number of an organisation called 'Parents Encouraging Parents' (PEP), who support parents in situations like ours. What they can do, I know not.

Neither do we know what we can do for Jeremy. We are utterly helpless. His future is out of our hands. The paediatrician prefixed "developmental problems" with "severe" for a reason. She believes that he will live nothing like a 'normal' life, whatever 'normal' means. If she had just said "developmental problems", then he might have a chance, in her judgement. Will he be able to wash, dress or feed himself? Will he walk or talk? Will he need help going to the toilet? Will he be able, *ever*, to look after himself, and make his own decisions? Or will all these things be done for him by someone from the State, or by a run-for-profit home? Who will protect him after we are gone? Yet he is still *my son* and I weep for him. He is so innocent, so unaware, and so vulnerable.

My anger-monster roars at the unfairness. I cannot stop thinking about the one-in-sixty-thousand chance of CMV inflicting so much damage to Jeremy's brain and trashing his life. He is the one child in a group of sixty thousand who was dealt the shit hand. Why did the dice land on penalty and not jackpot? For over forty years, my dad did the weekly football pools and never won a penny. My mum and grandmother went to bingo every week for years and never even won enough for the bus-fare home. In fact, I do not know anyone in my family who won anything by luck. Jeremy has inherited the family misfortune. Lady Bad Luck, the Law for the Below Averages, Sod's Law applies to us and our antecedents, to counterbalance good luck dispensed to others.

Tomorrow, we are setting off for our holiday. Right now, it is hard to get into a holiday mood. Yet we must, for Roxanne's and Victoria's sakes. We must show them that our three weeks away is something to look forward to and not dread. They are excited about staying in a Eurocamp site in France for the first time. It is their great adventure. We should be excited too, but our thoughts are on Jeremy and the next appointment at the children's hospital. What news will the coming months bring? But we must bury the worry, grief, anger and bitterness. We will don happy masks for our children, for the people we meet, and pretend that everything is fine.

# GONE CAMPING

We are in a large tent on a Eurocamp site in Brittany and the weather is glorious. But I do not really care about that, although blue sky instead of grey helps keep dark thoughts away. Yesterday we caught the ferry to Calais and drove four hundred miles in searing heat. With no air-conditioning, we travelled with the car windows down. Roxanne and Victoria sat either side of Jeremy in the back seat with luggage crammed in every nook and cranny. Somewhere near Caen, we pulled off the road and parked cheekily in an empty barn to shelter from the blistering sun. Then we piled out and had a picnic. Halfway through, the farmer turned up. I apologised, but he waved, wished us "bon appetit" and left. Our first meagre slice of good fortune for a while.

We reached our campsite after twelve hours of driving. Hot, tired and trance-like with the news about Jeremy still ringing in my head. Our neighbour in the adjacent tent handed me an ice-cold beer and introduced himself. He complimented me on my leather jacket, lying crumpled in the car boot. I bought it when Liz and I were holidaying in Florence in 1986, our last holiday of freedom, before the children arrived and our lives changed irreversibly. Our neighbour had a professional interest, he explained, being one of the few remaining tanners in Britain.

Our tent is pitched at one end of a semi-circular ring of tents and mobile homes, occupied by a mixture of English and Dutch families. The communal dustbins stand like sentries in the centre of the ring. Our tent has three compartments, Roxanne and Victoria share one and Jeremy is in a second, beside ours. We are spoiled by a fridge, power and lighting, and a water tap just outside the tent flap.

My sister and brother-in-law, Lorraine ('Lol') and John, and daughters Jasmine, Abigail and Emma, want to visit while we are here. We told them about Jeremy before leaving. For the first time, Lol and I talked openly about the death of her baby daughter. Some people find it difficult to talk to others who have suffered personal tragedies. I am, or was, one of those awkward people. I was afraid of saying something that would increase her pain. Now I grieve, and strangely, feel more comfortable talking to her about her bereavement. That must be about the only positive thing to emerge from the past dreadful weeks.

Liz and I phoned our parents before we left and told them what the paediatrician had said. My mum and dad listened to the news about Jeremy in silence. This is a new experience for them. They have always been able to help when I have been hurt. This time, there is nothing they can do. They cannot make Jeremy better. And that helplessness must hurt.

# THE DUSTBIN GANG

August 1992.

We are returning to England tomorrow. We have enjoyed unbroken sunshine for the entire holiday. Roxanne and Victoria mixed well with the other kids in our closely-knit community of tents and mobile homes. They are fully-fledged members of the 'dustbin gang', named after their HQ. They comprise a dozen children, between three and nine years old, Victoria being the youngest and Roxanne of five years, who hang-out by the communal bins, where all operations are planned and executed. Expeditions to the play areas, to the children's mornings with the campsite leaders and, of course at some point, to buy ice-creams and lollipops. They have been a light of bliss and happiness, illuminating the darkness.

Liz and I blended with other kids' parents and tried to have a good time and not be too much of a downer to everyone else. How much effort that took! We tried to be sociable. We pretended that all was well but sometimes our masks slipped. I was quieter than usual, broodier. My state of mind made it difficult to talk to anyone.

We have told some of our fellow campers about Jeremy, only because it was an inevitable result of normal conversation between parents:

"How old is he?" - "Just over four months" (*so far, so good*).

"Is he sleeping well?" – "No" (*unexpected answer alert!*)

"Is he feeding well?" – "No" (*sound the alarm bell!*)

"How's he coping with the heat?" – "Terribly, he won't drink anything" (*change the subject!*)

Each unexpected answer revealed the full picture, piece by piece. But God bless them, they have been more supportive and sympathetic than I could have imagined. Strangers can be angels as well as demons. But, with no previous experience of having a one-in-sixty-thousand son, I do not know what to expect from other people. Maybe we have been lucky with our group? It sounds odd, but I *want* to believe they were put here with us for a reason, to help get us through the mess we are in and give us *hope*.

Returning to England tomorrow will be a return to bliss-less reality. I hope the car does not start. I do not want to go back to that hospital for more knife-twisting torment, to be told about the things that Jeremy will never do, will never be. Nor to my work life, where I must present a fictional happy, no-problem-is-unsolvable attitude in front of customers, peers and managers, where I must suppress my anger, depression and grief. God protect my work-mask, lest it slips and reveals my true feelings. I have not been to work since that dreadful day when we were given Jeremy's prognosis. Now I must prepare for the inevitable and awkward pleasantries, "how was your holiday?" "How's the little one?" "Did you have nice weather?" Holding on to my mask, I will smile and give pleasant responses. Pretend to be happy, be professional, then take off the mask and go home to the *real* reality.

Before we left for France, the paediatrician booked a CT scan for Jeremy. No doubt, more tests will follow the scan. What is the point? They cannot do anything to make Jeremy normal again.

# NO WALKING OR TALKING

We have been home for three weeks and the news about Jeremy has spread like a bush fire. Relatives and friends want to talk and help. The phone has not stopped ringing. Liz always answers. I run whenever it starts shrilling. I cannot talk because there are no words to describe how I feel.

Why are women so much better than men at talking about their feelings? Is it because society equates emotion with weakness and being in control with strength? Any demonstration or emotional outburst from a man is a no-no. Men wear masks and pretend they are not fazed by anything. But I *am* fazed, seriously and deeply. Without words to untangle feelings, all that remains is an emotional mess.

A support organisation called 'Parents Encouraging Parents' (PEP) contacted us shortly after we returned from holiday. They offered to put us in touch with other parents who have been through what we are going through. "You are not alone," the PEP volunteer said. So, Liz met a mum with a seriously disabled girl, and I met another volunteer, a fireman with a disabled boy. But our conversations never grew beyond small talk. He persisted politely, gently and selflessly, but could not break through my barrier of pain, grief and confusion. He reached out his hand to help but I was not ready to grasp it.

Things have gone from bad to worse since we returned

from holiday. We took Jeremy to the Atkinson Morley Hospital in Wimbledon for a CT scan, so the paediatrician at the children's hospital could build a 3D image of his brain. Fortunately, he was asleep when we arrived – he prefers to do most of his sleeping during daylight hours. They laid him on a sliding table, attached some pads to his head and slid him into a tube. A man wearing a white coat sat at a computer screen, as the image appeared in sections, like slices of a cauliflower.

A few days later, we returned to see Jeremy's paediatrician for the results and a more detailed prognosis. We dropped Roxanne at Primary School and Victoria at Pre-School in the morning, as usual. We must be a normal, happy family for them. Julie knew about our meeting at the children's hospital and offered to collect the girls after school, in case we were in no fit state to do so. Gratefully, we accepted and left for our dread-full appointment.

Optimism and hope vanished long before we shuffled into the paediatrician's office. The news would be bad, but far worse than I imagined. The virus had "eaten away" the inner core of his brain. Laying the CT scan images over her desk, she pointed at the damaged area - a large black hole. She compared it with a normal brain scan to illustrate what should have been there, had the virus not got there first.

"The black spots," she said, "are deposits of calcium that may cause additional problems."

Silence from across the desk.

"The motor functions, situated at the back of the brain, have been severely damaged too."

She waited a moment before asking, "you know about cerebral palsy?"

Both a question and statement.

"Excessively high muscular tone or stiffness, shaking, and general inability to control."

More silence.

"The scan also shows that his cerebral cortex has been

smoothed, so his intelligence will be severely limited."

Her words floated around the room. Jeremy would never be normal. The gates of mercy had closed on him for good. There would be no magic cure.

But the paediatrician had more, "given the extent of his brain damage, and I'm sorry to tell you this, but …." I wanted to switch off, change the channel, but could not speak or move.

"He will never walk or talk and will need full-time one-to-one care for the rest of his life."

Liz stammered, attempting to say something sensible, rational, seeking hope, muttering something about CMV, the virus that had vandalised Jeremy's brain while he was defenceless. Then the paediatrician delivered the *coup de grace*, "and, of course, he still has the virus."

Something snapped. A brain half-eaten, calcification, cerebral palsy, never walking or talking and NOW … NOW … the thing that caused it all is still there?!

I leaned forward, "you mean it's still *there*? Inside his brain?"

"I'm afraid so," she replied.

"And is it still damaging him?"

"Quite probably."

Deflated, beaten, my eyes filled with tears of indignation, rage, and pity for my tortured son, while he stared absently.

Life can be so cruel, unfair, unjust and evil. There was a one-in-sixty-thousand chance of my son sustaining severe brain damage from CMV. I looked at Jeremy, at his innocence and wondered what he had done to deserve such savagery. Suddenly overcome with love for my beautiful son, I wanted to protect him and slaughter the thing inside that was, right then, eating his brain. My rage would be a laser beam, burning through his skull and vaporising the virus. I would do *anything* and *everything* to protect him no matter how impossible. *I* would repair the damage that the virus had done, nobody else would, so *I* would.

But the paediatrician had not finished, "it's also probable that he is having epileptic seizures," she said.

Liz sobbed, struggling to stay composed, be logical, analyse the possibilities. She has always been better than me at thinking clearly in difficult situations. I over-react, while she drives through with cool reason, and asks the questions that need asking. But, this time, she could not. Her confusion threw me off-guard. I was a punch-drunk boxer flailing against an invisible opponent – a tiny virus killing my son slowly – and her words were hammer-blows, knocking me senseless.

The paediatrician continued, "I would like to book him in for an Electro-Encephalogram, or EEG, to measure his brain activity."

"More tests," I uttered, pointlessly.

"I'm afraid so," she agreed, "the next few weeks will be testing for you too."

We left the children's hospital just as we had a few weeks earlier, numbed, stupefied, two zombies and their baby. Inside my head, I heard "never walk or talk," "care for the rest of his life," "eaten away his brain" and "still damaging him" over and over. How much more pain can there be?

# WHAT'S HE STARING AT?

October 1992, five weeks after the paediatrician added 'possible epileptic' to Jeremy's growing list of ailments.

"Epileptic seizures can be life-threatening, especially prolonged ones", she warned.

Once again, Liz and I booked a day off work as holiday, left Roxanne and Victoria with Julie, and took Jeremy for an EEG appointment at the Royal Surrey Hospital. We are accustomed to wandering along long corridors with our baby son now, seeking departments we would normally avoid. First came radiography for the X-ray, then haematology for his blood test, radiology for the CT scan a few weeks ago, and neurology today.

Thankfully, the test was painless. No needles, just a simple task of sticking a cap of electrodes to his bald head and keeping him awake. A technician explained that brain wave patterns change during sleep, "mostly theta and delta waves, as that's when alpha and beta activity ceases, and we want to look for spikes across all frequencies."

"Spikes?"

"Seizures show up as a burst of high amplitude waves."

A series of lines traced on a screen at his desk, like an oscilloscope taking voltage readings.

A few days later, we returned to our least-favourite office for his ever-worsening prognosis, where the paediatrician confirmed her hypothesis that Jeremy has epilepsy.

She treated us to a lecture about the main types of seizures. The most common is *grand mal*, the kind that many people have either experienced or seen at some time in their lives, where the sufferer crashes to the floor and shakes uncontrollably. Then there are *petit mal* seizures that can be difficult to detect. The victim drifts off and stares into space. They are often mistaken for a bout of inattentiveness and daydreaming.

"The results of his EEG indicate he is most probably having temporal lobe seizures," she explained.

I asked my first sensible question in four months of visits, "what will that do to him?"

"No one really knows for sure, but they are associated with hallucinations, feeling frightened and disoriented," she suggested, "and the jerking movements that accompany the unusual brain activity indicate he is having what's known as tonic-clonic attacks."

"What's that?" Liz asked.

"It's when the initially localised seizure spreads to the whole brain, leading to stiffening of the muscles and spasmodic movements."

Her words registered. *That look* in Jeremy's eyes just before the twitching started. Pupils expanding, eyes glazing over, looking through me at something else. What was he staring at? Could he see something frightening? He looked utterly terrified, like being on a bad acid trip. I want to comfort him, re-assure him that he is safe.

"You say that you can recognise the symptoms of his seizures?" she asked.

"Yes," I said, "he usually goes very still, he stares through me, then he starts twitching."

"How many times a day do you notice it?"

"About six or seven."

Liz added, "then there's the times during the night, when he's up crying – you can add more."

"Then, it's *really* imperative we start controlling them as soon as possible," the paediatrician urged, "that's far too many."

She explained that a seizure starves the brain of sugar, which can lead to coma and death, in prolonged cases.

"Unfortunately," she said, "finding the right medication and level of medication to control them is more art than science, it's a trial-and-error process."

Not for the first time, we stared blankly, like two *petit mal* sufferers.

"So, we will try one medicine and gradually increase the dose. And if it fails to control the fits, then Jeremy will try an alternative. We should try Tegretol as an anti-convulsant first because it's often effective in younger patients."

The virus is still there, eating his brain, as we discuss medicine to counteract its destruction. Why was Jeremy chosen for such a brutal start to life before he even drew his first breath? Why not pick on one of the many more deserving candidates? There are so many injustices in this world. Why do despotic and narcissistic maniacs have such fantastic lives? They are rewarded for oppressing, torturing and murdering with praise, obscene wealth and privilege. They have perfect children, some of whom continue the family legacy of torturing and subjugating their people. Idi Amin, Nicolae Ceaușescu, Josef Stalin, Saddam Hussein, Pol Pot - the list is endless. Yet innocents, like my son, who has not harmed anyone or anything, is the one being punished and suffering.

Few of my work colleagues know about Jeremy. No one has asked me about him, except during the first few weeks after his birth, before his condition was known. In those happy days, the questions were the usual ones, "boy or girl?" "How are mother and baby?" "How much did he weigh?" I dread anyone asking me about Jeremy now because I would not know what to say. I might break down in front of them.

But my job deflects thoughts away from what is happening to him. Over the past few weeks, a tornado of emotions swept through my mind and re-arranged my priorities. I no longer feel pressure at work. There are more important things in life than missing a deadline. Work is an opportunity to forget about my home life – it is a convenience, an escape. But I make sure I do not work stupid hours and am home in time to bath the kids and read them stories. And when I am home, I forget about work. I lead two lives, neither of which interferes with the other.

Liz works part-time, so she has little respite. When she is not working and I am at work, she copes with Jeremy on her own, something I have never done. We are lucky to have a wonderful helper, Julie, who looks after Roxanne and Victoria when we both work. She takes and collects them from school, feeds and entertains them. She has been a massive support and is more to us than a child-minder.

There is no hope. I am resigned to Jeremy's fate. Nothing will ever be normal for Jeremy, us, or Roxanne and Victoria. Our cup runneth over with grief. My cup overfloweth with anger and injustice too. The sleepless nights continue, so Liz is too fatigued to be angry. But we will keep going. What else can we do?

# FITS AND STARTS

November 1992.

A month has passed since Jeremy started his Tegretol medication and it seems to be having an impact. His fits are not as frequent.

Now I know what to watch for, and just how life-critical it is, I look for the early signs of seizure. His pupils expand and darken, he stares, tenses up and becomes dead still, his breathing shallows. Then the twitching starts, and all hell breaks loose inside his head. He cries in utter terror and there is nothing I can do to stop the horror film sequence playing inside him. I hold him, stroke his head, and say soothing things like, "it's OK, I'm here," "it will be over soon" and, for some peculiar reason, "I know, I know," when I do not, I do not. After three or four minutes the twitching subsides, his eyes return to normal and drowsiness kicks in. The look in his eyes before a fit is burned in my memory forever. I will never forget.

He sleeps at random times and wakes after two hours at most. An hour, perhaps two dozing before we are woken up by his crying. Liz gave up breast-feeding him months ago, so he is on the bottle now. His cot is beside our bed so that we can hear when he wakes, between four and six times every night. We are zombie parents.

We took another day's holiday to visit the British Institute for Brain Injured Children (BIBIC) in Somerset. The organisation offers advice and training on intensive therapy for children with a range of conditions relating to brain injury.

"A child with brain damage can be taught basic movement skills by intensive repetition," claimed the BIBIC consultant, "we have a few children with similar conditions to Jeremy who are participating in our therapy programme, with promising results."

"Let me arrange for you to visit one so you can see what's involved," he said.

For the first time, a ray of hope beamed down on his tortured head. Maybe he could thwart his paediatrician's prognosis, prove her wrong, and be shown how to co-ordinate his limbs.

A week later, we treated ourselves to a second day's holiday in Walthamstow, north-east London, to visit the home of a two-year-old girl with severe brain damage. Her dad greeted us at the door and ushered us along a hall to a small room at the back of the house. We squeezed around a sturdy pine table and sat down in the far corner while dad disappeared to fetch his daughter. A table with no chairs, is this where the therapy will be given? But why had the doors to the room been removed? The answer came when the man reappeared carrying his floppy daughter, like a long rag doll, into the room and laid her carefully on the table. Was this what Jeremy's future looked like? Should we take off the doors to make it easier to carry him about the house?

A cool breeze whispered through French doors leading to a long garden. Soft rain pattered on the paving stones outside.

"We keep the doors open to let the air in, as it can get a little bit hot in here," he explained, "as much for my benefit as for Charlotte's."

"Two people are needed for each hour-long session," he continued, "an hour on, then an hour's rest for Charlotte, then another hour for nine hours every day, seven days every week."

Five sessions per day, thirty-five every week. The girl lay still on the table while dad stroked her hair lovingly.

"My wife or I are one of the therapists, but sometimes the second is late, usually because of traffic or for personal reasons." He glanced up at a large clock on the wall.

"If my helper doesn't arrive soon, then I'll need to wake her up."

On cue, a key rattled in the front door and a middle-aged woman entered the room.

"I am so sorry," she began, "my car refused to start ... and then ..."

She stopped mid-sentence, sighed, and leaned towards Charlotte, "and how are you my little petal?"

A smile flickered across the little girl's face, and the woman clapped her hands in delight.

"Ah, bless her," she said. All her troubles vanished with a brief and precious smile.

"Shall we start?" said the man.

Facing each other, they took hold of one of Charlotte's feet and placed a hand under a knee.

"Ready?"

One slid the girl's foot along the table and pushed up a knee, while the other straightened the girl's other leg, simulating the act of walking.

"Up ... down ... up ... down," they chanted, like a mantra.

For an hour, the two performed the motion metronomically. The man transformed from father to therapist, determined and focussed, yet driven by a deep love for his daughter.

Afterwards, he explained, "intensive therapy demands one hundred and one percent dedication."

"We have a team of fifty volunteers, mostly family members and close, now even closer friends, who we co-ordinate and communicate with."

"How much of your time does that take?" I asked.

"We have nothing to spare - nine hours every day goes

on therapy, then more time feeding, cleaning and medicating Charlotte. What's left isn't much, and that's spent on keeping the rota going."

"What happens if someone doesn't turn up?" Liz asked.

"My wife and I are the substitutes."

Charlotte's upright leg slid down the table. Was that a conscious decision or just gravity doing its work?

"Is the therapy making a difference?"

He regarded his daughter for a few seconds, "sometimes she twitches a leg, then nothing for a while, changes in fits and starts. But who knows? She may have accomplished that without therapy, so I'm not sure."

Never raise hope, we had learned that after a few weeks of crushing blows.

"We must leave, so she can rest before her next session. I hope you found this session helpful."

He lifted his daughter up and carried her out the room.

The diabolical traffic gave plenty of time to discuss options. Should we sign up to the programme or not?

"Results aren't guaranteed," Liz said, "he didn't know if the therapy was working."

"Where would we find fifty volunteer therapists from?" I added, "would we have time to co-ordinate them all, hold down two jobs and look after Roxanne and Victoria?"

"True, the girls would suffer."

"Even now Jeremy takes up far more attention than a normal baby would."

The radio played quietly in the background as the we moved, in fits and starts, along the motorway. The BBC news said something about the Queen's *annus horribilis*. We had something in common with royalty, after all.

"I'm sorry, but I don't think we can," Liz concluded.

"I'm sorry too," I agreed, passing a chance to give Jeremy greater independence. Choosing one child over another is always difficult, yet millions of parents do so every day.

*"No, you've had your turn, now it's your sister's."*

*"Let her watch 'Beauty and the Beast', you watched your video yesterday."*

Such choices teach a child that life is not stacked in their favour. But this choice was different. There was no lesson for anyone, no right and no wrong, just one child's future sacrificed for two others. A gamble that things would be less bad for all if we took this path. Would we regret our decision later? What if? What if? The guilt we feel for making the choice will never disappear – it will visit in fits and starts.

# JOB

December 1992.

I read the 'Book of Job' from the Bible, hoping to understand why Job suffered so terribly, having led such a devout life. I wanted to know why Jeremy must suffer before he has even had a chance to live. The book is a parable about freedom of choice. Job is a kind and pious man who loses everything in a bet between God and Satan. Would he also lose his faith, and his goodness, when he is the victim of a sequence of terrible tragedies? In the end, Job's faith prevails, and he is rewarded with a happy life for ever after.

At only nine months, Jeremy has not made any choices, so what he has done to deserve his suffering? If his prognosis is accurate, then he will *never* have the mental capacity to choose - right or wrong. So why does God allow my son to be tortured with terrifying fits? There is no answer. Small mercy has been granted by Tegretol medication. The frequency of seizures has reduced, but it will take time before they can be controlled fully. An emergency rectal tube containing Diazepam, a powerful sedative, will knock him out when fits are prolonged. Man-made solutions to an unjust and evil condition.

Whereas Job could choose between right and wrong, Jeremy cannot and never will. But *I* have a choice, Job taught me that. I can refuse to accept Jeremy's condition, pretend it does not exist, and lose my faith in him and in everything else. Or I can turn my negative energy - anger, bitterness and grief – into positive, and help him lead the best life he can.

This revelation was reinforced by a trip to the Deaf Centre in north London, after the paediatrician speculated that Jeremy had hearing difficulties. We waited in the reception area, full of foreboding. Minutes later, a family burst into the room, bubbling with life and bringing a breath of fresh air. Mum carried their disabled daughter, followed by dad and their five other children. Like the girl who received intensive repetitive therapy a few weeks earlier, their daughter was motionless – little more than a floppy doll. The parents owned no car, so had relied on four separate bus journeys to arrive at the Deaf Centre from south London. Dad explained that they lived in temporary housing with two bedrooms, while their local Council sought permanent accommodation. Mum fed her daughter liquidised vegetables from a baby bottle, as they laughed and chatted to their children. Their devotion, tenderness and quiet determination convinced me that it is possible to lead a full life and remain a strong family, even with such hardship. Like Job, they chose to fight for the good of their defenceless little one and were thriving.

On our way home, Liz and I discussed how fortunate we were in comparison. No matter how badly off we think we are, there are others who are worse off. That thought is not *schadenfreude*, not intended to bring comfort - it is a wakeup call, "quit feeling sorry for yourself, stop being angry, get on with it!" If that heroic and loving family can manage, then so can we. We can be like them. Without even being aware of it, they slayed my anger-monster.

# FIRST BIRTHDAY

March 30th 1993.

Many one-year-olds are crawling, babbling words and some are toddling. Not Jeremy. He cannot crawl, talk or toddle and probably never will. But he can make noises, which his speech and language therapist calls "vocalising." And he recognises us. With a lot of persistence, he may reward us with a glance or even a smile. Although he has not changed much in a year, *we* have. Without knowing it, Jeremy has transformed our families' and friends' attitudes to the disabled. He has become their unofficial ambassador, breaking down barriers wherever he goes. That is a gift we cherish.

We go to shul (synagogue) on Saturday mornings. Shortly after the news about Jeremy blazed through our community, a dapper elderly couple, Hettie and David, approached us after a service. They asked about Jeremy's condition with no inhibition and enormous sensitivity. They explained that their granddaughter had a learning disability.

I asked a question I could never have asked a year earlier, "how do you feel about that?"

"Oh, we love her just as much as our grandchildren," Hettie answered, without hesitation, and David beamed with pride.

We always sit close to each other in shul now, comrades-in-arms, strong in our mutual understanding.

Jeremy has had all kinds of tests and check-ups in his first year. His fits are fewer and further between. He has one or two on most days, always noticeable and distressing to watch. All we can do is cuddle him until the fit subsides. Julie, our child-minder, has become an expert at detecting them. A few days before his birthday, we were told that he was finally clear of CMV, and no more damage was being done to his brain.

No one taught us how to summon the will to carry on, as each test revealed more problems. Microcephalic, learning disabled, cerebral palsy, the presence of a persistent and destructive virus, temporal lobe seizures, tonic-clonic attacks and partially deaf, they kept on coming. We learned how to keep going with Jeremy by taking one step at a time, making sure of his way ahead in life. We never lost our love for him. Rather, our love grew stronger, to compensate for the weight of his handicap.

I still believe Jeremy's mood changes when he hears music, just as I thought before knowing about his condition. Put on the cassette player in the car and he immediately goes still, as if he is concentrating, trying to understand the sensation in his ears. The same change comes over him when he hears the shul choir and congregation sing.

We often take Jeremy out for walks, especially to the forest. His eyes dance as he gazes up at the leafy canopies, mesmerised by the shapes of the branches and how they move in the breeze. Maybe because trees occupy a large chunk of his vision space, he cannot help but notice them. But I like to believe that he has developed a love for trees as a personal choice.

If I ever win the lottery, I will buy a forest, hire an orchestra and a choir for Jeremy's birthday, and throw a concert in the woods.

# SMALL SIGNS

Children shoot up so quickly. Blink an eye, and you will miss the signs of their progress - first words, first tottering steps, first potty-time, first spoonful guided into mouth. Our two daughters, aged seven and five, climb reliably towards sunlight and ultimate independence. Already they have reached heights beyond Jeremy's limits. But their twenty-month-old sibling has sprouted a few green shoots. He can almost sit up unsupported, roll on to his tummy and back, and has become a fully-fledged dendrophile. Leafy Surrey has more trees than any other county in the UK, so he is spoiled for choice.

At just twelve pounds, Jeremy has a chronic weight problem. He refuses food and drink for days, then binges. A little black diary beside our kitchen table, donated by the children's hospital, contains a meagre record of when he ate and drank. The nutritionist wants us to watch for a pattern. Does he prefer a particular time? Is his location important – kitchen, lounge, in his buggy? What about the surroundings – with siblings buzzing around noisily or peace and quiet? But right now, we cannot see anything obvious.

We keep a second diary to record his doses of Tegretol anti-convulsant. The diary is red because his life depends on it. The paediatrician stressed the importance, "missing a dose is a good way of inducing a fit, and you don't want that." He hates his medicine, so we squirt the white syrup into his mouth with an oral syringe, against his will. Some days he consumes more medicine than food. And when we take him out, an emergency bag with Tegretol, Diazepam, oral syringes, nappies, bottle for drinks, water and diaries accompanies him. If we forget anything, then we go back for it, no matter how far along the road we have gone.

Attracting Jeremy's attention is like catching a rare butterfly. Waving, jumping up and down, or clapping hands is more likely to make him turn away than settle his gaze. A calmer strategy may yield a sidelong glance, but never a full-on stare. The glance lasts for no more than a second, so the attention-seeker must be vigilant. Unfortunately, many are not, so they fail to receive the reward they so richly deserve for their efforts. So we watch for them. If they miss it, we cry out, "you got *the look*!"

Jeremy wears a hearing-aid, as recommended by the children's hospital and Deaf Centre, even though we know he can hear. He is not stone deaf, maybe slightly hearing-impaired, because he reacts to some sounds, especially music. He listens to me when I sing in the choir and is quite happy, which is surprising, considering no one else is.

Liz reminds me to "look for the signs of progress, no matter how small." We look for the minutest grain of evidence, blow it up to mountainous proportions, then tell the world about it. The signs are small and sweet, we take them and coat them in honey.

# BUREAUCRACY

March 1994.

The postman stuffed a twenty-page form through our letterbox. A Statement of Education Needs (SEN) for Jeremy, dispatched by the Local Education Authority (LEA). They want to determine a school placement for him. Credit to them for starting the process two years before the national entry age for schoolchildren. The form demands statements from an armada of specialists, including the paediatrician at the children's hospital, the physiotherapist, speech & language therapist, nutritionist, occupational therapist and psychologist. We have been granted a whole page to write about other needs that they may miss. Bureaucracy, but necessary.

The LEA will want the cheapest option. They are a public body, strapped for cash. They want to place him in a state school and expect the teachers to cope, but that would be a disastrous mistake. They are more likely to decide on a local special needs school, with teachers who know how to work with children with profound and complex disabilities. The best we can hope for is a place in a Jewish special needs school, where Jeremy's cultural requirements would also be met. But the LEA are unlikely to consent to that because they conflate culture with religion and will make no concessions on those grounds.

Our one page swelled quickly to six, with an essay about why being Jewish is far more than just religion. We elaborated on the Jewish way of life, the "sights, sounds and tastes" unique to each festival and life event, such as Passover, Bar Mitzvah, and so on. Many secular special needs schools will not know the rules of 'kashrut' - what he can and cannot eat - the festivals he celebrates with his family and Jewish community. They will be unaware that he does not observe Christmas or Easter. Continuity between his life at school and at home is crucial to his development. When he is eighteen and leaves the education system, we will be asked to justify a placement in a full-time Jewish care home. The words we write in his SEN will echo through the years.

# NORWOOD AND THE VILLAGE PEOPLE

April 1994.

There is a Jewish special needs school in the middle of a forest, only ten miles from us. The school is part of the Ravenswood 'village', a buzzing, vibrant community of a hundred and ten adults with learning and physical disabilities, that no one in the heart of the UK's commuter belt knows anything about. Liz discovered it through a close friend in our synagogue. Our struggles with Jeremy, and two young daughters, have not gone unnoticed.

Norwood is the charity who manage the village and the Annie Lawson School. Their mission is to care and support children and adults with conditions like Jeremy's. Two testing years have whizzed by, but we cannot rest for a minute. The pressure is on from the LEA. We must find a school that can cater for all his needs, cultural as well as physical and learning. The LEA will want Jeremy to go to one of the local schools, who may not provide all the facilities that he will need. We are ready for battle.

One crisp spring morning, we drove twenty minutes up the road to Ravenswood for a meeting with the Annie Lawson School's Head Teacher. The village is set in Swinley Forest, a half-mile down a private road with open views across fields. Jeremy watched in fascination at the tall pine trees sweeping past. The receptionist led us to a waiting area with a small kitchen and pointed out the tea, coffee and biscuits.

A middle-aged lady with Down's syndrome bounced into the room to make a coffee. Singing happily, she filled her cup. Then she turned her attention to Jeremy.

"Hello, what's your name?"

He made no noise. She looked at us, "what's his name?"

"Jeremy," I answered, "he can't talk, but he knows you're there."

"I'm Jenny, pleased to meet you Jeremy," she grabbed his hand and shook it.

"How old?"

"Two," Liz replied.

"What does he like?"

"He loves going for walks, especially in the trees, and music," I answered.

"When's his birthday?"

"It was just two weeks ago, on 30th March," Liz said.

"What's his favourite colour?"

"Red," we both answered in unison.

She thought for a moment, all the while looking at Jeremy with concern.

"What football team does he support?"

"Liverpool", I said while Liz cried out, "Manchester United."

"Hooray," she said and ruffled his hair.

Then, cup in hand she said, "goodbye Jeremy, it was nice to meet you," and left the room. A short and sweet encounter, with no hint of awkwardness.

The village is a galaxy away from the hustle and bustle of life a half-mile outside, where no one has time for anyone else. Care and respect for the individual takes priority. If anyone ever wants to get away from it all, then the village is the place to be.

# TOUGH LOVE

July 1994.

We lost the battle with the Local Education Authority, despite our passionate plea for Jeremy to attend the Annie Lawson School in Ravenswood Village. They declared that he would attend the local special needs school in Camberley, starting September this year. They rejected our preferred placement on "religious grounds", disregarding our words in his statement, where we argued that Jewishness is a cultural need, not a religious one. It could have been worse - they could have gone for the cheapest option and bunged him in a regular school.

Jeremy still sleeps badly, waking two or three times every night. He is also louder and heavier, despite being chronically underweight for a two-and-a-quarter year-old boy. We moved him into a bedroom next to ours, so we can listen out for his fits. He eats and drinks irregularly although his diet has expanded to sandwiches, without crusts, smothered in a thick layer of creamy butter and Marmite. High fat and protein by any means, under orders from his nutritionist. We hand-feed him by tearing off chunks and popping them into his mouth. He has been diagnosed with reflux, so the poor lad often regurgitates what he eats. Obviously uncomfortable, he moans and shakes his head from side to side, spraying saliva coloured with Marmite onto his feeder's clothes. I suffer from mild reflux, a burning sensation in the throat caused by stomach acid rising up the oesophagus. Whereas I understand the cause of my pain, Jeremy does not. He feels pain without reason.

Because he eats and drinks at odd times, his toileting is irregular too. He is doubly incontinent, so he wears large baby-sized nappies, which we change six or seven times daily. Like his eating habits, his toileting is binge-based, so he will go for three days without any movements and then, like the proverbial bus, three will turn up in rapid succession. We must take a minimum of three clean nappies, change bag and mat, pseudo cream for preventing rashes, sterile wipes and nappy bags with us, even if we are just popping out to the local shops. There is little worse than the filthy looks from shoppers while Jeremy sports a soiled nappy. They do not know that changing facilities for the disabled are non-existent. So, we take him back to the car and change him there, as discreetly as possible.

Every meal comes with a garnish of medicines. Tegretol for his seizures, Ranitidine for reflux and, the most recent addition, laxative to help relieve constipation. He will not take these in pill form, so we must force them into him with an oral syringe, which he hates. It is tough love.

# POSITIVES AND NEGATIVES

October 1994.

Jeremy started at Portesbery, a local special needs school in Camberley, last month. Julie takes him in the morning, and I take Roxanne and Victoria to their schools. Then I shoot off to work, where I lose myself in mundanity. I talk to friends and work colleagues more freely about Jeremy now.

Six months ago, Steve became a first-time dad. With delight and pride, he told everyone about his baby son. Five months later, he shuffled into my office, head bowed, and slumped into a chair opposite my desk. Normally, Steve would charge in with a challenging question, usually about AI. Instead, he sat still and silent, staring down at his hands.

"What's up?" I said.

"How do you manage with Jeremy?"

"Is this today's tough question?" I replied.

More silence.

"God knows how, we just do, somehow. We have no choice, we have to manage."

"I'm sorry," Steve said.

"What for?"

"I've just had some bad news, that's all."

I leaned forward, "what's happened?"

"My son has had hearing tests – he's completely deaf."

"I'm so sorry Steve," I said, "when …"

He looked up suddenly, tearfully, "why does this happen?"

"There's no answer matey, it just does."

"There has to be a reason, it's so unfair," he blurted, then looked down again at his hands.

Stuck for something to say, to console him, "we're dads-in-arms now, united by a common aim – to love our sons and give them the best life."

Did he just tremble?

"You must look for the positives, no matter how small they are," I offered.

"Accentuate the positives," Steve sniffed, "and eliminate the negatives."

Then there is Rob, another work colleague I confide in about Jeremy. Rob is a cheerful, highly intelligent and healthy chap who works in the same department as me. We are like-minded, sharing a common sense of humour and taste in music. Once or twice every week, Rob pops in for an update on Jeremy's condition. He joked that the updates are "downdates" because the news is often bad. His delightfully upbeat and ironic humour helps. But everything changed one day when, like Steve, he slumped in the chair opposite.

"Well? How's Jeremy?"

"He's coming along," I gave my stock reply and then added, "he looked at me the other day, as clearly as he's ever done before."

"Excellent!" said Rob. But there was a muted tone to his response.

"What's up? Are you OK?" I asked.

Rob frowned, an uncommon expression for him, "I think I have multiple sclerosis."

"How do you know?" I asked.

"Just basic things, like tingling, being uncoordinated and occasional loss of balance," he said.

"That might be just the job, working here does strange things to me too," I joked, rather poorly.

Rob gave a half-smile, "No, this is different. I've spoken to my GP, and he wants to conduct tests."

I did not see Rob again for a few weeks. When he reappeared, he pulled up a chair and grinned, "So, how's your boy?"

"He's taking small steps forward, you know, more smiles, eating better, more eye contact," I replied, "but, what about you? Where have you been?"

"Tests," Rob answered, "tests and more tests."

"So, do you have MS or not?"

"Yes, confirmed by MRI scan," he admitted, still looking remarkably cheerful for someone who had been awarded a debilitating illness that would, most probably, lead to complete loss of mobility and independence.

Rob then said something that will stay with me for the rest of my life, "you know, you and I are at opposite ends of the spectrum."

"What do you mean?"

"You look for small signs of progress in your son, and I look for small signs of regress in me."

# ANOTHER LEAP

December 1994.

Liz and I want to grow the family. She worries about having another baby, believing that she "left the spring chicken club" at the ripe old age of thirty-seven.

"I want another baby, but suppose the virus comes back?"

"Lightning doesn't often strike the same place twice," I re-assured, "and you must take it easier, have lots of rest and eat well."

"I'll take my maternity leave earlier."

"It will be difficult," I said, "we'll have a newborn to nurture, as well as Jeremy and the girls."

"You'll have to help more."

My sister Lorraine lost her second child to an unsolved cot death. Ten years passed before she found courage to try for another baby. Having a child is a leap in the dark. You never know what will happen, cannot predict what your child will become, whether they will be happy, achieve fame or bring something positive to others' lives. It is both daunting and exciting. Life is full of risks and bringing a new life into the world is the greatest risk of all. Sometimes it works out well and sometimes it does not. Forget about fame, good looks, super-intelligence and wealth, the health and happiness of our children are the only things that really matter.

# JD

February 1995.

When we go out in the car, Jeremy sits in the front seat, beside me. It will be his third birthday next month, so he was promoted from the back. The view from up front is better. He looks out of the window, thumb in mouth, at the trees passing by. Occasionally, he will see something and chuckle or vocalise, and I reply with the same sound. Our man-talk time. For some reason, I began dropping his name into our conversation, abbreviating it to "JD," maybe because it sounded cool.

"Yes JD."

"Errr" (vocalisation).

"I couldn't agree more, JD."

Chuckle.

I continue the conversation while pushing him in his buggy through the shopping centre, despite concerned looks from people.

"So, JD," I say as we enter Waitrose, "shall we have curry tonight?"

"Errr."

"I'll take that as a yes," grabbing a root ginger and some green chillis.

"Goidy-goidy."

"That's a new sound JD," I said surprised, "but you're right, the red chillis are hotter."

# PUMA FOREST

March 1995.

A puma has been spotted in a nearby forest, where I take the kids for walks. The animal was reported in the local newspaper, so it must be true. A large black creature was seen by several locals on a few occasions, so I have renamed the area 'Puma Forest'. The alleged puma was observed hanging around some trees beside a forest track. When not visiting my mum and dad or relatives at the weekend, we take the girls and JD out for walks there, because the trees fascinate him, and for healthy exercise. I am surprised we have not been eaten yet.

To reach Puma Forest, we park the car opposite a derelict house on the main road to Deepcut, tread carefully along the aptly named 'Dog Poo Alley', turn left at the end, past the disused air-raid shelter where the zombies live, hack through 'Bramble Jungle', and turn right on to a forest track. Pushing JD's buggy through the mud while scanning the branches above for pumas-in-waiting can be tricky, but he appreciates the effort and excitement.

Now almost three, JD sits up unsupported and communicates with a wider range of sounds. He may be way behind developmentally, but Liz and I are delighted with whatever he can accomplish. Small steps are better than none. His delightful and infectious smile is worth the hours of effort trying. Hearing his attempts to speak tell us he knows we are here and that he wants to tell us something. The ingenuity of the human brain to express emotion is amazing. Tone, duration and pitch offer a limitless supply. I can distinguish between his happy, angry, bored and "I'm interested" noises. We talk incessantly in the car together. Our conversations are nonsense to eavesdroppers, but precious for rapport.

# EXTENSION

May 1995.

"We'll really have to build an extension," Liz said.

"Why?" I asked.

"We'll need it - now that number four is on the way," she announced.

The best news in years. The previous three years had been a fuzz, a fog of random memories, carrying JD uphill, climbing over obstacles one by one. He had been born into a world made for the able-bodied and minded. Now number four was on its way. He would be a big brother to look up to.

We would keep the news quiet, until Liz was sure that everything would be fine. Baby must be declared fit, healthy, and above all, free of the brutal and evil CMV. She would set a date for a first scan, in June or July, and then make an official announcement.

"It will make a change for JD," Liz said, "he won't be the centre of attention anymore."

"True, but we're going to need a lot of help during the first few months."

"I think we'll have to tell Julie," Liz said, "she'll guess anyway."

"I agree, she'll need to know, so we can work out how we get three children to three different schools and care for a new-born at the same time."

"I'll do the caring for the new one," Liz volunteered, "I will be his or her mum, after all."

"About that extension…," I began.

# ESCAPE TO FRANCE

June 1995.

"Shall we go somewhere warmer for our summer holiday this year?" Liz asked.

I thought about the places we had been in previous years - France, Spain, France and France again. Before that, Cornwall twice and Scotland in 1988. Last year in Vendée, the weather had been terrible, so no opportunity to make sandcastles, float JD on the sea in his inflatable boat and eat beignets on soft beaches.

"Let's go to France," I suggested enthusiastically, "only further south."

"How far south?" Liz asked.

"How about Biarritz, near the Spanish border?" I answered, "there's a long sandy beach, it's warmer than Vendée and the Pyrenees are close by."

"Sounds good, we could drive up to the mountains if we get bored paddling in the sea."

JD never held us back from anything we wanted to do. Liz and I were adamant that he should never be denied access to anywhere or do the same things that most people his age can do. JD and the girls love holidaying *al fresco*, sleeping under canvass, where the tent flaps are open to the small friends they make so quickly. So, we booked eighteen days in August on a Eurocamp site in Bayonne, with a boat crossing to Bilbao.

"How long does it take to sail from Portsmouth to

Bilbao?" Liz asked.

"Thirty-six hours," I answered.

"Enough time to get the lift from the car deck to our cabin," she said, with a touch of irony.

She referred to the short ferry crossings from England to France. Getting from the car deck to the passenger decks, located three of four levels up, can be done by stairs or by one of two lifts in the centre of the boat. We have enough stuff to fill a lift, but they are often occupied by able-bodied passengers clutching large cases of beer or wine purchased from the duty-free. So we stand by the lift door and make ourselves conspicuous to elicit the maximum guilt from the thoughtless.

I lost my rag once when a lift door slid open to reveal the occupants, crammed inside like sardines, carrying sacks of perfume and tiny daysacks. I asked pointedly, "can anyone walk?"

Blank stares, some tinged with panic, others just blank, pretending we were not there.

Access to lifts in public places is just one of the mobility obstacles we are still climbing.

# (STAR) TREK TO THE MUSEUM

July 1995.

Mobility is a big issue for us. If we want to go out for the day, which we often do, it takes thirty minutes to get out of the house and on the road. Time flies changing JD's nappy, putting on his coat and shoes, folding his buggy, packing his change bag, preparing Marmite sandwiches in case he gets hungry, checking the medicine bag, then loading him and the buggy in the car. Roxanne and Victoria chip in if they feel like it, usually by carrying a bag or two.

Our expanding family and special needs call for a bigger car. I asked my employer to replace the Ford Granada because it will not do anymore. So, the company offered me a delivery vehicle, a large diesel-powered Midi van, with sliding doors. It is noisy and accelerates to a top speed of eighty miles per hour in two minutes, downhill and with a fair wind behind. Despite a lack of power, it is the most practical car we have ever owned, with three rows of seats and a huge loading space behind. And the sliding doors make it easy to lift JD in and out.

Today, we drove into Kensington for a Star Trek exhibition in the Science Museum. The Midi van transformed into a teleporter full of noisy children with ages ranging from eleven years (JD's cousin Andrew) to three years (JD). Andrew loves JD - he is always so concerned about him, maybe because he knows that boys must stick together when outnumbered by girls. I parked the new company car in a disabled bay right outside the Museum entrance. Roxanne, Victoria, JD, Andrew, Andrew's sister Rebecca, my sister-in-law Debbie, the buggy and beloved Marmite sandwiches all piled out of the van and beamed on to the bridge of the USS Enterprise.

For an hour we were the lead characters from 'Star Trek'. JD unwittingly played the role of Mister Spock, Andrew charged around as Captain Kirk, Rebecca as Uhuru, Roxanne as Counsellor Deanna Troi and Victoria as visor-wearing blind Officer La Forge, slipping her pink hair band across her eyes as a convincing prop.

# LOST AT SEA

August 1995.

Our trek to the exhibition four weeks ago was a dress rehearsal for our trip to a campsite in Bayonne a week later. It took little time to load the cavernous Midi van, but that was its only advantage. Noise from the screaming engine on the two-hour drive to Portsmouth for the Bilbao ferry crushed all hope of singing along to the Food Tape. The latter was a recording of a BBC radio programme with songs from the 1950s and 1960s, quirky and different, such as 'Pass the Peas', 'Hot Banana' and 'Do the Duck'. The kids love them - when they can hear over the racket from the engine.

We are proud owners of a disabled blue badge, so we rolled on to the car deck in the first wave of passengers. By the time we had parked and extracted JD's buggy, change bag and nappies, medicine bag, Marmite and overnight bags, the lifts were occupied by the passengers from the second and third waves.

The ship's purser escorted us to our cabin to check its suitability for JD. We had booked a cot, despite his mature three and a half years of age, so he could not roll on to the deck at night. Through the two portholes in our cabin, a few feet above the waterline, we played spot-the-fish before exploring the boat. We found the canteen first, serving traditional British food of curry, pizza, pasta and burgers. As a treat, we ventured upstairs to a piano restaurant for an early taste of French cuisine with full waiter service and live entertainment, a medley of jazz and classics from the pianist in residence.

The noisiest place on any passenger ship is the children's play area, not the engine room, as one might think. Small people throw themselves fearlessly on to brightly coloured plastic balls while other, usually smaller, people burrow beneath, and inevitable accidents ensue. The area is surprisingly popular with parents too, despite the cacophony, chaos and danger to their offspring. Liz and I unleashed Roxanne and Victoria into the ball-pit and watched for a few moments. I carried JD in and sat among the balls, picking them up and showing them to him, but he was much more interested in the hyperactivity. He chuckled as children hurled themselves, screamed and threw tantrums. One child stopped and stared at JD, not quite sure, his thoughts written on his face - as they are with adults who see JD for the first time.

*Could be a toddler* (he is small for his age, about the same size as an eighteen-month-old).

*But he is dribbling a lot, and toddlers don't do that, unless there's something wrong with him* (JD has no control over his swallowing reflex, so saliva accumulates and, occasionally, flies out when he shakes his head).

*There is something wrong, he is shaking his head, and his hands are curled up* (one of the signs of cerebral palsy).

"What's wrong with him?" the boy asked, one more question than many adults ask.

His courage to ask merited an honest answer, "he was very ill when he was born, and his brain got damaged."

Curiosity unsated, he followed up with a more difficult question, "why?"

The boy was too young to know about viruses, or fate, so I gave him the best explanation I could, "that's a hard question to answer – but everyone is born different, some are boys like you, others are girls, some grow to be tall, others stay small. But inside we are the same."

He looked at JD for a few seconds, "Oh," he said and left.

The noise from the pit rose as more children piled in. As we deliberated over pulling the girls out, Victoria disappeared.

"I can see Roxanne," said Liz anxiously, "but I can't see Victoria."

I scanned the ball-pit. There were about forty children, and none were her. We called Roxanne over and asked her if she knew where her sister was.

"Nope," she replied, then added, hopefully, "can I go back now?"

I put JD in his buggy and returned to the ball-pit and sifted through the plastic balls looking for Victoria, to no avail. Liz asked other parents if they had seen a five-year-old girl carrying a Minnie Mouse coat, her favourite item of clothing. She and mouse-coat were inseparable, even though she had out-grown it three years earlier. Mouse-coat was not in the ball-pit, so we inferred she was not there either.

"We can ask someone to make an announcement," I suggested.

Grim thoughts ran through my head as we raced to the purser's desk. Perhaps she had found her way to the outside deck and fallen overboard? Or lay injured somewhere?

"Children don't go missing at sea because there is too much to do on board," the purser explained.

"It happens a lot," he continued, in a bored tone, "we'll make an announcement for you."

"Will Victoria Smith please make herself known to a member of the crew, your mummy and daddy are worried."

We continued our search, by dividing and conquering. I took JD aft, while Liz took Roxanne for'ard. Our strategy was to search one half of a deck each, meet in the middle, go up a level and repeat.

After ten minutes searching, we heard welcome news over the ship's tannoy, "will the parents of Victoria Smith please report to the purser, your daughter has been found."

We spotted Victoria, clutching her precious mouse-coat tightly, fingers in her mouth. A crew member explained that she had been wandering around duty-free. We never found out what she had been shopping for.

The boat docked the following day, after an uneventful night. JD slept well for a change, the gentle swell of the ocean lulling him into a deep sleep. We breakfasted in the regular canteen, ignoring the glances from the curious, as we forced two oral syringes of Tegretol into JD. A few tables in front, I watched a man feed his disabled son with a spoon. The man was in his fifties, about fifteen years older than me, and his son was in his late teens. Their bond was palpable, eyes locked, telepathic exchanges through facial expressions, sounds and gestures. Was I looking through a glass at JD and me?

# ALL FINE AND BEAUTIFUL

September 1995.

There is no denying that Liz and I are worried about the baby's health. CMV began forging a path of destruction through JD's brain six months into term, then kept going for months after his birth. The probability of the virus striking again is much greater than "lightning striking twice." I chose that metaphor a year ago to reassure Liz because, like her, I wanted a fourth child. When she became pregnant, I nagged her to work less, eat better and sleep more. The first two were more achievable than the last, especially as JD still sleeps as erratically as a newborn baby.

Liz's mid-term scan was due in September, shortly after we returned from holiday. She saw the midwife as an extra precaution, who told Liz that she had built-up a stock of antibodies from when she first caught the virus.

"But things can still go wrong," Liz fretted.

The midwife and doctors must have heard. They treated her with more sensitivity than usual and took extra steps to show her that our baby was, "just fine and beautiful."

# FEEDING THE CARPET

October 1995.

"We will need another carpet soon," I said to Liz, staring at the remnants of what had been in JD's mouth just a second before. The contents had been ejected and propelled a couple of feet away on to our lounge rug. A light brown stain of Marmite diluted with dribble and half-chewed bread and butter had formed.

"You should feed him in his chair," Liz replied, "that's what it's meant for."

Surrey Care Services gave us a chunky feeding chair for JD this week. Although the right size for a chair, it weighs as much as a double bed. Made with high quality wood, it has straps for holding him in, pads on the back rest and arms, and a sturdy wooden tray that slides over his thighs. A beautiful piece of craftsmanship. The only design flaw is that JD does not want to sit in it. He wants to sit on our lap, or on the floor, as he always has done, and be fed from there. He lets us know in no uncertain terms, by shaking his head from side to side and crying out. He has a healthy temper, just like the rest of us.

If only he was aware of the effort that went into making that chair. First, the physiotherapist and occupational therapist determined the optimum size and shape to maintain a good posture and one that would, at the same time, encourage him to feed himself. That meant he must sit at eye-level, so he and his feeder could communicate better. Then, Surrey's finest carpenters were given the brief, and toiled for hours to produce what JD thinks is as comfortable as a bed of nails.

"Well, at least the stain will match the others," I said, trying to stay positive, while regarding the blotches left from other little incidents. There were two reddish purple splodges of Tegretol anti-convulsant liquid that JD had refused to accept from his oral syringe. I counted at least three other Marmite-wine stains. Our carpet resembled a Jackson Pollock painting. In a few weeks' time we will put it on the market and see if we get any offers.

Our house is not like other peoples' houses. Since JD's prognosis became clear three years ago, all house rules went out the window. Everyone must eat together at the dinner table, except JD, who can start there and finish on the kitchen floor, or lounge floor, so he can look out the window at the trees. Everyone must finish their mains before pudding, except JD, who can eat anything to help increase weight from his current eighteen pounds. Everyone must go to bed at a sensible time, except JD, who can go to bed after he has bathed, changed and asleep, which is not as soon or as often as we would like. We try to maintain some semblance of order in our house, we try, we really do.

We also have two cats, Ponsonby and Tabsworth, who pussy foot carefully around the chaos, avoiding human contact if possible. We cannot get rid of them – they are part of our family now, having been with us since the year 1 BC (Before Children). So, we will live with the chunks of cat fur that tumble over the kitchen lino and stick to the food stains on the carpet.

Let me be frank – our house is a complete tip. I am too ashamed to invite our friends over. Other peoples' houses are immaculate. Pristine carpets, clean and hoovered, clutter-free, ordered and manicured gardens. I am too scared to visit our friends' houses in case JD throws up on something. So, our social life has crashed, except for the occasional synagogue event, like a Bar or Bat Mitzvah party. Anyway, we are usually too knackered for socialising and there are not many people who could babysit JD.

We are slowly accumulating more equipment for JD. Apart from the feeding chair, we have been given a standing frame to help his muscles develop and maintain an upright posture, instead of the skewed posture he adopts when he is sitting on the floor. We are resigned to the fact that he will never walk, but the frame will help prevent future problems caused by his lack of physical movement. When not in use, it hides a particularly colourful food stain on the dining room carpet, whilst occupying another square metre of precious floor space.

# LITTLE SISTER

December 1st 1995.

Memories of our last visit to the Maternity Ward returned, as we drove sedately over the speed bumps to the hospital a few minutes after midnight. We had to find someone to look after Roxanne, Victoria and JD while we were at the hospital. Julie, our child-minder, was the only person we trusted to look after our seriously disabled boy. She knows how to medicate him, can see the impending signs of a fit and knows how to help JD through them, how to change him, feed him, and so many other how-tos we cannot explain.

"We'll call you when something happens," Liz said to Julie as we left the house.

Roxanne's and Victoria's births had both been marathon affairs – each lasting over twenty-four hours. JD's had been super-fast, due to his light weight and small head, although we suspected nothing at the time. So, we expected another long delivery. But the contractions intensified quickly, the midwives popped in and out, taking measurements, "six centimetres," then "seven centimetres," like a submarine on a dive. I did my best to help, as most fathers do – stay conscious, hold hands, encourage, mop brow. Apart from delivering the baby, there is not much more a father can do in a Maternity Ward.

At half-past five in the morning, Georgina Alma

Carmel arrived in the world, after only a few hours of pushing. Immediately, the midwife measured her head size, weighed her, and assured us, "she's fine – her head size is normal, maybe a little on the big side, and she weighs six pounds eleven ounces."

Relief swept over Liz's face, followed by joy. I think Liz saw the same expression on me, "thank God," we said in unison.

Roxanne, Victoria and JD now have a little sister to look after. Georgina has been born into a family with a special needs brother and we wonder how much that will affect her. Unlike many other children, she will not get as much attention as she should, and there is not much we can do about that. I hope she will adapt to her unique circumstances and, above all, know we love her as much as her siblings. Another new life and another uncharted journey begins.

# A RIDE IN AN AMBULANCE

March 31st 1996.

JD and I rode in an ambulance on the day after his fourth birthday. Completely unplanned and we wished it had not been necessary. Liz's parents, Reg and May, drove two-hundred-and-fifty miles from St Annes-on-sea to spend quality time with baby Georgina and their other grandchildren over the week of Passover. We just finished lunch and washed up when JD started to fit. I saw the usual signs - a look of terror in his eyes, shallow breathing followed by the terrible twitching and uncontrollable jerking. I cannot suppress a sickening feeling of helplessness when I see JD so distressed at something I cannot see, hear or understand. All I can do is hold him, speak softly and calmly.

I do not know what triggered the fit – it could have been the bright sunlight outside, lack of sleep the previous night, no one will ever know because JD cannot tell us. Normally, his fits last between two and five minutes, but this one kept on going, for over ten. As a last resort, we administered Diazepam with his emergency rectal tube. There is nothing worse than pinning my son down while Liz removes his nappy, unwraps the pre-filled syringe and injects the contents in his rectum. All the while he looked at me, his pupils expanded transformed into deep pools of black, soaked in fear. The Diazepam was supposed to knock him out, but it had no effect, so we phoned for an ambulance. Then JD stopped breathing and began turning blue.

"What do we do?" I shouted in panic.

"I don't know!" Liz screamed, cradling Georgina in her arms.

"Is he going to die?" Roxanne asked anxiously.

"No," we snapped.

In desperation, I gazed out of the kitchen window and prayed silently for the ambulance, while May and Reg prowled about trying to find something to do. They were helpless, just like us, unable to do anything but watch the drama unfold. In that moment, I saw their pain.

The ambulance pulled up, blue light flashing. I darted out of the house carrying JD in my arms with Liz in pursuit. Suddenly, he gave a sharp gasp and began breathing. Maybe jolting him up and down while running resuscitated him. A healthy pink flooded into his face. From inside the ambulance, the paramedics checked him over and insisted on taking him to the hospital as a precaution. As the doors closed, Liz urged me to call her from the hospital as soon as possible, and the ambulance sped off.

Liz spent an uncomfortable night in the over-heated children's ward while the medical team kept him under observation. He was discharged in the morning.

The next day, the week ground to a start, with visits to customers, meetings to attend, presentations to give, reports to be written, and far more important things to do at home.

# THE PAEDIATRICIAN CALLS

Liz found herself back in the children's ward last night, this time with five-month-old baby Georgina, who had developed a chest infection. A month earlier, it was JD's turn to stay in an over-heated ward while I looked after his three siblings and Liz's anxious parents.

Memories of our last encounter with JD's paediatrician are painful ones. She proclaimed news of JD's condition when he was four months old.

"He will never walk or talk," she said then, brutally and honestly.

A few weeks later, she told us, "he will need one-to-one care for the rest of his life." Again, delivered without pulling any punches. More weeks passed and she informed us of his epileptic seizures and the virus that still infected his brain. We dreaded those visits to her clinic. But we accepted that honesty hurts, especially when it concerned our precious child, so we understood she had little choice but to be direct. There was no room for pussyfooting, but her bedside manner could have been better.

The morning after a sleepless night, Liz waited beside baby Georgina in the children's ward. Her condition had improved, and she was expecting Georgina to be discharged after the paediatrician had passed around the ward. Six other children lay in cots with anxious parents waiting to be inspected. The door flew open, and JD's paediatrician entered with a posse of junior doctors and nurses scuttling in her wake. Liz watched as she approached the first bed and the parents leaned forward in anticipation. She spoke and the parents' faces whitened, mum reached for a handkerchief and, with tears rolling down her cheeks, held it to her face. Dad sat expressionless and frozen in shock.

The paediatrician moved to the next bed and studied her notes before speaking. The pattern was repeated only, this time, both parents held their faces in their hands after she had departed. Each visit lasted only a few minutes and terminated with every parent visibly distraught, Liz explained. Eventually, the paediatrician approached Georgina and Liz, looked at her notes, then with a broad smile of recognition announced, "oh, hello Jeremy's mum! I didn't expect to see you here!"

On this occasion, we were the lucky ones who escaped brutally delivered news, and Georgina was duly discharged.

# THE CASE OF THE MISSING WARDROBE

July 1996.

"It's not fair!" protested Roxanne, "why should she get a room with a clothes cupboard?"

"She" was Victoria, Roxanne's seven-year-old younger sister, who was due to inherit our old bedroom, with its integrated wardrobe, when our house extension was completed.

A frantic six months had passed with the house in disarray as builders knocked down walls, put up new walls and stud partitions, and trampled about, upstairs and downstairs. Brickie, Chippy and Sparky came and went, leaving their handiwork behind – a two-floor extension. Liz and I moved into the new upstairs bedroom, bequeathing our old room to Victoria. Roxanne lost her wardrobe, demolished to pave the way to our new bedroom.

All the kids have their own rooms now, even little Georgina, for the first time in her eight months. For four years, we shared our sleeping quarters with JD, and then with Georgina. JD moved into the box room next door nine months ago, to make way for his little sister. He will not move to his new room downstairs until he has added a lot of weight and becomes too heavy to carry. We have two baby alarms, one for Georgina and a second for JD, so we can react quickly to any fits he may have during the night.

In the meantime, we arbitrate between Roxanne and Victoria, on the case of the missing wardrobe.

"I'm older than her!" Roxanne continued.

"Well?" Liz interrupted, "what's that got to do with anything?"

"I've got more clothes than her," Roxanne answered, "*and* they're bigger!"

"So?"

"Well, I need more space to keep them," she concluded.

We could not fault her logic, but we had discussed the impending move months before, and both girls had agreed to it. Maybe we did not mention the bit about sacrificing part of her room for a greater cause. Sibling rivalry was alive and well in our household, much to JD's amusement. He vocalises and shakes his head at the antics of his sisters, especially when a full-blown row is raging.

# DOUBLING UP

August 1996.

Our first holiday with two cots - one for JD and a second for little Georgina. We doubled up on everything, as though we had twin babies instead of one. Two cots, two buggies, two change bags and two sizes of nappies, two change mats, two sets of food for the seriously small, and so on. Then we added six suitcases stuffed with clothes, toys, beach towels, beach toys, and loaded everything into the Midi van. Liz and I sat up front, Victoria and JD in the middle, and Roxanne and Georgina in the back row, with the luggage behind and on the unoccupied seats.

We are seasoned campers in France, but this year we upgraded to a caravan on a campsite near Deauville on the North coast. JD still wakes up frequently in the night and, as he has grown bigger, so has his voice. From inside a tent, his crying would wake up others sleeping under canvas, so we opted for a deluxe thirty-foot caravan with three bedrooms, a kitchen, toilet, shower and dining area. The thicker walls should help muffle his cries at night. Roxanne and Victoria shared one bedroom, JD slept in one of the cots in the other room, with the baby alarm, and Georgina slept in the second cot in our bedroom.

We brought the cots outside at daytime, so that JD and Georgina could enjoy the sunshine, and JD could watch the tree branches sway in the breeze. The older girls were independent enough to amuse themselves for most of the time, making friends easily and running off on a promise to "be back for lunch," and then forgetting. Continental campsites are perfect for children. Liz and I drifted into our holiday routine where JD and I hunt and gather food from the shops while Liz looks after Georgina.

We visited the beaches along the Normandy coast, but often arrived well after the other beachgoers. The best spots are reserved for those who can be away two minutes after uttering the suggestion "let's go to the beach." We, however, can take as much as an hour to get away, so our journeys must be planned days in advance. Fortunately, we were spoiled by plentiful disabled parking bays with the wonderfully worded put-down, *"si vous prenez ma place, alors vous-pouvez prendre ma handicap"* (*"if you take my place, then you can take my handicap"*) emblazoned in big blue letters. Not once did we experience what we see so often at home – rows of disabled bays occupied by cars without blue badges. A few carefully chosen words can be an effective deterrent.

The beach tent was a crucial piece of equipment, shielding JD from sand blasts and for privacy while changing his nappy. He lay happily on a soft beach rug beneath the tent roof, illuminated by the bright sun, watching it ripple as the wind gusted by, and listening to the waves, splashes and screams of children. Simple things we take for granted are so significant and meaningful to him that we cannot help but notice them ourselves.

# NEW MEDICINE

November 1996.

"Two fits every week is still too much," said the paediatrician.

"Should we increase the dose?" Liz asked.

"No," she replied, "we've tried varying the dosage already. I would suggest a different medication."

We looked concerned, so she continued quickly, "Epilim or sodium valproate, I think would be best."

"So, when should we start him on it?" I asked.

"It's not that simple. He will need weaning off Tegretol while gradually increasing his Epilim dosage. The good news is that Epilim is available in crushable tablet form."

Great. More chemicals for my son. Sometimes, he eats more chemicals than proper food. But the anti-convulsant is, by far, his most important medicine. He will "almost certainly fit" if he misses just one dose, according to his paediatrician. Medicating JD is the most stressful part of our day, and of his day, I suspect. Mornings are the worst because he must be ready, suited and booted, by eight o'clock so Julie can take him to school. It is such a terrible rush. Roxanne and Victoria have had to be less dependent on us for the basics, like getting themselves up in time and making their own breakfasts. But, if JD is late waking up, then food, drink and medicine must be tipped into him with minimum spillage.

We try so hard not to show any sign of stress in the

mornings. If we do, then it is picked up by the kids, including JD, who will refuse to cooperate if he thinks he is being hurried. But I think that is something that most children do anyway. JD is a rebellious child, in his own quiet way.

# WHO ARE YOU?

February 1997.

"It's busy today," I said, pulling into Warwick Services car park.

We were in the Midi van on our way back home after a long weekend with Liz's mum and dad in St Annes. Heavy traffic on the M6 and M40 convinced me that everyone on the planet was migrating south. All ten disabled bays by the service station entrance were occupied.

"It's very unusual for all of them to be taken," said Liz, "I wonder if they all have blue badges."

"I could have a look," I suggested.

"One of these days, someone will get aggressive with you," she replied. She was right. My habit of challenging anyone parked in a disabled bay without a blue badge could land me in a prison cell or in a hospital bed. Many offenders had been rightfully chastened, so I hoped. On one occasion, I confronted a tattooed white van man, built like a pocket battleship and with hairs on the palms of his hands,

"Err, excuse me," I said boldly.

"Yer, wot mate," he replied.

"Do you have a blue badge?"

He froze with his back to me, and for a moment, I considered the possibility that he would drag his knuckles off the ground and use them for a bout of facial reconstruction. Instead, he just walked off without answering. Counting myself lucky, I whispered meekly, "well, I'll take that as a 'no' then."

On this occasion, we waited in the Midi van behind the row of parked cars in the disabled bays, desperate to get out so we could feed JD and the kids. After two minutes, a perfectly mobile twenty-something couple approached a car. The man jangled some keys by the driver's door.

I got out of the van and approached him. He froze. Looking up at his six feet plus, I asked, "do you have a blue badge?"

Looking down his nose, he replied, "and who are you?"

His tone made me snap, "it doesn't matter who I am – do you have a blue badge?"

He smirked and opened the door while his partner clambered into the passenger seat.

"I have a seriously disabled boy in my van behind you who needs to have his medicine and I can't give it to him because you are taking up his parking space," I screeched.

They sat in their car while I ranted outside, "perhaps you would like his disability as well as his parking space?"

And with that parting shot, they drove off, with a cloud of shame raining down on them for all to see.

# IS THIS YOURS?

August 1997.

For a change from our annual two-week camping holiday, we stayed for five days in a log cabin on the Euro Disney resort, a few miles East of Paris, with a four-day pass to the theme park for the rides and full Disney experience.

While Roxanne and Victoria were trusted to look after each other on the more daring rides, Liz, JD, Georgina and I hopped on the gentler ones. The teacups were a hit, as was the Pirates of the Caribbean, with its star-studded Planetarium ceiling and special effects. We re-convened at the Rainforest Café for a pricey junk-food lunch, except JD, who supplemented his with Marmite sandwiches while vocalising his approval of the décor with extra-long "aaaahhh" and "errrhhh" sounds.

I tore off a chunk of sandwich and popped it into JD's waiting mouth.

"Look at that boy, mummy," exclaimed a young boy, holding his mother's hand.

Mummy said nothing.

"What's wrong with him, mummy?" the boy persisted.

"Shhh," said mummy, and hurried past with the rest of the family in tow.

We are used to children staring at JD in amazement, or asking questions about him loudly, for their parents to field. His disability is more obvious, unlike when he was younger and indistinguishable from other small children. He looks like someone with a physical and learning disability now. He dribbles continuously and shakes his head from side to side. His hands are folded over, like a praying mantis, the tell-tale sign of someone with cerebral palsy. But he is still my son and I really do not care about how he looks; I care about how he feels.

Euro Disney is a nightmare for parents but a dream for children and, it seems, for the many childless adults too. After only two days, Liz and I were Disney-ed out. There was only so much glitz and junk food we could take, especially when it was in our faces and on our plates "twenty-four-seven". But we soldiered on, knowing it was the kids' holiday too. Judging from the expressions on other parents' faces, that was their experience too.

With great relief, we packed up and left for a second campsite in the French countryside, a *proper* campsite, near Saumur in the Loire valley. Like last year, we booked a caravan, out of consideration for the neighbours. And, just like previous years, we took JD and Georgina out shopping in the morning only to return and find our caravan stuffed full of Roxanne's and Victoria's friends. On one memorable day, we counted seventeen children, of all shapes and sizes, crammed into our bedroom. I shut the door quickly and sought refuge in the tiny galley kitchen.

"Hallo," said a small voice, "who are you?"

The voice belonged to another one of their many friends, a grubby little girl of about six, helping herself to a glass of juice from our fridge.

"I'm the proprietor of this fine establishment," I replied, sweeping my arms around the caravan with a dramatic gesture.

She gulped down the juice, blinked at me, and fired her parting shot, "you're weird," and disappeared into the bedroom with the other children. Georgina, an early toddler, followed her into the room clutching her La-La Tellytubby toy preciously.

"Well, that's them sorted for the rest of the day," Liz said.

The weather was excellent, and JD spent many happy hours outside rummaging around the forests, shopping and mingling with his sisters' new friends. The swimming pool was less popular with him because the water was too cold and there was nowhere to lie him down safely.

On our penultimate day, we lost Georgina, and to make matters worse, we did not know we lost her until someone else found her.

"Have you seen Georgina?" Liz asked, with panic on her face.

I searched inside the caravan, under the beds, inside the small shower cubicle, in the kitchen cupboards, then outside and under the caravan. Roxanne and Victoria hurtled outside, "we'll find her," they yelled as if they were embarking on a hunting expedition.

As they were about to leave, the grubby girl I had such an unrewarding conversation with arrived, holding Georgina's hand.

"Is this yours?" she asked, nodding towards Georgina, dummy in mouth and La-La held against her chest.

"Could you leave it over there, please," I said, pointing to the caravan doorstep.

The seriousness of the episode hit us both. It could have ended far worse. We were lucky. How could we let our twenty-one-month-old daughter just walk off like that? Most of our time and attention is given to JD and too little to our other three children. We must learn to spread ourselves about more.

# BREAKING DOWN WALLS

September 1997.

For three years, JD has been at a special needs school, Portesbery in Camberley, where he mixes with other children with learning difficulties. It is a big school, considering its one hundred pupils are all one-in-sixty-thousand children, like him. They start their education at two years of age and leave at nineteen, when they transition to adult care services. He attends every weekday from half-past eight until half-past three. Julie collects him at eight o'clock and Liz or I bring him home after work. During the week, he has regular physiotherapy and hydrotherapy to help muscle development and encourage better posture, to compensate for the time he spends sitting and lying down.

Despite these benefits, we stated our case for him to attend the Annie Lawson School, a Jewish special needs school with equivalent facilities to Portesbery, but our Local Education Authority saw differently, on cost grounds. Every year for the past three years, we lost our argument for the same reason. They do not consider "religious grounds" strong enough to justify the extra cost. So, we looked elsewhere to provide a Jewish education, to top-up his secular education. We found the solution in the most obvious place – the Jewish Sunday School, known as 'cheder', at our synagogue.

Today, JD started his first day at cheder, where he

mixes with other Jewish children. It is a bonus for him to be among his extended family at North West Surrey Synagogue (NWSS). I take his older sisters there every Sunday morning, so one extra small person in the car makes little difference. Apart from that, JD loves riding in the car and going to synagogue. Every time he sees the trees lining the car park, he grins toothily and chuckles. It has become a second home.

His cheder class has six children aged between four and five years, one of whom also has special needs. Creative methods are needed to catch and maintain JD's attention since he is often in his own world. Debbie, JD's cheder class teacher, has more than enough skill, care and patience to cope.

Even though we could not convince the LEA to place JD at the Annie Lawson School, receiving his formal Jewish education at NWSS is an opportunity to break down walls. Walls that separate those with disabilities from those without disability, from the mainstream, the normal, the fortunate. In fact, it is vital to stop the walls being built in the first place. That means bringing JD out into the open where he can be seen. It means talking about him, encouraging others to talk to him and ask questions about him, not holding him back from any of the things that everyone else does, even though he may not be able to do them by himself. This must start at the earliest possible age, by socialising with small children who have no preconceptions or biases. Children ask questions if they do not understand or if they see anything that is not normal. The answers, provided they are given and given properly, help them to understand that it *is* normal. Walls are built when people with disabilities are kept out of sight and no explanations for their condition are asked for and, therefore, ever given. They become a mystery and something to be avoided. This is a chance for JD to be in a class with other children, who will ask about him, understand him and interact with him. It will be an experience that will be beneficial to JD and to them, giving them a better understanding of disability, and encourage them to care and not stare.

# A RIDE IN THE FOREST

Late September 1997.

JD is having a big impact on his sisters. A few weeks ago, his ten-year-old sister Roxanne suggested we enter Norwood's annual cycle ride and raise some money for the charity. Liz and I were shaken from our belief that he would go through life with us fighting his battles, not his sisters. It was a wake-up call that they cared for him and wanted to do something to show it.

"Can I come too?" asked Victoria, "I can cycle as good as her."

"As *well* as, not as *good* as," I replied – I am a stickler for proper English.

"Yes, but I want to go too," she said hopefully.

"There's no cheder in the morning," Liz interjected, "so you could take them, and I'll look after JD and Georgina."

"Good idea, my mum and dad could come over and help," I suggested.

So, that was the plan for today, cast in stone weeks ago. Just like everything else we do, it needs planning weeks in advance.

With three bikes bundled in the back of the cavernous Midi van, Roxanne, Victoria and I arrived at Norwood's event tent, just outside the grounds of Broadmoor Hospital. We handed over our registration forms and donations, collected our T-shirts and listened to the safety briefing. An equally cavernous Range Rover would follow behind, in case there were any accidents.

The weather forecast was good for the first day of an English Autumn – warm and overcast. We followed the track into Swinley Forest with Roxanne in front and me following Victoria. I estimated we would need about three hours, plus or minus an hour, to complete the fifteen-mile circuit. The thirty other riders soon passed us, some of whom looked a bit too serious for the event, wearing top-of-the-range mountain bikes, lycra shorts, re-hydration bottles (*aka* 'water bottles'), and streamlined crash helmets. The Range Rover struggled to be as slow as us.

The going was good until we came to a long dip in the forest track. I led the way, freewheeling down the slope, with Roxanne behind and Victoria following. I saw the quagmire of mud at the bottom of the dip thirty feet before I rolled into it, and shouted, "keep pedalling through, whatever you do, don't stop." I pushed through to the other side, stopped and turned around to shout words of encouragement. Roxanne stood up on her pedals and pumped her way through the sticky mud.

"Well done sweetie," I said.

Victoria's progress was more cautious. She stopped half-way through the mud and toppled over to one side. I squelched over and pulled her out with a 'shloop'.

Plastered on one side with viscous, treacly mud, she screamed, "it's not fair!"

Sometimes, there is no justice in this world. She was doing a good deed for Norwood, the organisation who could care for her brother in the future, and a mudpie in the face was her reward. I consoled her as best as I could and gestured to Roxanne to wear a serious face.

"Is she OK?" asked the driver in the Range Rover.

"I think so," I said, "just a bit shocked."

"Would she like a lift in the Rover?" he offered, "you can come along too if you like."

Victoria stopped screaming and her face lit up, "yes

please!" I loaded her bike into the back and agreed to meet her at the finish line.

Norwood's publicity team took a snap of us at the end, with me beaming from ear-to-ear. My two daughters sacrificed a Sunday for their brother. As JD grows, so do my worries for his future. But his sisters will be there for him. Just because he is different, he is still afforded the same love and attention as his more independent peers are by their siblings.

# EATING OUT

December 1997.

Eating out is Grandma's and Grandpa's treat. Every year after Boxing Day, we drive two hundred and sixty miles up north and stay in a hotel near Liz's parents' seaside apartment in St Annes. We are joined by Liz's brother David, sister-in-law Rosalind, and their four nippers Rhiannon, Madeline, Lydia and Arthur, who come up from Bedford. With eight small children and six adults, it is an ear-shattering and expensive lunch in Salter's Wharf, paid for by Grandpa. The massive pub is the only place in town that can cope with JD's special seating, changing and feeding requirements. He needs plenty of room, well away from other diners, unless they relish unexpected side-orders of airborne semi-masticated and dribble-coated chunks of bread and Marmite.

It takes oodles of time to feed JD. Liz and I have an arrangement whereby one of us feeds him while lunch goes from hot to luke-warm, and the other eats theirs while it is hot. Then we swap over. This year was different because two-year-old Georgina needed assistance as well. So, after JD and Georgina had finished, we tucked into our cold roast beef, Yorkshire pudding, roast spuds and congealed cold gravy. Hot dinners are a thing of the past, as are unhurried meals. We eat quickly, while we can, stuffing our faces as if it is our last meal on Earth, while preaching, "don't bolt your food!" to our children. I can demolish a full plate in two minutes - a habit I cannot break, even when I am away from the kids.

Our reward for eating out is to see how much JD enjoys the lively surroundings. He will occasionally eat something from the main menu, usually donated by Liz or me, provided it is cut up into small chunks that can be swallowed without chewing. Unfortunately, more enjoyment means more headshaking and more unwanted little food packages hurtling across the room. To protect other diners, we equip ourselves with a tower of muslin towels. We wrap one about his neck, one on his lap and distribute others over his buggy as a shield.

Our priority is to make sure JD eats as much as he can. He is grossly underweight for a five-year-old boy, so we let him have his own way and sit him on the floor if that is what he wants. It is not ideal, but if it works, then it is a success.

# THE QUIET COMMUNITY

March 28th 1998.

Turn back the clock six years to a time when we knew no one with a serious learning or physical disability. We never asked questions about them and were unaware of the thriving community that loves, protects and supports people with disabilities. Occasionally, we would see someone in a wheelchair being assisted by a carer, but we never thought about how well they managed. They mingled briefly with the mainstream community, and then disappeared quietly from sight.

JD changed all that. We have become full lifetime members of the quiet community. He opened its doors and showed us that every member has a unique, often heart-rending and tragic, story to tell. He has many friends at Portesbery School, who we know and talk to. We have met other parents in similar situations to us, struggling, coping, leaning on others at desperate moments, carrying on with grim determination and *never ever* giving up.

We are acutely aware of how different the quiet community is. Our public transport system does not make it easy for JD to use the same trains, busses and airplanes as the mainstream. Access to play areas, parking, shops and swimming pools is more difficult and time-consuming. But, over time, we have built friendships with people we otherwise would have never met.

Today, JD celebrated his sixth birthday, two days early.

His best friend Stephen, from Portesbery School, and his carer, Kate, came to his party. Our hallway was turned into a parking lot for buggies as we sat at the table filled with tuna mayonnaise, Marmite sandwiches and birthday cake. In a darkened room, the cake was carried in, glowing with six sparkling candles.

Kate burst into song, "Happy birthday to ….."

"Ooo," Stephen said, eyes closed.

"Happy birthday to … ."

"Ooo," he repeated.

We finished the song together, with Stephen completing each line.

"Can Stephen talk?" I asked.

"No," Kate replied, "but he likes finishing things."

Stephen is physically larger and heavier than JD, but that is no surprise, given that JD weighs only twenty-two pounds. Stephen can obviously hear but is blind and has low muscle tone, so his arms and legs flop like a rag doll.

"What's Stephen's condition?" I asked. In our quiet community of carers, "condition" is a general term covering a broad range of physical and learning disabilities. Any question about condition also implies the cause of the disability, so the answer is never short.

"He was brain-damaged at birth," she answered, "and a few months later, his mum died in a car crash."

Six years ago, if someone had recounted such a tragic tale about the boy I sat next to, I would have drowned in awkward silence or changed the subject. Like JD, Stephen would be helplessly dependent on others all his life. And his mother was no longer there to love him. And how on Earth did his dad cope with the double tragedy? I was stabbed by sorrow for Stephen.

"His dad's alive and well," she added, spooning cake into Stephen's mouth, "but he's away a lot."

"What does he do?"

"He works for a Formula One racing team and goes to the Grands Prix, he's in Brazil at the moment."

JD and Stephen sat beside each other tucking into cake, with our assistance, as we talked.

"Errrr…," JD vocalised.

"Ohhh…," Stephen replied.

Their vocalising swung back and forth, with the occasional chuckle for variety. We did not know what they were talking about – maybe they shared a mutual appreciation of the chocolate cake. But it was good to hear them practice their conversational skills. The weather was kind, so we put the garden rug and pop-up tent in the garden and laid them side-by-side. JD has a slight advantage over Stephen - he can crawl slowly, occasionally over-balancing and tumbling forward. He can also reach out and grasp objects. This time, Stephen was the object of his attention, and he grabbed him by his T-shirt. They clearly like each other's company.

They are among a quiet community of soulmates.

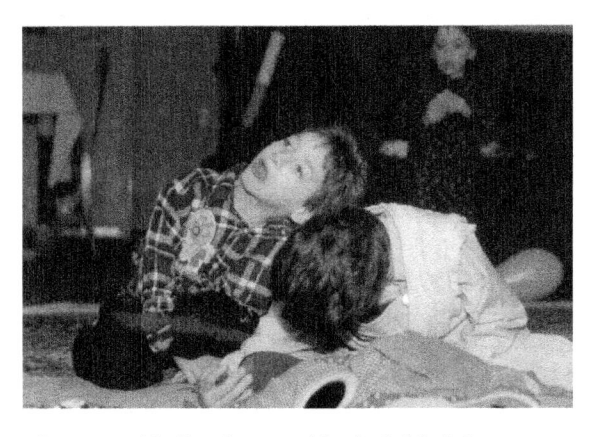

Jeremy with Stephen on his sixth birthday party

# SUN, SEA AND KINDNESS

August 1998.

Summer holidays are always something to look forward to, even if Liz and I need another one after returning. But holidays are for the memories they make, so the effort is worthwhile. Our choice of location depends on several things – it must be warm, easy to get to, provide ample parking right next to our accommodation, be near a hospital in case JD has a seizure, and popular with the kids. We also like to spend time on a beach or have easy access to a warm swimming pool. These are the minimum requirements for someone with JD's condition.

Over the years, we have had some good holidays on campsites in France. Driving has never been a problem. The children travel well and enjoy listening to the 'Monsters, Cats, Spiders and Flies' and 'Food Tape' CDs in the car. The roads in France are much clearer than the English roads, so the journey there and back is part of the fun. And the food and wine are better and cheaper.

This summer we spent two weeks in a caravan on a Eurocamp site on the west coast of France, a few miles from the Côte Sauvage ('wild coast'). A long wide sandy beach dished up monster-sized waves for adults and surfers, and lakes of warm seawater trapped by sand banks for the girls, JD and me to paddle and float in. But getting on to the beach involved a lot of huffing and puffing. Dragging a pushchair with a six-year-old disabled boy, five large beach towels, beach tent, beach boat and a heavy change bag proved to be easier than pushing it over soft sand in the full heat of day. I managed on my own, while Liz and the girls carried the picnic basket, beach toys and other accoutrements to our chosen patch of Blighty-a-la-plage-de-France.

JD would not go anywhere near the big waves. He let me know that by vocalising his unease and wrapping his arms about my neck tightly saying, "get me outta here!"

"OK JD, you win – they are a bit dangerous," I conceded, "it isn't called the wild coast for nothing."

He basked in his inflatable boat, bobbing gently on a lake, looking cool in sunglasses, with the roar of distant waves and cries from ice-cream, peanut and fritter sellers in his ears, "a la glace! Chouchou! Beignets!"

Leaving the beach at the end of the day was as much of a struggle as arriving. A middle-aged man pulling a pushchair loaded with disabled boy in sunglasses, a stack of towels and a tent across a wide expanse of sand, is a rare sight. Inclined at a forty-five-degree angle, my arms locked on the pushchair handles and my eyes faced the sand. Suddenly, a group of French sun-seekers sprang to my aid and carried the pushchair with all its contents a hundred yards to the beach boards and bid, "bon vacance."

Such random acts of kindness are manifestations of the 'JD effect'. I am convinced that he unwittingly promotes international co-operation and détente by being in the right place at the right moment.

Kindness knows no borders.

# GRANDPARENTS

March 1999.

I often wonder what our parents feel about our struggles with JD. I catch glimpses from the things they say. Liz's dad and JD's grandpa, Reg, frequently adds, "…when he's bar mitzvah, PG" ("PG" is his abbreviation of "Please God") when we talk on the thirty-minute drive to synagogue together. It is a telling thing to say - he wants JD to lead as normal a Jewish way of life as possible. He wants him to be accepted by his Jewish community and, most importantly, Reg wants to be there to see it happen at his bar mitzvah. But JD is only seven years old, so he has six years to wait before that event, if indeed, it ever happens.

My mum and JD's nana, Kathleen, likes to remind me of how handsome JD is. She wants me to see the positives, no matter how small they are. It is her message of hope to me, that all is not lost, that he is still someone to love. It is her responsibility, as my mother, to support her child in whatever way she can. Showing me hope, and therefore encouragement to continue, is her way.

Parents never stop worrying about their children, Liz and I know this is true with our four. The worries change as they age, but they are always there. When they are babies, it is simple. The maxim 'happiness is a full belly and an empty botty' often works when they cry. The problem is at one end or the other, but it is frustrating when that does not work. When they are small children, parents worry about them for different reasons. Are they climbing the stairs? Can they reach the hot stove? Can they toddle out the front door? As they become more independent, we worry more and more about their *feelings*, as well as their health and safety. Are they happy at school? Will they be safe staying out until eleven o'clock on a Friday night? What will our worries for our children be when they are adults? The only clues I have are from what I see in Reg, May (Liz's mum), Basil (my dad) and Kathleen.

We worry about JD as if he were a baby, because he has a lot in common. He cannot communicate his problems and is not mobile. Our biggest worry are his fits because they are life-threatening. And our parents worry about us worrying about him. The difference between our worries and theirs are that they cannot do much to resolve them, except say the things they do, in the hope it will make us worry less.

Last Wednesday night was the first night of the Passover festival, known as Seder night, or 'Jewish Christmas' because it is the biggest event in the Jewish calendar. It is traditional to have a big meal with family and friends, at which we read the story of the rise and fall of the Jewish people in biblical times, sing songs, perform strange customs, drink four cups of wine and eat unfamiliar food like boiled eggs in salt water, raw horseradish and parsley, unleavened bread or 'matzah'. We always have Seder night at home with the children, Liz's mum and dad, my mum and dad, Liz's brother's family of six, and the occasional guest or guests. There were twenty people at our Seder on Wednesday. I lead the Seder at the head of the table, with JD by my side and Reg on the other. There was plenty of opportunity for Reg and Kathleen to express their hopes.

"So, who knows what the four questions are?" I asked, referring to the four questions that are always sung at the start of the Seder.

"Will JD be bar mitzvah?" someone answered, a little flippantly.

"Yes, PG," said Reg.

"He's certainly handsome enough to have one," added my mum.

# RE-BOOTING THE GAWPERS

September 1999.

We take JD out as much as possible – he gets restless and bored when indoors for too long. He plays with the curtains beside the patio door, looking forlornly at the tall pine trees, the sky and clouds, telling us where he would rather be. He comes to synagogue and gets lots of attention from our friends there. He has plenty of walks, attends all the family get-togethers, and goes shopping – both the *real* kind when we buy stuff, and the *pretend* kind when we flit from shop to shop with no intent to buy, or "grazing," as Roxanne calls it.

Shoppers react to JD in a variety of interesting ways. Many do not even notice him, which is pretty normal. Some see him and pretend they have not, possibly because they do not know how to engage with him. Others glance at him, then their eyes roam up to me, trying to determine why he is the way he is. Some will stop and talk to him, which is an absolute joy. Then there are the gawpers, individuals and sometimes entire families who freeze on the spot and stare at the creature from another planet. Either they are oblivious to their behaviour or just do not care. They do not see JD as a person, but as some kind of rare exhibit.

Gawpers demand special treatment to shake them from their stupor, not for their sakes', but for JD's. I do not like being stared at, so why should he? Something must be done. Here are some tips.

First, try the 'circus treatment'. Stop pushing, stand still and call to them, "roll up! Fifty pence to see the rare exhibit!"

If that fails, then apply the 'reverse goldfish'. Kneel beside JD, point at the gawpers and say, "fascinating aren't they JD? Regard their plumage!"

If neither treatment effects a cure, then we exercise the 'joinem' remedy, from the maxim "if you can't beat them, join 'em". Spin JD around, scan the horizon and cry out, "what are they staring at JD?"

Thankfully, I have never deployed all three. But when successful, the gawpers snap out of their trance and carry on, as if they have been re-booted, like a computer.

# THERAPY WITH HORSES

April 2000.

JD has a team of therapists to keep busy. He sees a physiotherapist twice weekly at school, who helps his physical development. The speech and language therapist encourages his communication and choice-making skills using various techniques like eye-pointing, sign language, picture cards, a 'Big Mac' device – a large blue button that says "yes" when pressed and a red button that says "no." Liz and I attended a Makaton sign language course at his school last week. We learned some basic signs, like "hello," "goodbye," "good," "not good," "please," and "thank you." We practice them on JD and his friends at his school whenever we can.

He also has a music therapist, hydro-therapist and aromatherapist, who stimulate his senses with sound, water and smell. He has a reflexologist who helps him to balance and maintain a good posture. His occupational therapist instigated weekly trips to the Riding for Disabled Association stables in the Royal Military Academy in Sandhurst. As a result, JD can ride a horse, which is more than many able-bodied people can do. He can sit upright on a saddled pony, wearing a riding hat and riding boots, hold the reins and trot around the paddock for fifteen minutes, flanked by two helpers.

He has had so much therapy in six years at his special school, and the results are evident. We celebrate the slightest improvement. Every weekday for the past two weeks, Liz took JD to Finchley for his annual assessment at the Bobath Centre. They conducted an intensive assessment of his capability – what he can and cannot do and developed a programme of interventions to help him progress.

"You have a very clever son," Liz beamed when I got home from work on Friday.

"Why?" I asked, "what's he done?"

"His physio said, 'that boy has potential'," she said proudly.

"Why?" I asked sounding like a broken record, "what did he do?"

"She sat him on a wheelie chair and called to him."

"And?"

"He wheeled over to her!"

"What?!!"

"Not by much, but enough to qualify as a response and movement with purpose," she concluded.

This little action might not sound like it is worth raising a glass to, until one thinks about the processes that went on inside his head. First, he balanced himself on a wheelie chair with no sides or back. Secondly, he noticed the physiotherapist. Thirdly, he understood that she was beckoning to him, "oh, she's signalling to me." Fourthly, and probably the hardest part, he worked out the correct response, "she wants me to move forward, now how do I do that?" Finally, he worked out how to execute that response, "if I move my foot and push back, then I should go forward – like this – now, repeat on the other side." He worked all that out by himself.

My clever son. I am proud to be his dad.

# BLOODY STAIRGATE!

September 2000.

"Bloody stairgate! It's going to make me late," Roxanne complained, clambering with difficulty over the three-foot high obstacle barring her way downstairs.

Half-past seven on weekday mornings is when our house is at its most frenzied. Four children, ranging in age from four to thirteen, need to get to three different schools at the same time. JD was upstairs, crawling amidst the chaos, breakfasted and medicated already, waiting to be washed and changed, as Liz searched for Georgina's clean school uniform. Roxanne was right, the stairgate was a "bloody nuisance," but essential to prevent JD hurling himself down thirteen steps and a potentially serious injury. I often wonder if he senses danger or has a fear of heights, like I do.

Our family bathroom is the source of many battles for occupation. I picked JD up and carried him to our ensuite for a wash and scrub, just in time to see Victoria walk into the family bathroom, emerge a second later with Georgina in her arms, and deposit her outside. The door slammed shut and, in unison, the lock turned, and a scream of protest filled the narrow landing.

"I was there first!" four-year-old Georgina shouted through the door, beating it with her clenched fists.

"Well, I have to walk to school," came the reply from inside, muffled by the sound of teeth being brushed frantically.

"Er-her-her," chuckled JD at his sisters' antics.

"It's not funny Jeremy!" yelled Georgina.

Our three daughters have learned how to get along with each other and find peaceful resolutions to their conflicts. Liz and I are often pre-occupied with JD but, despite this handicap, they manage very well.

"Byeeee," came a shout from downstairs, as Roxanne rushed out of the house for her mile-long walk to school.

"See you later sweetie," from me and, "have a nice day," from Liz, too late.

I laid JD on our bed and turned on the TV for Telly Tubbies, a favourite of Georgina's and JD's. The deflection tactic worked. Georgina sat next to him while Liz consoled and dressed her. But nothing could help me brush JD's teeth. He kept his mouth firmly shut, turned his head away and swatted at the toothbrush. He resists all forms of restraint, even when it is for his own good. It is easier to brush his teeth and cut his nails after his evening bath when he is relaxed and drowsy. With time running out, I gave up, and mopped his face, neck and hands with a warm flannel to remove all traces of dribble.

"Julie will be here soon," Liz reminded me, "do you need help dressing JD?"

"No, it's OK," I answered, "are you taking Georgina to school, or am I?"

Liz and I have a flexible caring routine, and often take turns walking Georgina to school, four hundred yards away, while the other waits with JD to be collected by our child-minder Julie and driven to his special needs school.

"I will today," she replied, "will you still be here when I get back?"

My work is a fifteen-mile commute that can take between twenty and sixty minutes, depending on the M3 southbound traffic. Today, I needed to be in work for a ten o'clock meeting. I organise my meetings to be between late morning and early evening, so I can be home to help relieve the pandemonium. Once upon a long time ago, I was ambitious and wanted to be the company guru on AI, but children intervened, and my ambitions transferred from work to home.

"I need to leave by nine," I said, as I removed JD's soiled nappy, wiped him with an antiseptic tissue and slid a clean nappy underneath.

"OK, I might not see you until this evening then," said Liz, taking Georgina by the hand, "I must go to work straight after dropping Georgina off."

Liz returned to part-time working a few months after Georgina was born, nearly five years earlier. Four children and a mortgage needed regular feeding, and my income alone was insufficient. Besides, it gave Liz the opportunity to pursue her career in IT and forget about JD's and our other children's difficulties. We agree on many things, especially that we go to work for a rest.

I kissed Georgina on the cheek, and they headed downstairs, just as the front door opened.

"That'll be the door," I said to JD, "probably Julie."

"Er-her-her," JD chuckled, practicing his new sound.

Meanwhile, Victoria was still in the locked bathroom, making meticulous preparations before revealing herself to the outside world. Liz de-briefed Julie in the hallway downstairs and left, completing our daily changing of the guard ceremony. Shortly after, Julie came upstairs and gently persuaded Victoria to hurry. I picked JD up, wished Julie a hurried, "good morning," and carried him downstairs. Together, we put on his coat, leg splints, shoes, strapped him into his wheelchair, and checked his schoolbag for emergency Diazepam, eating and drinking record book, spare nappies and pseudo cream.

"All set?" I asked.

"We're ready to go," Julie answered, and turned the wheelchair about to face the front door.

I ruffled JD's hair as they rolled out the door, and up the path to Julie's car.

"I'm going to be late," announced Victoria from behind me.

"Would you like a lift?" I offered.

"I wouldn't have been late if that bloody stairgate hadn't been there!"

# CRAWLING

January 2001.

I am playing the guitar again, twenty years after my last pluck and strum. I want to make a real go of it and teach myself to read music, so I can play proper tunes, instead of sounding like a busker falling down a flight of stairs. JD encourages me. He crawls into the piano room, twenty feet from his favourite position by the lounge window, to see what is making such a racket. Then he arrives at my feet, sits up on his knees and grabs me with his left hand, never with his unused right. He either wants me to stop or wants to play the guitar too. Of course, I let him strum, ensuring that he does not hook his fingers around the strings. He often crawls over to his sisters, Victoria and Georgina, during their piano lessons, as if he wants lessons too. Whatever his reasons are, he responds well to music, as he has always done since birth.

The guitar and music books accompany JD into the bathroom every evening. He lies in the warm water and listens to my attempts at playing and singing at the same time. His eye contact is more prolonged, and he crawls around with a sense of purpose, as if he has worked out how to track sources of interesting sounds. It is another small step, or shuffle, along the long road to reach his full potential.

# THE BEAUTIFUL GAME

July 2001.

"It's Jeremy's turn," declared JD's team captain, placing the baseball bat on his lap and cap on his head.

Summer week at our synagogue means seven days of fun, games, songs and sleepovers for a Jewish community of children aged from eight years upwards. The teenage helpers plan and execute the week's most vigorous activities. This afternoon, they took advantage of the good weather and led an exodus of little ones to the nearby park for a game of rounders, or "it's baseball, but not as we know it," as the American contingent called it.

One of JD's namesakes propelled JD four hundred yards to the local park to join a disorderly line for team selection. The two captains, both named Jeremy, stepped forward to make their choices. JD was picked first on the basis that "the probability of victory was directly proportional to the quantity of Jeremys in the team." I wheeled him over to line up behind his captain. Children jumped up and down in excitement, and a few yelled, "pick me, pick me," as the selection continued. One ingenious small girl announced, "I'm Jeremy!" and was promptly chosen.

A helper placed four mats on the grass at equal distances, to form a square about fifteen yards across. Another tossed a fifth mat on the grass a few yards from first base, to mark the batter's place. JD's team fielded first, and his captain wheeled him to third base. I sat on a picnic rug off-pitch to watch. The batting team jostled for position behind the first batter, shouting out encouragement. The game started.

"Strike one!" shouted the umpire, not called Jeremy.

The bowler fed the ball, under-arm, to the small boy, clasping a bat half his size with both hands and swinging wildly.

With a "thwack!" the ball flew between second and third bases. Three out-fielders ran to fetch it. The boy hurtled towards first base, bat still in hand.

"Drop the bat!" came a collective reminder from his team, as the second batter stepped on to the mat.

Meanwhile, the out-fielders converged on the ball. "Third base! Third base!" urged the captain of the fielding team, standing beside JD. A boy picked it up and threw it as hard as he could, but it rolled to a stop, five yards short. A girl collected, carried it to third base and placed it in JD's hand. But it was too late, the batter had reached it safely. The game continued, the bowler adjusting his pace according to the size of the batter. The larger they were, the faster it was bowled, and the further it went when struck.

Another ball was struck with venom, and it sailed between second and third bases, falling mid-way between JD and the out-fielders, thirty yards back. JD and his captain turned around and raced after it, towards me. His face creased with laughter as the wheelchair bumped and clattered over the uneven grass. The captain picked the ball up and placed it on JD's lap, spun his wheelchair around and ran back, just as a covering fielder reached the vacant base and shouted, "Jeremy, throw it! Throw it!" I thought he meant JD, as did his captain, who ran all the way back, then wrapped JD's hand over the ball and handed it to the fielder.

Football, soccer, or 'the beautiful game', as it is called sometimes, could not be compared with this game. JD, my profoundly disabled boy, who would depend on others for the rest of his life, a member of the silent community of the disabled, never noticed, recognised or acknowledged, was accepted as an equal player, a member of their team. This was the *real* beautiful game.

# BACK PAIN

February 2002.

Only four weeks until JD's tenth birthday, but a casual observer would never guess he was that old. Much more like a three-year-old, if they judged age by size and weight. They might estimate his age at about six months, if they went by what he can do physically, verbally, and intellectually.

He sleeps upstairs in a bunk bed with a wooden bar along the side, to stop him rolling out. He wakes up every night, usually at that moment just before plunging into deep sleep. Then the alarm crackles into life and hauls us back to wakefulness. I think he is excited or happy about something, although we do not know what. He squeals with delight, chuckles, and bounces up and down on his knees on his bed. But he will inevitably start moaning, crying out and, ultimately, self-harming if no one goes to him. He makes a lot of noise for someone so small, but he is a lot bigger and louder than any baby I know.

JD has high muscle tone, meaning that his muscles are in an almost permanent state of tension. He clasps his arms close to his chest and his legs stiffen like poles when we change him. That is not conscious resistance, but his natural state. His arms and legs must be threaded through the sleeves of his clothes, or pulled through like long thick needles, if the muscle tension is too great. Most children have learned to dress themselves by the time they are JD's size or, at least, cooperate when being changed. But he has not learned that he cannot sit in his pyjamas all day, or go to bed in shirt, trousers and shoes. He may never learn, but we still try and explain the necessities of life to him.

"JD," I said as he lay on his bed, "I'm going to change you now because we must be out of the house in fifteen minutes."

"Errrhhh," JD vocalised. Being an optimist, I interpret his response as, "OK." If I were a complete pessimist, it would just be a noise. But that would make any conversation pointless, so I carried on.

"Good, so you know resistance is futile JD?" I joked, "we're going to cheder and the car leaves in fifteen minutes – be in it."

"Er-her-her," JD's possible laugh.

It is so easy to forget about posture when changing and lifting him. Bending over is a sure way to strain or pull a muscle, and Liz and I have done that many times, just as I did today – again. It was the classic scenario, where I had to take JD and Georgina to cheder (Jewish Sunday school). Liz fed and medicated JD while I loaded the car with his medicines, change bag and spare clothes, harried his siblings and got myself ready, just in time to carry him upstairs to wash and change him. Posture forgotten, I bent over and lifted him off the bed, and immediately felt a familiar stab of pain in my lower back. I knew the cause and knew it would take days to subside.

"Oh bollocks," I cursed at the shock and at my carelessness, "that was stupid."

On previous occasions, it had been when lifting him out of the car, out of the bath, and picking him up off the floor. The pain is a hindrance to getting anything done quickly - not that we could ever do anything quickly anyway. Every movement must be planned carefully when in pain.

"Too late now," I said, clutching JD close to my chest, with his head over my right shoulder, left arm over his back and right arm supporting his thighs.

"Now I need to turn through one hundred and eighty degrees, don't twist my upper torso, I must use my legs to turn around slowly."

"Now descend the stairs, one step at a time, slowly."

The word 'slowly' accompanies every action. So, we were late for cheder today - again.

# BIG BLUE BALL

May 2002.

We are the proud owners of a big blue ball, three feet in diameter. It rests in our lounge, taking up precious floor space, but it is another essential piece of equipment to help JD's limited mobility. We bought it on the recommendation of his physiotherapist, who spends an hour each day helping him improve co-ordination, flexibility and strength. She lies him on his back over the ball and rolls it gently back and forth and side to side. It must help his balance when horse-riding, which is what he does so well every Thursday evening.

Liz nagged Social Services about JD's habit of head-banging at nights. We think that it is another sign of his frustration because he cannot tell us what is upsetting him. All we can do is hold him and lie down with him until he settles. He sleeps in a normal bed with one long side against a wall, so there is a real possibility of him beating his head on solid brick or against the wooden bed frame. That prospect terrified us, and it must have galvanised Social Services into action. Within two weeks, they instructed two retired carpenters to design, craft and fit padding on his bed frame and against the wall. JD now sleeps in a padded bed. It has done nothing to prevent his self-harming habit, but at least it has removed one of the many dangers that arise as he grows.

Three more pieces of equipment for JD arrived in the

last month. First came a bigger standing frame, about the same size as a comfy armchair, but heavier and taller. An octagonal and mirrored ball pit arrived the following week, which also resides in our lounge. JD kneels at its side, staring at his reflection among all the brightly coloured plastic balls. It becomes the centre of his attention, unavoidable because of its size. But capturing and holding his attention is exactly what it is meant to do.

The final piece of equipment arrived last week - a tricycle with harnesses for strapping him in, clips to keep his feet on the pedals and a little pouch containing tools for adjusting. He went out on his inaugural ride yesterday in fine weather. It took fifteen minutes to fasten him to the saddle, clip his feet to the pedals and strap the helmet on his head, amidst a great deal of protest. But all resistance stopped when he started moving and felt the new sensation of rotating legs.

There is little unoccupied space left in our house, even with the extension built six years ago. But lack of space is a small price to pay for JD's wellbeing. When family or friends visit, we wheel the frame and tricycle into the music room, next to the piano, and roll the ball into the extension. And when they leave, it all rolls back into the lounge again.

# THE LADY IN DARK GLASSES

August 2002.

Why are there are more adults than children in Euro Disney? Parents could have a great time if they deposited their kids at the entrance, then scarpered off to see the sights of Paris and collected them later? The queues would be so much shorter, and the kids would have more rides. We were OK because we waited in the disabled queue for only a few minutes, while the able-bodied queued for over an hour. Separate queues for people like JD are one of the few perks of having a disabled child. In fact, they are much more than perks – they are essential. JD gets bored if he is still for too long, especially in the heat, and beats himself up. How many families standing in the long queues looked with envy at us, as we whistled past, wondering why JD was treated differently?

The campsite in Euro Disney is a village of log cabins. The area was deluged in rain and thousands of bright orange slugs slithered over the wooden veranda, the doorstep, pavements, and left slime trails on windows. To escape the luminous slug invasion, we popped to the indoor swimming pool for a dip in the hot jacuzzi. JD made happy noises floating on his back while being massaged by bubble jets. A lady in dark sunglasses watched for a short while and waded over, drawn to him by his infectious laughter. I held JD upright, half-floating in the water to face her, while she dropped under the water, and bobbed up with a "boo!" JD laughed hysterically at her antics. For ten minutes she entertained him, deriving as much joy from him as he did from her. She was worth hundreds of the Goofys, Minnie and Mickey Mouses patrolling the site who tried, heroically, to elicit a response from him, receiving no more than a cursory glance.

# VIGIL

November 2002.

"I think he's fitting at night," Liz said.

"It's possible," I said, "drifting off to sleep might trigger a seizure."

Sleepless nights are the norm in our house and have always been, ever since JD was born. Some people at work think I am exaggerating when I tell them.

"Burning the midnight oil again, Laurence?", one colleague suggested, when I arrived bleary-eyed and late one morning.

"Too much wine last night, I suspect," someone else said, then laughed.

If only they could understand the reality of caring for a severely disabled child.

I gave up protesting years ago. Only parents and employees with new-borns or 'problem children' are granted special dispensation. Our situation with JD is too alien to their experience. When I try to explain, they stare blankly or change the subject, which is understandable, because I was like them before JD changed everything.

But Liz bears the brunt of JD's wakefulness - she gets up to him in the night more often than me. Of course, it is vital we check on him because epileptic seizures deprive the brain of oxygen, and JD's brain has sustained enough damage already. If he is fitting at night, then we might need to increase his dosage of Epilim to let him, and us, sleep normally. But things are never that simple. Changing his medication "may not be necessary," explained JD's paediatrician, "we must confirm whether he is having seizures first."

So, his paediatrician set up an appointment for a sleep EEG at nine o'clock in the morning at the Royal Surrey Hospital in Guildford, with strict orders to keep him awake until then.

"We must run the test while he falls asleep," the paediatrician said, "so he must be tired when he arrives at the hospital."

"That should be no problem," Liz replied, "he'll be awake for most of the night anyway."

"But you *must* make sure he's really tired before the test starts," she emphasised.

"I'll have to keep him awake until the appointment then."

"I'm afraid so," the paediatrician agreed, "it will be an all-night vigil for both of you."

Afterwards, Liz and I discussed logistics. Who would participate in the vigil and who would stay behind with JD's sisters? Clearly, the one staying behind would be the one drawing the long straw. They would sleep while the one with the short straw struggled to stay awake and amuse JD through the long night. But, in her typical self-sacrificial manner, Liz volunteered.

"I'll do it," she said, "I can take him to the new twenty-four-hour Tesco in the night." She sounded almost enthusiastic.

"He'll like that – JD loves shopping," and so it was agreed.

I dozed off to sleep at one in the morning to the sound of Liz reading and singing to JD in his room. I did not hear her dress him two hours later, carry him downstairs, load his essential medicines, changing gear, spare clothes and lift him into the buggy and slip out the front door.

There was no JD there in the morning to feed,

medicate, wash and dress for school, just his three sisters, who do not need me anyway, since they can dress themselves, feed themselves and walk. So, the house was unusually calm at breakfast time. It was like a holiday, apart from having to go to work, fresh-faced for a change. I reminded myself that the opposite was the case for Liz, who spent the night wheeling JD up and down the shopping aisles while struggling to stay awake. By now, she would be with JD at the hospital waiting for his EEG.

Liz was crashed out on the bed when I returned home that evening. She reported to Julie that everything went according to plan. JD was wired up for his EEG and promptly dropped off to sleep during the test, as required. They monitored his brain activity for two hours, and no retakes were necessary.

"My clever son," I said, "he passed a test first time."

# BIKE

December 2002.

The Jewish festival of Hannukah, the Festival of Lights, falls around Christmas time. It commemorates the recapture of the Temple from the occupying Assyrians in Israel in 168 BCE. It is traditional to buy presents for family and friends at Hannukah, but Liz and I decided that JD's present would be combined with his birthday present at the end of March. The unusual decision was taken because his present was big, expensive, and useful - a custom made and beautifully engineered 'Duet' tandem bike.

The Duet is an adult-sized wheelchair with a clip-on bike frame. JD is strapped in the wheelchair, and I pedal from behind. The bike has seven gears, a small maintenance kit, a dynamo, lights, reflectors, mudguard, bell, handlebar-operated brakes and tough Perspex covers to stop him sticking his fingers in the wheels. We ordered the contraption from London Recumbent Cycles in Dulwich, having made several journeys to make sure it would be right for him.

His special bike arrived this week and I could not resist taking JD for a spin at the earliest opportunity. Waiting until his birthday would waste valuable fun time. We took only short excursions, owing to bad weather. The bike is easy to pedal while on level ground but much harder on even the slightest incline. JD is still terribly underweight for a ten-year-old boy, thirty-one pounds, or the same as an average three-year-old, which is heavy enough to make a difference, especially as the bike weighs a hundred pounds.

On an unusually warm and sunny English winter's day, I loaded JD's special bike into the car and headed to Swinley Forest for a longer trial. Our five-mile trip along gravel tracks was a spectacular success. JD chuckled constantly, as we freewheeled at twenty miles per hour downhill past pine and birch trees. Turning his head and looking up at me, his eyes said, "faster, faster!" and the faster we went, the louder and longer he laughed. His present has transformed him into a speed demon.

# DO THE CAR WASH

July 2003.

For the past eleven years we have holidayed on campsites in France. This year, we discovered our favourite - Le Brasilia, on the Mediterranean coast near the Pyrenees, close to the Spanish border.

In one of the most intense heat waves on record, we drove nine hundred miles from leafy Surrey to Canet-Plage, near Perpignan. The thermometer read thirty-seven Celsius when we left and climbed to forty-three at Toulouse. Fortunately, the car's air-conditioning rendered us oblivious to the raging furnace outside. Our cool little bubble whistled through Venusian temperatures without a complaint from its passengers. The 'Food Tape' CD followed the 'Monsters, Cats, Spiders and Flies' CD and world peace between Victoria and Georgina was maintained by judicious positioning of a clothes rack to keep them apart. By two o'clock in the afternoon everyone wanted feeding, so we pulled into an *aire* (service station) near Toulouse for a bite to eat.

We opened the car door and stepped into a Turkish bath. Liz and the girls headed quickly for the oasis of the restaurant, while I brought JD out to the intense heat and humidity. But there is no way to be quick about transferring an eleven-year-old severely disabled boy from a car to a wheelchair and loading his change bag and medicines. Nothing can be overlooked. Is he strapped in properly? Are his feet away from the wheels and on the rests? Fifteen minutes later, we rolled into the restaurant to discover it was just as hot and humid there as it was outside. JD was too lethargic to eat or drink, refusing all attempts by shaking his head.

"He must drink something," I worried, "otherwise he could have a fit."

"Let me try," Liz said. We swapped seats, but JD closed his eyes, and his head rolled back.

A child's scream outside grabbed my attention. A group of small kids ran through an unused car wash twenty yards away.

"I have an idea," I said, and strapped JD back in his wheelchair and headed outside, with Roxanne, Victoria and Georgina following.

We raced over a small lawn towards the car wash. A blast of cool water from several side jets immediately washed away his lethargy. Running through the car wash a second time prompted fits of laughter. After his third trip, he shook his head, bounced in his seat, wanting more. A convoy of children followed us while a crowd of parents stood by. Car washes have many uses.

# HE COMMUNES WITH GOD

April 2004.

We take JD to shul (synagogue) for Saturday morning services. About fifty people attend, and there is plenty of singing. Liz and I want JD to show his support for his Jewish community, just as his sisters do, by attending services, cheder (Sunday school), Bar and Bat Mitzvah celebrations and by following the customs and traditions of Judaism. No one bats an eyelid when he crawls around the synagogue floor and vocalises his delight loudly during the services. He is always welcomed with warmth, dignity and affection.

We sit in our usual place near our two dapper friends, David and Hettie, and within seconds he is off on his travels around shul. He crawls over to his favourite people, sits up on his knees and talks to them in his unique way. Occasionally, he lies in front of the Ark, where the Torah scrolls are kept, as the service continues around him. He is happy in shul, and everyone is happy to see him too. Maybe he loves the singing, or being with his extended family, or perhaps it is the atmosphere of calm, peace and joy. We know that JD feels something special there.

When the Torah scroll was taken out today, he crawled in front of the Ark for a close look inside. The Ark symbolises the 'Holy of Holies' in the Temple in Jerusalem, where the Ark of the covenant, the two tablets of stone given to Moses by God resided. Some Jews believe that the Ark contains the *Shekhina*, or Divine Presence of God. JD stopped there for a few minutes, still and silent, studying the small chamber. After the service, one of our friends remarked, "he communes with God."

It is strange that the Ark draws his attention every week. Perhaps he is captivated by the silver-plated scrolls, the latticework on the inner doors, the *Ner Tamid* ("the eternal light") glowing over the entrance, or something else, who knows? So, maybe, just maybe …

# LAS RAMBLAS

July 2004.

"How good is your Spanish?" Liz turned to Victoria sitting in the car seat behind, next to JD.

"I think they speak Catalan here, mum," she answered.

We were on a daytrip in Barcelona, after driving from our favourite campsite, Le Brasilia, in Canet-Plage in France, a hundred and thirty miles north. Leaving three hours earlier on a warm sunny morning, we crossed the Pyrenees, into hotter and stronger sunshine. The air-conditioning in the car was a blessed relief.

"Do you think you could ask someone where we can park?" Liz persisted.

"Maybe in Spanish, yes," Victoria replied, "they'll probably speak both languages anyway."

"How about asking for disabled parking?" I asked, hopefully.

We were on the outskirts of the city, passing a confusion of signs to places I never knew existed. Liz scanned the map frantically for directions. Meanwhile, JD sat contentedly in his car seat, fingers in mouth, watching out the window. "We'll need somewhere to change JD too," Liz said.

"Hopefully, we'll find somewhere secluded, where he can be changed without anyone seeing," I added. Finding somewhere to toilet him was another thing we must consider when we take JD out. He is a twelve-year-old boy whose dignity must be maintained. I pulled the car over to the side of the road, so that a queue of vehicles could pass. I turned on my hazard lights and waited for a local to walk by.

"We must be close to Las Ramblas," Liz said, tracing her finger over the map, "I think we're here." She showed me. If she was right, then we were only a ten-minute stroll from the Plaça de Catalunya, the start of the kilometre-long Las Ramblas, and its famous street performers.

We rejected two passers-by as "too touristy," one carried a camera and the other wore a small daysack. Then a man carrying a newspaper, bereft of camera and daysack, rounded a street corner. We agreed unanimously that he fulfilled the credentials for a local, so Victoria stepped out of the car and approached him. I could not hear but the man said something and pointed.

"Well, he seemed to understand you," Liz beamed at Victoria when she returned, "what did he say?"

"I don't know," she replied, "he spoke Catalan, but I think he said there was a disabled bay in one of the side-streets a bit further up the road."

After a slow crawl along a busy road followed by a queue of impatient motorists, we found a space, roughly where the local hombre had said. Easy to spot, light blue paint on tarmac with the universal wheelchair sign in yellow. I assembled JD's wheelchair while Liz laid him across the middle row of seats, changed him and rubbed high factor sun-cream on his arms, neck and face. His sisters held up a blanket by the open door to ensure his privacy.

"We must keep him cool," I said anxiously, as we ambled towards our target – the Plaça de Catalunya. JD shook his head from side to side, eyes half-closed, tell-tale signs he was feeling uncomfortably hot. Five-storey high apartment blocks and shops faced each other across a wide pedestrianised walkway, flanked by narrow driving lanes. I zig-zagged between dark pools of shade cast by two rows of trees lining our route, reviving JD, who laughed at the sudden changes in direction and cool oases.

What do two men and a skeleton on bicycles, Fidel Castro and an elf have in common? We found the answer in Las Ramblas. A skeleton and two men on bikes sporting top hats, moulded and dunked in liquid silver stayed as still as statues, even in the full heat of the day. We tossed a two-Euro coin into a tin bucket at their feet, stood back and watched them spring into life and pedal furiously, chains and wheels squeaking. JD tilted his head, furrowed his brow, popped his thumb into his mouth and considered the unusual spectacle. A crowd gathered and tossed more coins into the bucket.

A young Fidel Castro stood on a pedestal a few yards away. Dressed as a revolutionary, he burst into mimed animated speech when a coin clanged into the tin pot before him. Capitalism spurred him into action. We continued along Las Ramblas, keeping JD in the shade as best we could while weaving through tourists and shoppers.

Something bright green flashed a hundred yards further down the street. An elf adorned with leaves stood on a box, leaning forward on a long staff. We dropped a coin into a bucket at its feet and watched its fixed grin spread wide to reveal brilliant white teeth, transforming itself into absolute evil. The elf turned slowly to face JD and reached out to touch him, but JD was more interested in the leaves on its staff and grabbed a handful before the elf could react. The elf then turned its attention to Georgina, who shivered as one hand crept onto her shoulder while the other wagged pointed and painted fingernails at her threateningly.

We pressed on to the entrance to La Boqueria, one of Europe's largest indoor markets, to seek shelter from the oppressive heat. Bombarded with a kaleidoscope of colours, perfumes, and cries of stallholders, JD livened up immediately. We steered him through a maze of brightly coloured fruits and vegetables, heady spices and scent from freshly cut flowers towards a rolling rhythm of flamenco guitars.

"It's lunchtime," I announced, "let's see if we can find something tasty."

"JD's Marmite sandwiches will be toast if they stay any longer in the food-bag," I added.

We found a free table at a bar inside the market, near stallholders carrying pallets of fruit and vegetables and wading through a slow-moving sea of shoppers. A guitarist and drummer played in a corner while I pressed chunks of sandwich into JD's mouth. He vocalised loudly to compete with the sounds around him, while scrutinising the hanger-like roof of the market and eating everything put in front of him.

We never completed the ramble down Las Ramblas, being far too hot and uncomfortable for JD. Besides, we only drove there on a whim, drawn by rumours of its street performers. But we found somewhere more memorable.

# INCIDENT AT WAITROSE

October 2004.

"Will the owner of car registration number XXXXXX please move their vehicle," said the announcer over the tannoy, "it is denying access for a disabled user."

Saturday is the busiest shopping day of the week at our local Waitrose, and I could not find anywhere to park. JD and Georgina were helping me with the weekly shopping, and I was just beaten to the last disabled bay. The driver got out, said something to someone inside, locked his car and headed for the store entrance.

"Well, I'll be...," I watched from a few yards away, then climbed out and checked the owner's vehicle. No blue badge. A young boy, about five years old, sat unaccompanied on the back seat.

A car on my right reversed out of a normal parking space, not much use to someone who must lift a twelve-year-old disabled boy through a narrow gap without damaging the car parked alongside. The only thing I could do was half-park, turn the engine off, assemble JD's wheelchair, lift him out and strap him in, push him to a safe area, then park properly. Unnoticed, Georgina clambered out and ran over to the man and started to remonstrate. I glanced over to the entrance and saw my eight-year-old daughter battling for her brother against someone four times her size and five times her age.

"Do you have a blue badge?" I inquired, wheeling JD

alongside Georgina.

"No," he replied, "but the only place to park was at the back and my son didn't want to walk."

"Well, at least he has the choice," I stabbed out the comment, incensed, and rolled into Waitrose to seek the store manager.

I was a regular customer, easily distinguished from other shoppers, pushing a wheelchair, and pulling a large trolley behind. I worked out a system of shopping with JD years before. I asked a lady at one of the busy check-out counters if I could speak to the manager and, while riffling through the spices section, felt a tap on my shoulder.

"You wanted to speak to me, sir," said the manager.

"Yes," I was impressed with the speed of response, "there's a Jaguar with no blue badge parked in the disabled bay outside – is there anything you can do?"

"Not really sir," she answered, "it's managed separately by our contractor." She looked almost disappointed. I thought for a while, and then had a brainwave.

"How about making an announcement?" I suggested. Her eyes lit up – she was obviously as keen as I to do something to seek recompense.

"I could give you his registration number and you could just publicly name and shame the driver," I continued.

Within a few minutes, while at the fruit section near the store exit, I heard the announcement. I watched in satisfaction as the man froze, while unloading the contents of his trolley on to a counter.

"Well done dad," said Georgina.

The man spotted me and headed over.

"I had every right to park my car there!" he yelled, red with rage, or embarrassment, or both. All eyes turned to us, and a few shoppers tut-tutted their disapproval.

"Really? How so?" I responded coolly, relishing his histrionics.

"And another thing – you should never let your child

approach strange men," he added, struggling to justify his action, "you never know what could happen."

Several responses flew through my head at that moment including, "are you a strange man then?" Instead, I followed his line of reasoning.

"And where is *your* son right now?"

He answered truthfully, "in my car, safe."

"Are you sure?"

"Absolutely," he replied.

"Because you locked him in?"

He packed up suddenly and left under a cloud of steam and, perhaps, feeling guilty for leaving his son unattended in a locked car. Fifty pairs of eyes watched him scurry out the door.

That was payback for all the times I have confronted people who believe they have a right to park in disabled bays. They do not understand the difference that easy parking makes to someone with a serious disability and how much their selfishness restricts them. He made a fair point about Georgina having a go at him, on her brother's behalf, without me being there. But I was only a few yards away and I was proud of her for sticking up for him.

Later that day, I cooked the Saturday traditional nosh of seared tuna marinated in a blend of lemon juice, cumin, turmeric, root ginger, garlic, red chilli, fenugreek, chopped coriander leaves, on a bed of wild rice soaked in sesame oil. I placed the pestle and mortar on the kitchen floor, carried JD in, and pounded and mixed the spices before him. He sat on his knees and leaned forward, inhaling the perfumed aromas, and reached out to grab the pestle. I wrapped my hand over his and, together, we celebrated the fruits of our shopping labours.

# BAR MITZVAH

Saturday May 21st 2005.

JD is *bar mitzvah* ('son of the commandment') today. According to Jewish faith, when a boy reaches thirteen years of age, he is considered responsible enough to lead a Jewish way of life. He *becomes* bar mitzvah. Girls become *bat* mitzvah ('daughter of the commandment') at twelve years. To mark the event, the bar or bat mitzvah leads the Sabbath service and reads from Torah in front of a packed congregation and tearfully proud parents, grandparents and friends. The Torah is written in Hebrew without vowel marks, so it takes weeks to learn.

Over the years, we have been to many bar and bat mitzvah ceremonies. We celebrated Roxanne's and Victoria's and hopefully, will witness Georgina's in three years' time. The big question was whether JD could *ever* be bar mitzvah because of his profound learning disability. He may not understand the commitment to lead a Jewish way of life, but we know that he loves the traditions, customs, food, rituals and music. Rabbi Jackie feels the same way as us. When we broached the subject, her response was immediate, emphatic, bordering on indignant, "of course he should be bar mitzvah!" She could have taken the same view as some, "what would be the point? He would never understand," but she did not. She knew that JD was an important member of our Jewish community with the same right to be celebrated as everyone else. So together, we adapted the ceremony to suit his needs.

JD cannot talk or read. So, unlike other bar and bat mitzvah students, will not be able to read or chant from the Torah. But he loves books being read to him. How much he understands is debatable, but I believe that he responds to tone and emotion, not content. Rabbi Jackie and I agreed that I would read the Torah for him and point out the Hebrew words as they were spoken. Instead of the scroll staying on the bimah (the podium), which is too high above the ground for JD to see, we would photocopy the script and put it on a low table at his eye-level.

Planning, preparing for and rehearsing his bar mitzvah took months of effort and tons of support from friends. The build-up started in January and culminated today in front of a hundred and twenty people. JD read from the Torah scroll and pointed out the script with the *yod* ('hand', or pointer). I held the yod in his hand and guided it over the words as I *leyned* (chanted) the script. Normally, JD does not like anyone forcing him to do something, such as making him hold an object or move his hand. He resists, shakes his head, and cries out in protest at any form of restraint. But today, he was quiet, relaxed and *listening*. He sensed 'something big was going down'. He communed with God.

The reading lasted thirty minutes, with short breaks as relatives and close friends were invited to recite blessings at various points. My attention was on JD and the scroll, so I never looked up at our family and friends. I never saw the tears of joy on their faces. But I felt a glow around us and was certain JD did too. JD passed a significant milestone in his life's journey, a point that seemed inconceivable to us thirteen years ago. Even if he did not understand the significance, it was understood by everyone else. His bar mitzvah was as important to them as it was to us, and that meant *ha olam kulo* ('the whole world').

Our only regret was that Liz's dad, Reg, could not be

there. For years, he had said how much he was looking forward to JD's bar mitzvah (always followed immediately with "PG," short for "please God") when he accompanied us to shul. In February, he had a serious fall that accelerated his dementia. He was too unwell to attend but he was there with us, in spirit if not in person. It was a cruel twist to a truly special day.

Jeremy (aged thirteen) and me with Torah scrolls, Bar Mitzvah rehearsal in 2005

# NEW BEDROOM

July 2005.

At thirty-five pounds, JD is grossly underweight for a thirteen-year-old boy. But our days carrying him upstairs and downstairs and bathing him are numbered. He is louder now, which is a problem for everyone when he wakes at nights. Liz and I agreed that JD's bedroom needed to be re-located downstairs. So, nine years after building the extension, Mr Danieli our builder, returned to add the finishing touches. He bears an uncanny resemblance to Father Christmas and greeted me cheerily with a builder's handshake that nearly crushed every bone. After a short and thorough survey of the extension, he grasped our unique requirements for JD's new sleeping quarters.

"One door or two into the wet room?" he asked, referring to the ensuite. He suggested a wet room so that we could wheel JD under a shower instead of lifting him in and out of a bath.

"Two doors please," I answered, "one from his bedroom and the other from the hall in case we need to get him there in a hurry at daytime."

"Makes perfect sense," agreed Mr Danieli, pulling on his white beard, "and will the young lad be wanting a bath as well?"

"Oh, definitely," I said, "it's one of his little pleasures in life." Like most of us, JD loves to soak in warm soapy water. His experience is enhanced, as I frequently tell Liz, by my strumming on the guitar and singing, as he splashes about.

Two months later, we unveiled JD's new bedroom with ensuite wet room. Shortly afterwards, two men from Social Services arrived with the components for a huge new bed and spent half a day assembling it. The bed resembles a giant cot with padded sides to prevent injury when JD self-harms at night, a pneumatic pump for elevating and manoeuvring, and a padded grill on one side that can be lifted on and off for access.

The Social Services team returned a few days later and fitted a hoist to the side of the bath so we can transfer JD from a wheelie commode, also provided by Social Services. The downside is that he cannot lie in the bath – he must stay put in the hoist seat. On its inaugural use, he voiced his disapproval and frustration at being denied his fundamental human right to lie down in a bath, kick his legs and splash in the warm water. Ever since, I have shied from using it.

Best of all, his Jewish community chipped in and donated a multi-sensory corner for his new bedroom, as a gift to celebrate his bar mitzvah two months ago. Occupying a square metre in his bedroom, it has touch-sensitive pads that play sounds when pressed, a fibre optic ceiling panel suspended over his bed, and 'sparkle fibre strands', or thick strands of multi-coloured fibre optics. The gift came with a certificate signed by his friends at synagogue, a touching sign of how much he is loved.

JD moved in last week and the early signs are good. The baby-alarm we use to listen out for him at nights has not yet crackled into life, probably because he is still in the honeymoon period, where everything is new and interesting. Things might change when he is bored with his new bedroom, we shall wait and see.

# CAN WE PRAY FOR HIM?

August 2005.

No more camping holidays. We bought an apartment in Canet-Plage, a town on the Mediterranean coast thirty miles from the Spanish border, our favourite part of France. We are a four-hundred-yard walk from a long sandy beach that stretches to the Pyrenees, a natural border between France and Spain, from the Atlantic in the west to the Mediterranean in the east. Our apartment has a lounge with galley kitchen, a bathroom and toilet, one bedroom and a balcony overlooking a marina. One of a hundred apartments in a block, it is managed by 'Le Syndic'. Most of our neighbours are locals, either retired or working in nearby Perpignan. Maybe Liz and I will retire here too one day. The kids can also stay in the apartment if they ever fancy a cheap holiday.

We worked out the complex sleeping arrangements for six people on our first two-week holiday. Liz slept in the double bed with Georgina, while Victoria slept on a blow-up mattress on the bedroom floor. Roxanne preferred to be on the balcony, with more room and privacy. JD lay on a pull-out double sofa bed in the lounge, and I slept on a pile of sun-mats at the foot of his bed. To stop him going for a crawl in the middle of the night, we barricaded his bed with cushions, spare mats, suitcases and whatever else came to hand. This left him with only one exit to freedom – me, an insurmountable obstacle. He woke me up every morning between three and five o'clock with ear-shattering vocalisations. Inevitably, he spotted me lying a few feet away, crawled over, grabbed a fistful of my hair and chuckled triumphantly, "er-her-her," as if to say, "found you!"

At the height of the tourist season, the promenade at Canet bustles. Every evening, stallholders set out tables and marquees against a backdrop of golden sand and turquoise sea. After dinner, we made our way through the colourful and noisy market, stopping briefly to admire the odd trinket, "shopping for holiday presents," according to Liz. While slaloming JD through the crowds, I noticed a poster advertising a gospel choir concert in the local church. "Oh, let's go," I urged Liz, "it will be brilliant!"

The concert started at eight in the evening, which gave plenty of time for dinner and a mile-long stroll to the church in the old village. Liz was equally keen to expose JD and his sisters to a variety of different experiences.

"Consider it an essential part of their musical education," she added.

Two days later, we arrived at the venue twenty minutes early, bought tickets and took up space on a hardwood pew inside a fourteenth-century Roman Catholic church. Immediately, JD's attention was drawn to the high roof with impressive arches, decorations, murals and intricate stonework. The hall filled with two hundred guests, an announcer walked on to the altar-stage, picked up a microphone and began speaking.

"What's he saying?" Georgina asked, "I can't understand."

"We are in France, dear," Liz answered, "we are probably the only English here."

"And probably the only Jews, too," I added.

The audience cheered loudly and clapped wildly as the choir appeared on stage, resplendent in long crimson gowns and began singing 'O bonne journée' ('O happy day'), a 1960s hit sung originally in English by the Edmund

Hawkins Singers. Every song was rewarded with prolonged applause from an enthusiastic and passionate audience. Sung in French, I struggled to comprehend the lyrics, but loved the complex, rich and free harmonies. JD listened, completely still, with his fingers in his mouth, eyes looking heavenward – three signs of deep concentration.

During the interval, six young members of the audience approached us and enquired about JD. They wanted to know his name, age, where he came from and his handicap. We explained in poor French and simple English. Two of the group crouched down to face JD, one took his hand, and the other stroked his hair and spoke quietly to him.

One asked, "are you Catholic?"

"No, we are Jewish," I answered.

"Jewish!" one exclaimed, "then, why did you come here, to a Catholic event?"

"Because I love gospel music," I replied.

They thought for a few moments, and fussed over JD, who seemed to like the attention.

"Please, can we pray for him," their eyes filled with concern. How could we refuse? We did not know their motive, but I was touched by their desire to pray for our son's salvation.

They placed their hands lightly on JD's head, closed their eyes and prayed silently to the heavens, lips barely moving. JD's eyes fluttered and closed, his head slumped on to his chest, and he fell asleep.

# WHERE'S BIG SIS?

October 2005.

There are no crocodiles, piranhas or giant anacondas in Camberley. Maybe that is why JD's big sister Roxanne has gone to the Amazon rainforest for her gap year. She left home last month, to work as a teacher in a remote village in the Guyanan jungle, close to the Venezuelan border. I admire her sense of adventure but worry about her constantly. Does JD understand he will not see his oldest sister for a year? Does he worry about her too? He cannot ask us, so we do not know, although we have tried to explain it to him. We can only guess and look for the signs, such as changes in his behaviour.

He went for an extended crawl after supper this evening. That is usually when his sisters are around to play with or annoy. Victoria practices her 'Czerny exercises' on the piano, while Roxanne and Georgina do homework or watch the telly, or both. But this time, someone was missing, and we think he noticed. He shuffled first into the music room - Victoria, one! Then into the kitchen – Georgina, two! Back to the lounge – telly on but no one about. From there, he crawled thirty feet to his bedroom - through the lounge door, down the corridor, left turn and past his wet room. But the search proved fruitless. He stopped, put his thumb in his mouth and pondered.

All the time he wandered, I wondered. Was he looking for Roxanne? I could not think of any other reason why he was so active. I picked him up and held him.

"Don't worry JD, Big Sis will be back next year," I consoled, carrying him back to the lounge.

He wrapped his arms around my neck, laid his head against mine, and sighed.

# FONT ROMEU

December 2005.

We flew south to Canet-Plage, for our first-ever winter holiday. The French Languedoc is quieter than the Cote d'Azur, the playground of the rich, the famous and royalty but basks in an hour's extra sunshine each day and offers greater variety. Spain is only a thirty-minute drive away and the Pyrenees are visible from the sea front. The residents are proud Catalans first, and French second. Walk along any promenade in the region, and you will hear French, Spanish and Catalan.

The local cuisine is French with a Spanish twist - paella and salsa share the restaurant tables with escargot and crème caramel. One can breakfast on *tortilla de patata*, coffee and croissants on the beach while admiring the majestic snow-capped Canigou, then spend the afternoon in the Pyrenees looking down at the beach. We have often wondered what the view was like from the mountains, so we went to see for ourselves.

After two hours driving up hairpin roads, we arrived at Font Romeu, a bustling ski resort town in peak ski season, and parked outside the télécabine station. During the six-thousand-foot climb, the temperature dropped to minus twenty Celsius. Deep snow lay on the mountains, compacted ice glazed the pavements and long icicles suspended like daggers from over-hanging rocks. We stepped from the car in our jeans, trainers, woolly jumpers and coats, and mingled with the ski-set dressed in winter onesies, snow boots and balaclavas.

"Well, now we're here, we may as well see what it's like at the top," I suggested.

I carried JD in my arms up the steps into the station, while Liz took his folded wheelchair, and the girls lugged the change bag and snacks. A continuous stream of télécabines came down the mountain, rounded the semi-circular station platform without stopping, and then continued their journey back up the mountain. As each pod passed, a door slid open inviting passengers to climb into its narrow moving mouth. Perspex windows offered all-round visibility for up to six passengers in two bench row seats.

We watched occupants alight and grab skis from slots behind the pods, while waiting passengers slid their skis in and climbed aboard. Liz and I debated whether we could execute an operation as deftly with a disabled thirteen-year-old boy and folded wheelchair instead of skis.

"We won't know unless we try," we said in unison.

A télécabine door opened. Clutching JD tightly, I threw myself in, Liz tossed the folded wheelchair onto the back seat and Georgina, Victoria and Liz squeezed in, while the pod rolled around the platform at a walking pace. With seconds to spare, the door slid shut, and we launched into space.

For ten minutes, we sailed up the mountain beneath a clear blue sky, over pristine snow and treetops. I hoped for a glimpse of the Mediterranean, but white-capped mountains obscured the view. Enthralled to see trees from a different perspective, JD pawed at the Perspex window, trying to touch them and murmuring, "errhhhh" and "aaahhhh."

We alighted the télécabine like aliens stepping on a new planet. People milled around in expensive ski outfits, wrap-around reflective goggles, heavy-duty mittens and gear I knew not the name of. We slipped and skidded on compressed snow in our trainers and boots and clung on to JD's wheelchair for stability. In the unfamiliar environment, we were the ones with mobility problems, and he provided the support.

## WRESTLING WITH TENTS

July 2006.

Canet-Plage is overcrowded in mid-summer. We never even try to book a café or restaurant table, as all seats are taken. Even if we are lucky enough to sample the local cuisine, we end up waiting an hour, and JD cannot hang around for his grub when he is hungry. Families on vacation share the promenade with cyclists, so we must be vigilant to avoid catastrophic impact. JD and I seek refuge on the long sandy beach, which is quiet in the mornings. But come afternoon, crowds flock there like birds migrating south for the winter. And four hours later, they migrate back to the campsites and apartments.

The coast is always sunny but often windy, so the fine sand is whipped up into clouds that blast everything in their path. A beach tent is essential in such conditions but challenging to set up. A man and disabled boy grappling with canvas makes great entertainment for the lifeguards and promenaders.

"JD and I are off to the beach," I called to Liz, Victoria and Georgina, "who wants to join us?"

From our apartment balcony, the boats in the marina sat still on the water and the palm fronds hung motionless. A small group of children sat on the marina steps with their feet in the water. The conditions were perfect for playing in the beach tent on the soft warm sand and bobbing on the waves in the inflatable boat.

"You go on ahead," Liz answered, "we'll get there when we can."

"We could be here all day, eh JD," I said while changing his nappy, "with three females and only one bathroom."

He looked at me and grinned toothily, "er-her-her."

I strapped him in the buggy, stuffed five beach towels in the tray underneath, laid the long tent bag over the push-bars, packed his rucksack with nappies, cream, medicines and toys and slung the picnic sack over my shoulders.

"We're off," I shouted, "see you later." We wheeled out the door, down the corridor and into the lift.

The four-hundred-yard walk to the sea was windless until we rounded the corner by the local patisserie. Gentle wisps increased in strength to a steady blast of warm air by the time we stepped on to the beach-boards, five minutes later. Fortunately, JD was shielded by the buggy hood and a beach towel, which I re-oriented to prevent sand being blown into his eyes.

I scanned the beach for a suitable pitch – flat and not too close to the sea, to avoid salty spray – and dragged the buggy over the soft sand. Past years of beach holidays taught me that the tent must be positioned so that JD is shielded from both sun and wind. Exposure to either would be uncomfortable, even dangerous. Sunburn and sand must be prevented while maximising enjoyment. The back of the tent must face south to screen him from the sun, and against the wind. Thus, the sun would pass behind the tent at mid-day and JD would be protected for several hours, provided the wind did not change direction. On other days, we have had to return to base defeated, because the wind was too formidable, or the sun and wind had conspired against us.

"Now JD," I said, "comes the difficult part – and I'm going to need your help."

I unpacked the canvas tent and poles and crammed the

tent bag into the buggy to prevent the wind whisking it miles up the beach. Tossing the poles on the sand, I unfolded the canvas, lifted the rear buggy wheels, and slipped one corner underneath.

"You make fine ballast JD," I added, "now I can clip the tent poles together without the tent becoming a kite."

With his back towards the unfolding tent, JD could not see what was happening behind, but he appreciated the sudden appearance of the top of the tent over his buggy, followed by considerable rustling as the wind took hold. To the sound of chuckling, I pushed the tent poles through the loopholes, while talking piratical nonsense.

"It be a mere capful o'wind matey."

"Avast ye!"

"Land ahoy!"

"Goidy-goidy," said JD.

With the tent erected, I laid the beach towels, picnic and change bags inside and pulled the buggy to the side.

"Finally! Now you're ready to come aboard."

I lifted him out of the buggy and into the tent, on a beach towel as further protection against sand incursion, fastened his sunglasses and laid down on the sand in front.

"Job done," I congratulated him, "I couldn't have done it without you JD."

# A PROMISE

August 10th 2006.

As a change from tent-wrestling in the wind amid flocks of tourists, we drove up the mountains for a picnic. Why sit on the beach for three weeks in a region that has so much natural diversity? JD loves trees, and there are plenty in the nearby Pyrenees, *and* it would be calmer and quieter.

We aimed for Font Romeu, the same place we visited in winter, when the ground was frozen, and the trees were white with snow. The local weather forecast predicted another typical Languedoc summer's day, so we hit the road. The two-hour drive took us around the outskirts of Perpignan and on to the fast road towards Andorra. An hour later, and fifteen-hundred feet higher, we rounded the fortified walls of Villefranche-de-Conflent. The road climbed and twisted up the mountains and through the narrow market streets of Olette. The cars disappeared by the time we passed the eighteenth-century citadel of Mont Louis. A few miles further, we pulled into an empty car park on the edge of a forest, six thousand feet higher up.

We spread a picnic rug under a fir tree, and laid JD down to indulge in his favourite pastime studying branches. Sunlight beamed through the tree-tops and formed glittering patterns that danced over the forest floor. The forest is his heaven, being fed at the same time is another step up. I tore a chunk of tuna mayonnaise sandwich and popped it into his mouth, while his eyes flicked over the complex textures of the undergrowth, and the light sparkling through the trees.

A short distance away, a path led deeper into the forest towards the mountains. A post nearby described a route called the 'GR10', an abbreviation of 'Grand Randonnée 10' ('Big Hike 10').

"Maybe we could walk along the GR10 this afternoon?" I suggested.

"Huh?" three heads turned.

"What are you talking about?" asked Liz.

"This path," I pointed, "it's called the GR10."

"So?"

"Well, rather than saying we walked on a forest path, we could say we walked the GR10," I announced enthusiastically.

"So what? It's only a path."

"Yes – but this one has a name!"

Liz, Victoria and Georgina looked at me with puzzlement, not an unfamiliar experience.

Pressing the point, I continued, "it's like saying, 'I flew to the Moon and back', rather than 'I flew through space for a bit'."

"Errr," said JD keenly.

"Thank you, JD. You see – he agrees with me!"

"But we don't even know what the GR10 is," Liz said, "so I'm sure anyone we tell won't know either."

Eventually, we agreed that JD would want to walk in the forest, if he could say so, and that we should make the most of our hundred-mile round trip from Canet-Plage.

We set off along a gravel track through a coniferous forest, over a cattle grid, and past neat stacks of freshly cut logs. Fresh pine and perfume wafted through sharp clean air, and insects buzzed over summer gentians. Two thousand feet below, cows grazed on green meadows as we headed towards higher mountains standing two thousand feet higher. No cars, *boom-ching boom-ching* pop music, people, and no burger, oily beignet, or monoxide smells floating in the breeze.

"It's exactly the same as Swinley Forest, but different, isn't it JD?"

"Er-her-her," he replied, shaking his head, and chuckling.

After a mile, the track became steeper, rockier and rougher, so we turned reluctantly and made our way back to the car park. Beside the GR10 notice, JD fell silent, and his eyes locked onto mine, searching, probing.

"What is it JD?"

"Errr," he said.

"Did you want to go on?"

"Errr," he repeated.

"I'm sorry, but it's getting late, and the path was too bumpy."

"Mmmm," he sighed.

We looked into each other's eyes for a moment, and the words came out.

"I promise I will come back and walk the whole road for you," I ruffled his hair, "would you like me to walk the GR10 for you?"

He smiled - a promise was made and sealed. I knew nothing about the GR10, or what I would be letting myself in for. But he understood my promise, so I *must* keep it. I determined to find out where the forest track went. I would like JD to walk with me but must accept that it may be too difficult with a wheelchair. I might have to walk the GR10 without him.

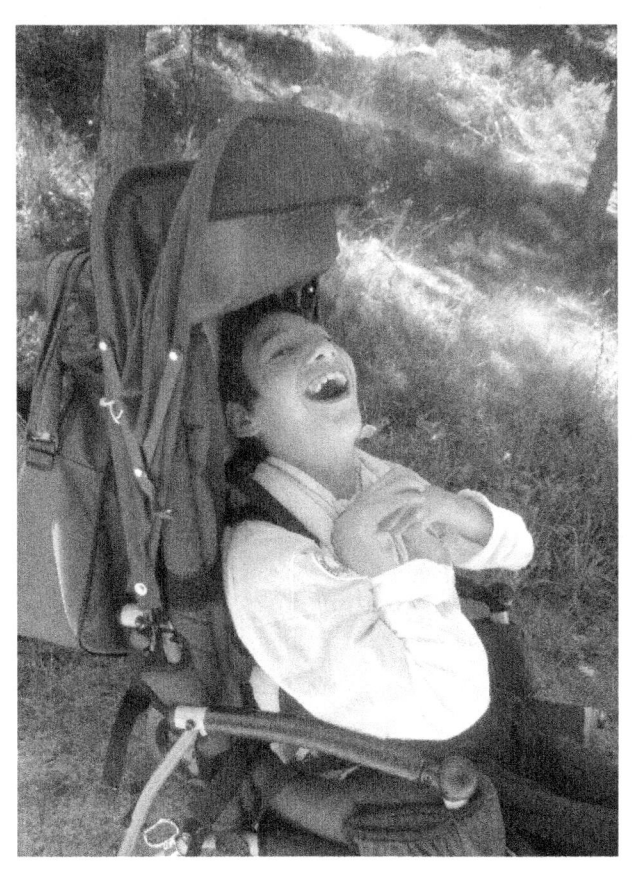

Jeremy (aged fourteen) on the GR10 in 2006

# THE WHITE NUNS AND THE SACRED MOUNTAIN

An eleventh-century Benedictine abbey sits in the clouds at three and a half thousand feet, nearly halfway up the Canigou mountain in the Pyrenees. The Canigou is sacred to the local Catalan population, dominating the landscape for miles around. Standing at over nine thousand feet, it was for many years considered the highest in the range, but that honour has fallen, or risen, on Pic Aneto, two thousand feet taller and two hundred miles west.

Liz discovered a brochure about the abbey buried among hundreds of leaflets, while ferreting around the Tourist Centre in Canet-Plage.

"Why don't we do something different today?", she suggested, sliding the brochure alongside JD's plate of Marmite-slathered bread.

I glanced at a glossy picture of the Abbaye de St Martin du Canigou, a complex of long, pink-roofed buildings perched precariously on a rock and surrounded by forest.

"Looks challenging," I said, "it's rather high up. How do we get to it with JD?"

"There's a paved path from a village below," Liz replied, "should be no problem."

Victoria and Georgina bundled into the car with JD, wheelchair, changing bag and medicines, picnic rugs, lunch, five litres of water and we set off for a forty-five-mile drive. We parked in the tiny village of Casteil at the foot of the sacred mountain ninety minutes later. A nearby sign directed us to a narrow tarmac path leading to the Abbaye, eight hundred feet higher up. I stripped down to shorts and t-shirt to prepare for a gruelling mile-long push in the heat and midsummer Languedoc sun. We strapped JD into his wheelchair, fastened the sun-hood, looped his change bag over the handles and headed on to the steep path.

The shade from overhanging trees disappeared and the slope increased. With arms outstretched, I pushed with my eyes facing the ground, occasionally raising my head to steer away from the edge. We hair pinned up the mountain towards the abbey, and the drop over the path grew. One moment, JD was shielded from the sun, and the next he faced it full-on. He shook his head and moaned, letting me know his discomfort. I removed my t-shirt and draped it over the front of the wheelchair hood for extra shade. Some overheated tourists climbed with us while a few fatigued ones lumbered down. After thirty minutes of puffing and pushing, two men appeared at my side, and whisked JD at a bristling pace the last quarter mile, carried him up some stone steps and deposited him in the cool abbey entrance.

They explained, "you had done enough, it was our turn", then disappeared inside.

Nonplussed, I turned to JD, "what just happened?"

"Er-her-her", he chuckled, out of the heat and blinding sun.

Liz and the girls caught up a few seconds later.

"Who were they?" Liz asked, "did you thank them?"

"I never had a chance," I replied. Random acts of kindness are the best kind, the giver does not bother to ask - they just do, and never expect anything in return. They are prepared to take the risk of the receiver reacting badly, which makes their act courageous, as well as kindly.

We arrived too late for an official tour of the abbey, but

a resident white nun offered to guide us personally because "we had made the effort to get here." She led us through the upper and lower churches, constructed in the early eleventh century, and around the remains of the cloister, with ancient carvings on tall marble columns. JD stared at the intricate ceilings, fascinated by the contrast of light and shade. In mixed French and English, our chaperone explained that she could not show us the burial ground of the abbey's founder, Count Guifre de Cerdanya, as it was out-of-bounds to visitors. She promised to take us to the church instead, on condition that we remain totally quiet while the white nuns prayed. I tried to explain, in my limited French, that while we would comply, we could not guarantee JD's co-operation.

Thirty white nuns faced the altar at the far end of the church, their backs to us. Not one head turned as they prayed with their heads bowed, while I prayed for JD's silence. Fortunately, his attention was taken by the arched ceiling and the sunlight beaming through the windows high above and along both sides of the narrow aisle. With his fingers in his mouth and eyes gazing upwards, he studied intently without a sound. Maybe it was the peace that kept him quiet, or perhaps he just sensed something big was going down, like key moments during synagogue services. We left as silently as we entered.

We ended our tour next to the shop, where we purchased a CD of a performance by the Community of the Beatitudes and listened to their joyful rendition of a medley of songs from the Jewish liturgy, as the sacred mountain receded in the distance.

# THE CACKLING LADY

December 2006.

"Fancy being a smuggler for the day JD?"

He lay on beach mats spread over the floor of our apartment in Canet-Plage, our bolthole from the dull grey English winter. The mats insulated him from the hard tiles as he crawled around. More importantly, they limited damage from head-banging during a temper tantrum. He ignored my offer, being content instead to play with the stuffed salamander toy he snatched from a market-stall in the summer.

Early 19th century villains, bandits and renegades crossed the France-Spain border through a pass known as *le Route du Trabucayres* ('smuggler's route'). Armed with 'trabucs' (muskets), they terrorised the region until they were rounded up and executed in 1846 by French and Spanish troops. A local magazine printed an article about their exploits that piqued my curiosity.

"It's a bit nearer than Font Romeu," I informed Liz and the girls, "only about two thousand feet up, but we'll still need to wrap up well."

"I doubt we'll be able to smuggle JD over the border," Liz quipped.

"Well, we won't know unless we try."

The thirty-mile drive was easy until the last few miles, along a narrow and tree-shrouded road that twisted and turned. JD dropped his salamander and laughed gleefully at the overhanging branches and foliage brushing against the car windows as we crawled towards our destination at the village of Las Illas.

We parked in a field beside a white building and unloaded the wheelchair, change-bag and picnic. Under a clear blue sky and with no snow in sight, we set off to find the smuggler's route.

"Keep your eyes peeled for a yellow sign," I said, "it's supposed to be somewhere near this white building."

The building was the Hostal des Trabucayres, a working hostel for hikers and the original smuggler's hide-out. During the Nazi occupation of 1940-44, it had been a refuge for Jews escaping France. But I did not know that at the time, neither did I know that we were searching for another section of the GR10, the route I promised to walk for JD four months earlier.

Victoria spotted the sign at the corner of the building, pointing along a gravel path leading into a forest behind. JD's wheels crunched as we took our first few steps, then froze on hearing a disembodied voice, low-pitched and crackling like the gravel. Its owner sounded close, talking to us in a tongue we could not understand. Liz and I looked to Victoria– she was the one with the penchant for languages.

Liz mouthed, "what's it saying?"

"Is it *parceltongue*?" I whispered, thinking of the snake-language from the 'Harry Potter' books.

Victoria guessed, "Catalan?"

The voice continued its incomprehensible monologue, then cackled. We looked around, then upwards to an open window and a muscle-bound arm perched on a ledge. The arm moved and waved, and another cackle came from inside.

"Bonjour?" called Liz hopefully.

"Ola?" called Victoria.

I rolled forward a few yards until I could see the occupant. A middle-aged lady wearing a colourful headscarf, grinned toothlessly at us and waved her arm towards the smuggler's route. Baffled by her behaviour, we said, "au revoir madame" and continued into the trees.

Pushing a wheelchair on loose gravel is as tough as pushing through sand. But worth the effort for JD to enjoy his favourite kind of environment. For the first hundred yards, the gravel track divided a paddock fence from light forest. Then it climbed gradually and rose above the mud and mulch on both sides and expanded to a platform wide enough for two wheelchairs. Two hundred yards ahead, the path turned and disappeared behind a clump of large rocks. From beyond, we heard a dull clanging.

Seconds later, a herd of monstrously sized cows with curved horns and heavy bells on their necks appeared. They ambled nonchalantly towards us, like a slow-motion stampede. The bovine wave front spread across the entire path and ten feet on both sides. Either we gave way to them, or they to us. Beasts like these were not acquainted with good manners or consideration for the disabled, so I hopped down into the muddy ground to test the going for a wheelchair. Liz, Victoria and Georgina could scramble to safety easily enough, but I doubted JD's chances. The step from the path was too high and the earth too boggy to push or pull him through. We turned and fled back the way we came with the Pyrenean monsters in cold pursuit.

JD chuckled hysterically as we bumped and clattered along the path with thudding hooves and clanging bells behind us. The cackling Catalan lady cackled louder at the window of the white building as we passed beneath her.

"Just because we couldn't understand her, doesn't mean it wasn't important," Liz concluded while we headed home.

"Aaahhh", murmured JD.

"JD's words precisely," I said.

# WALKING TO WALK

April 2007.

She referred to a device resembling a zimmer-frame but equipped with a seat, harness and wheels, that would encourage JD to experience the joy of movement. A walker would also help him maintain a good posture and prevent his scoliosis - curving of the spine - from worsening. At fifteen years, he had adopted an unnatural posture when seated, preferring to lean rightwards and aggravate his condition. If left unchecked, he would need major surgery to straighten his spine and prevent damage to his internal organs, a risk that must be mitigated.

"How much does a walker cost?" I asked, with a spoonful of rice and tuna marinated in lemon, ginger, coriander and chilli, poised two inches before JD's waiting mouth.

"About five hundred pounds," she replied, "but Social Services won't pay because they say he doesn't need one."

"His physiotherapist says it's necessary to help him develop, grow and strengthen his muscles," she continued, "and I think he needs one too."

There were plenty of good reasons to splash out. Physiotherapist plus mum over-rules Social Services every time. But it was a lot of money.

"Can we afford to buy him one?" I asked. Liz handles all our finances, so she knew better than I.

"Yes, but we would need to economise."

And that is where we left the matter until later in the week, when Georgina, JD's eleven-year-old sister, announced that she was going to raise the funds required for her older brother by walking all thirty-two miles of the Basingstoke canal.

"My friend Holly wants to walk it too," she insisted, "and we've already made the sponsorship forms for you to sign." She handed over two hand-written pieces of paper, with neatly drawn columns, headed 'Name' and 'Amount', with our names written under the first column.

Liz glowed with pride, while I fended off a tear. She was a fighter, and I had seen that look of determination on her face before, notably as a feisty eight-year-old confronting an adult man for "taking my brother's parking space" in Waitrose car park.

So, Georgina, her friend Holly, and I would walk the canal from its western end, the Greywell Tunnel, to the river Wey, at its eastern end. We would make the attempt over a weekend and hope for good weather. The two girls raised three hundred and sixty pounds over the following weeks, by cajoling school-friends, their parents, Liz's and my work colleagues.

We considered taking JD as well but were uncertain about the weather and how to manage his complex logistical requirements, such as changing him, feeding, or indeed, whether he would resist being incarcerated in his wheelchair for over eight hours without a break. In the end, and with regret, we decided against it. We also needed to start early on both days, and as we knew only too well, there is no such thing as an early getaway with JD.

Liz dropped us off at Greywell, near North Warnborough, at eight o'clock. We spent a few minutes peering through the eastern end of the mile long Greywell Tunnel, sealed off owing to its partial collapse in 1932. It is home to one of the largest bat colonies in Europe, although there were no signs of their presence, apart from a strong ammonia-like odour and crystal-clear water. A few hundred yards further, we passed the ruins of King John's Castle, built in the early thirteenth century, later becoming a hunting lodge, before falling into ruin in the 17$^{th}$ century.

The two girls maintained a brisk pace and a brisker chatter, while I admired the view that only a canal can offer as it cut silently through the countryside, villages and towns. I had taken JD many times along canal paths, by wheelchair and on his special bike, and recognised their attraction. Pea-green languid water bordered by shaggy grasses and ferns, instead of hard black tarmac roads and dirty grey pavements. The smell of damp earth and wood, instead of noxious car and diesel fumes. The soporific sound of flowing water and splashes of herons, instead of beeping horns and rumbling wheels. One urges "slow down, listen, look," and the other presses, "go quickly, get there and get out of my way!" But canals do not often take us where we want, so we are compelled to use the frenzied and far less enjoyable modes of transport.

After eight hours and nineteen miles of walking on our first day, we arrived at Mytchett Place Canal Bridge, where Liz collected us. The long day did not affect the girls, who laughed and talked excitedly in the car, while I nursed an aching shin that had intensified during the day.

JD and Liz dropped Georgina, her friend Holly, Holly's mum and I off in Woodham the following morning, at the closest point to the eastern end of the Basingstoke Canal. We conceded that we must walk the last mile of the canal twice, to and from where it joined the river Wey. The canal and river meet beneath the M25 – the outer London orbital - that towered on fat grey concrete stilts over green fields on the far side of the river. The riverside scene, ducks and geese floating serenely on glittering water, and the rushing, rumbling and clattering sounds of metal on tarmac and steel thirty feet above us, were a reminder of days long gone.

The sun warmed our backs as we pressed on, with the sound of traffic never far away, but soon forgotten. By mid-morning, we had passed through busy Woking town centre without being aware it was there. A few barges glided by, their owners waving and calling out cheery greetings.

Our friends, Alan and Nili, had arranged a baseball and barbecue event in the afternoon for family and friends at Frimley Lodge Park, adjacent to the canal at our official end, mid-way between its eastern and western ends. Liz, Victoria and JD would meet us there for fun, food and games. It would be a fitting end to the walk, and we did not intend to miss it. For the final four miles, I limped and gritted my teeth with the pain in my right shin. "Why only one shin, not both?" I complained, while the girls skipped, ran and chattered along, unaffected by the thirty-two miles we covered in two days.

Georgina and Holly were on their second burger when I hobbled into the marquee. Alan thrust a cold beer in my hand and slapped me heartily on the back.

"Well done, old chap," he said.

"Old chap" sounded strange coming from someone with a Californian accent.

"Yes, well done, old chap," echoed Nili, sounding even stranger in a Bronx accent. JD lay stretched out on a picnic rug vocalising happily at the surrounding trees and sounds of leather on willow, US-style. I laid beside him on the rug.

"You know JD, you are a very lucky chap."

"Er-her-her."

"Your sister has just walked thirty-two miles for you, so you can learn to walk."

"Every path of opportunity for you must be explored," I added.

A sign beneath a canal bridge we passed moments earlier summed up the sentiment - 'In the middle of difficulty, lies opportunity.'

# HAILSTORM AT FORT LAGARDE

July 2007.

From a rock eighteen-hundred feet up in the French Pyrenees, Fort Lagarde overlooks the border town of Prats-de-Mollo, twenty miles from the Mediterranean coast. King Louis XIV claimed the fort in the late 17th century, and later Vauban re-enforced it to defend against Spanish marauders. Our apartment in Canet-Plage is within easy reach and a visit would make a welcome change from lying on a beach sardined with roasting tourists and cars eructing fumes into the summer haze. Heat infects JD with lethargy, so a trip to the cool mountains would be a perfect antidote.

We parked in Prats-de-Mollo village centre, and bought a bus ticket to take Liz, Victoria, JD, Georgina and me up a mountain to the fort. Our eyes flicked from the fort roosting on top of a vertiginous slope, to a dented and rusting bus standing at the bus stop, and the driver emerging from a bar with a half-smoked Gauloises wedged in his mouth. He loaded JD's wheelchair in the hold, and with a collective gulp, we boarded. JD sat beside me up front, Liz and the girls sat behind and a dozen more passengers took their places.

"Oh the wheels on the bus go round and round, round and round," we sang, and stopped instantly when the bus shuddered to a start, growled and began its ascent up a narrow road. The gears crunched while the driver wrestled with the steering wheel and gears to negotiate a particularly tight hairpin. My knuckles turned white when we rolled backwards before the driver succeeded in ramming the gear into place and resuming the climb. The wheels on the bus were never more than inches from certain doom on a three-hundred-foot climb that lasted eternity. I suddenly longed for the safety of the beach. JD however, remained unperturbed and chuckled as the bus rocked around impossibly tight corners.

We arrived at a flat-topped summit with the fort before us. Legs shaking, we clambered off the bus and reclaimed JD's wheelchair. A rocky path led a short way to the fort entrance where we were treated to a period costume drama. A re-enactment and explanation of the history of the fort was in full flow, led by a glamorously moustachioed Musketeer on horseback, surrounded by a cast of costumed actors and horses. Suddenly, two men in Napoleonic dress appeared at our side, lifted JD plus wheelchair and carried him into the fort, up a flight of stone steps and on to the battlements for the second act. The moustachioed Musketeer played the lead role, explaining the action to an audience of forty amid swordfights and musket fire. Meanwhile, a cloak of grey cloud swept over the mountains and the temperature plummeted.

Suddenly, the heavens opened and hurled down marble-sized balls of hail. The audience, dressed for summer in shorts, t-shirts and light frocks, scrambled for cover. Without interrupting his whirlwind of words, the moustachioed Musketeer whipped off his hat, plonked it on JD's head with, "pour votre protection Monsieur," and continued with the play.

After five minutes lashing by frozen pellets, the hailstorm ended abruptly and the same two Napoleonic men carried JD down the steps outside to the walls of the fort, for a dressage. Still sporting the Musketeer's hat, and with a thumb in his mouth, he watched the horses parade by, each rider tipping a feathered hat.

# ARRESTED BY THE ARMY

March 2008.

The stranger at the next table tore off a chunk of pita, folded it and scooped up a generous layer of an oily paste into his mouth. He turned to us and grinned, revealing two absent front teeth and said, "too much humous gives you gas" and burst into laughter. He patted his portly belly for emphasis.

We were in one of the many humous bars in Haifa, famous for outstanding street food. A few days earlier, we flew to Ben Gurion airport to visit Victoria, seven months into her gap year in Israel. We knew that a five-and-a-half-hour flight with a sixteen-year-old disabled young man would be challenging. El Al gave us seats right up front, so that JD and I could lay safely on the floor between Liz's feet and the bulkhead, reading stories and playing with his precious salamander.

One of the few perks of flying with JD is being onboarded first via a special lift, then offboarded and fast-tracked through passport control while able-bodied passengers queue. The privilege meant we were first to arrive at the car rental desk and collect the keys to our hire car, an MPV large enough to accommodate six passengers, wheelchair, eight days' worth of nappies for JD, his medicines and four large suitcases. We calculated the nappy count carefully several days before and verified the total more than once. He must be changed six times every day at least, so we would require forty-eight, plus an extra twelve in case he caught 'Delhi belly'. Thus, three packets, each with twenty nappies, filled one of our suitcases.

We played dodgems on the twenty-mile drive from the airport to our hotel in Tel Aviv. Cars came from every direction, cut us up along the congested main road into Israel's capital city, at junctions and around confusing one-way routes. Israeli drivers gave no quarter and honked their horns after a millisecond of hesitation. Two hours later, we checked in to our hotel north-side of the city, with JD still chuckling at the pandemonium.

A few days later, we re-located to Nahariya, eighty miles north of Tel Aviv, close to the Lebanese border, to re-unite with Victoria. She was staying in Shlomi, a small village three hundred feet up in the hills, eight miles away. Hezbollah terrorists shelled the area on numerous occasions, most recently two years earlier. Despite the vastly different geopolitics, Shlomi compared well with many small villages in the south of France. Low brilliant white buildings with salmon pink terracotta roofs, in a peaceful setting surrounded by garrigue, or low-growing vegetation, and no sign of bomb craters. We met Victoria in a local park, where JD spent several minutes studying her before finally acknowledging that she was indeed his long-absent sister.

JD and I drove her back to Shlomi in the evening, after eating together as a complete family for the first time in seven months. On our return to Nahariya along a deserted road in the night, two soldiers signalled at me to stop. All movement at that time of night so close to the Lebanese border was suspicious. They approached the car, one on each side, rifles ready.

"Shalom," I said, winding down my window, passports in hand.

"Goidy goidy," said JD, fingers in mouth.

A soldier inspected our passports and glanced at the

blue disabled badge in the front window.

He asked, "are you enjoying your stay in Israel?"

"Wonderful," I replied, "we have just seen my daughter and his sister in Shlomi."

The other soldier leaned to JD and waved. In response, he was treated to a prolonged sidelong glance.

"It's not every night you get stopped by the Israeli Defence Force, is it JD?" I asked, a mile further down the dusty road.

"Er-her-her," he chuckled.

# THE WESTERN WALL

Walking through Jerusalem's Old City is like walking through the Bible. History seeps from every stone. In the 19th century, the area was divided into rough quarters, one each for Muslims, Christians, Jews and Armenian (Orthodox) Christians. We were staying a half a mile from the Jaffa Gate, one of eight gates into the walled city, and planned to welcome in the Sabbath at the Kotel (Western Wall). We would walk to the Jaffa Gate and then stroll a half-mile through the Armenian and Jewish quarters to the Kotel.

On an unbearably hot and humid evening, we passed through the gate and realised immediately it would be an uncomfortable journey for JD. With no suspension, his wheelchair juddered violently along the cobbled streets. I stopped to study my guidebook and plan a smoother route. Stuck for a solution, I asked a passing Chasid (Orthodox Jew) and his son for advice, suggesting a route through the Arab Suq markets.

"No," said the man emphatically, "it is far too dangerous at night, especially for Westerners."

Flummoxed, I asked, "is there a better way?"

He continued, "you must come with us."

Without hesitating, he picked up JD's wheelchair on one side, his son lifted the other and they marched off at a bristling pace.

We chased them with JD riding two feet in the air. My

eyes fastened on the two hatted gentlemen dressed in jet black carrying my son and swimming through a sea of like-costumed men with their families, all destined for the Kotel. In Hebrew, the man yelled "make way!" as they transported JD like King David, up and down stone steps and through narrow passages for half a mile. Suddenly, our destination appeared before us and they lowered him back to earth, bade us "gut shabbos" ("peaceful Sabbath") and vanished.

"That was an impressive act of tzedakah," Liz said. (Tzedakah, or 'loving kindness and charity', is an important principle of Judaism.)

"And I didn't even get a chance to thank them," I said regretfully.

"Tzedakah just gets done," Liz added, "it's as natural as breathing – no thanks are expected or given."

The Kotel is the holiest place on Earth to the Jewish faith. Built over two thousand years ago by King Herod, the sixty-foot-high wall divides the Jewish quarter of the Old City and the original Temple, now within the Arab quarter. Facing the Kotel, the golden Dome of the Rock peered over the top. Two hundred worshippers sang, chanted, shouted and danced with joy before the Wall.

Liz and the girls headed for the women's section, and I wheeled JD into a covered area, where the cacophony of sound was loudest. Bookcases full of prayer-books faced the ancient Wall, the most sacred of sacred places in the Jewish faith. For a few seconds, I looked about, wondering what to do, before picking a book off a shelf.

"Well, we're here JD," I said, "what shall we do now?"

My question drowned in waves of song and prayer. A line of ten bearded Chassidic Jews dressed in black like the two men who carried JD from one end of the Old City to the other, ringlets beneath wide-brimmed and furry 'Cossack-style' hats, *davened* (rocked back and forth) a foot from the Wall, clutching miniature prayer books.

JD stared at the Wall, six feet in front. I wheeled him

closer, then took his hand and placed it on the rough limestone. I began singing the 'Shema', an ancient Hebrew prayer that declares belief in the unity of God, words that had been chanted by JD's ancestors for hundreds of generations. The thick stone and low roof muffled the sound of my cautious singing. Terrified of reciting one word incorrectly, my confidence began to wane. Two Chassidic gentlemen appeared on either side of us and joined with the chant. I shut my eyes and held JD's hand on the Wall, and the words of the prayer returned. Time stood still while we chanted together. My senses sharpened. Why is the Wall so smooth and warm when it should feel rough? Why is JD's hand so relaxed, even with his arm fully outstretched? Did I just hear a bird sing from somewhere? There is a musty smell from the books and a dry powdery taste from something else, maybe the Wall?

I opened my eyes. The two men were no longer there. They disappeared as quietly and mysteriously as they appeared. How long had I held JD's hand against the Wall? Surely, no more than a minute? A timeless minute if there can be such a paradox. Yet JD tolerated it, so he felt the same wonder, power, of something undefinable. Only once before, at his Bar Mitzvah was he so still, quiet and focussed. I replaced the prayer book, wheeled him outside and reunited with Liz and the girls.

We left the Old City through the Dung Gate and followed the city wall back to where our spiritual adventure began. Even now as I write, I try to make sense of what happened. Science would explain our experience as something generated from within, purely emotional responses and nothing to do with any mystical Being. But I believe that JD communed with God. He drew out the goodness that lies in all of us not once, but twice that magical evening – two men lifted him across the Old City to the Wall and then two more lifted us through prayer at the Wall. The Wall was his destiny.

# THE DEAD SEA

The Dead Sea is a giant hot salty bath. You cannot drown. Wade out to three feet depth and your feet will be lifted away from under you. Thirty-five percent salinity prevents any organism from prospering, except the hardiest bacteria. Unfortunate fish washed into its northern bank from the river Jordan perish quickly. At one thousand three hundred feet below sea-level, it is also the lowest point on Earth.

On another baking hot day, we drove from Jerusalem to Ein Gedi on the west bank of the Dead Sea, a three-thousand-five-hundred-foot drop in altitude. Soapy stones lined the shore, so not wanting to take any chances, I sat down and shuffled towards the water with JD on my lap. Had he been a healthy weight for a sixteen-year-old boy, instead of a mere forty-four pounds, a dip would not have been possible without assistance. As we drew closer to the sea and the sound of rippling waves became louder, he clasped his arms tightly around my neck, preparing himself for a cold shock. Then we slipped into hot water, and he burst into laughter. I waded out further, struggling to stay upright, while watching oily patterns of blue and green swirl on the surface. I laid him on his back, making sure water did not get into his eyes, nose or mouth, and his weight was taken from me.

"I could cast you off to Jordan," I joked.

"Er-her-her," JD chuckled, hot water lapping over his

shoulders and chest.

Afterwards, we drove thirteen miles along the west bank for a trip in a cable car one thousand feet up to the ancient fortress of Masada. In 73CE, the occupying Roman Army laid siege to the fortress to crush nine hundred and sixty Jewish rebels. Rather than submitting to the victorious Romans, the Sicarii men, women and children committed mass suicide by self-immolation. Only five women and children remained alive, according to the account of Josephus.

On the exposed summit, the sun beat down fiercely onto baked red sand. With the temperature in the mid-forties Celsius, lethargy overcame JD, his mouth dropped open and he shook his head slowly. We darted between pools of shade cast by boulders in a vain attempt to keep him cool. He refused drink, even though thirsty. In desperation, I squirted water into him with an oral syringe, ten millilitres at a time. Massada was not a success. The place is too barren, hot, dusty, ruined buildings and has too few people for him to watch. But he was with us, and even though he may not like everywhere we take him, we will never know if he does not go.

# RESPITE

October 2008.

"I can't go on much longer," Liz struggled to speak, after spending another night grappling with JD's challenging behaviour, a euphemism for beating himself up when unattended. The alarm in our bedroom is unnecessary because he is so loud, and our room is directly above his. But we keep it on so we can get to him in time. His safety takes priority over our sleep.

His night-time ritual is the same as it was when he was a toddler, not that he ever toddled. Dinner and medicine in the evening, followed by an hour or two in the lounge, or playing the guitar, then bath, story and bed. He is usually tucked up by half-past nine. I read to him for about thirty minutes while he pulls his quilt cover over his head, sticks his fingers in his mouth, watches and listens. So far, I have read him 'The Hobbit' and started the weighty 'Lord of the Rings' tome, about a thousand-and-a-half pages of wizardry and fantasy. Last thing at night, I kiss him on the head, slide the giant padded cot front on his bed, turn on the baby-alarm, turn off the light and whisper, "night night JD, sleep tight."

On most nights, he sleeps for a few hours before waking. After that, he is up and down until breakfast, at six o'clock. I compare him to a new-born baby, only one that weighs forty-five pounds and is five feet tall. Liz is up to him most nights and sometimes I hear her crying with tiredness. Then I get up and lie down with him in his cot-bed. Liz and I dream of a good night's sleep, or we would, if we ever had time to dream. And when the night is done, we start the day with bright, happy smiles for Georgina and work.

About ninety percent of our energy is exhausted on JD. The rest is spent on family, home and work. We have no social life to speak of, apart from synagogue, and our friends, Alan and Nili, who live nearby. Sadly, they are returning to the USA at the end of the year, and we will miss them sorely. But Social Services threw a lifeline and provided funding for some evening respite care, an hour on three weekday evenings. A volunteer comes to our house and looks after JD, while Liz and I prepare meals, help Georgina with her homework, or do what normal families do – whatever that is.

There are a couple of volunteers who are well-matched for JD. We can tell from the way he responds to them, the side-long glance and barely noticeable smile he gives when they appear in his peripheral vision space. They are positive, bright, laugh a lot, and he reacts positively to that. They talk to him, and he vocalises in return. The other volunteers do not know what to do and spend most of their time following him around when he crawls in search of Liz or me. I know they mean well, but they do not have the necessary experience and lack the right skills. We try and explain to them, by which time, half the hour-long session has gone.

Life must go on, with or without respite.

# EMPIRE STATE OF MIND

July 2009.

Faraway places are further away for some. They are more out of reach for JD than most seventeen-year-olds. Medicines, nappies and wheelchair add bulk to the 'one bag only' restriction. In some countries, he must present a doctor's note as evidence that his anti-convulsant and other drugs are legal. He cannot communicate so someone else must talk for him, make sure he does not self-harm or crawl around confined spaces like aircraft cabins, as well as feed and change him.

Sea and air are the only long-distance travel options. JD has been on overnight ferry crossings to France before, but a two-week transatlantic journey would exhaust us before the holiday had even started. He would need two large suitcases of nappies for each month spent afloat. Flying is obviously much faster. But on long-hauls, we can pass time watching films, listening to music, reading and playing games, whereas JD likes shuffling about on his elbows and knees and introducing himself to people. Left alone, he would happily grab a stranger and dribble on them. Then there is the problem of 'number ones and twos'. An aircraft toilet is meant for one person at a time, but it is a three-person job for JD. And as an aircraft climbs and descends, the cabin pressure changes and we ease our discomfort by yawning or blowing, JD does not understand so he beats himself up. Yet despite his disability, he *will* do what other teenagers do. He will go with us, no matter where, and we will surmount each obstacle as it comes.

The challenge started with planning our eight-hour flight to New York and three-week camping holiday in the USA. E-mails and phone calls to the travel agent, the airline company and camp sites checking and double-checking the fine details. Nothing could be overlooked.

We asked every camp site the same question, "Will there be a mattress on the floor of our log cabin for our disabled son to sleep on?"

"Sure," they said.

"Can you guarantee this?" we responded, "because our son will fall out of a bed and injure himself."

"We confirm that all our cabins are equipped with spare mattresses," they replied.

"Can he take Marmite sandwiches through security at JFK airport?" we asked the travel agent.

"That's an original question," she replied, "is there a special need for Marmite?"

"It's the only food our son will have with his medication."

"Well, it shouldn't be a problem then."

"What are the seats like in the aircraft?" we nagged, "economy seats won't do because our son will want to lie down."

"That won't be possible," she said, stating the obvious, "you will be more comfortable in business class."

"Sounds expensive, especially as he won't be able to sit by himself. He will need one of us with him all the time."

"One carer can accompany him at economy class rate," she informed us gleefully, after checking with the airline, "and I've been assured that there will be a safe space for him to lie down in."

"Well, it looks like JD and I will go business class," I said, "and Liz and the girls will fly bucket class."

"Maybe we can swap," Liz suggested, "but I'd be happy

to stay in economy, at least I'll get some unbroken sleep."

Just before take-off, the cabin crew upgraded Liz so she could sit near JD and me. Our concerns and fears for his safety on the flight were mitigated by two camper style seats facing in opposite directions with a partition that could be raised and lowered. JD sat by the window, with room to lie down safely.

Toileting him was our greatest challenge. While I held JD upright, Liz pulled down his pants, removed the soiled nappy, cleaned him with antiseptic wipes and gave the all-clear, so he could sit down. All the time, I was half-out the door bearing his full weight. Anyone passing by had a clear view of proceedings.

We caught the early flight so we could drive in daylight from JFK airport to our campsite in Allentown, Pennsylvania. Landing and disembarking at noon, we spent anxious minutes in the passport and security queue worrying about Marmite sandwiches. The USA has strict controls over food brought into the country. Would they confiscate and destroy them? We braced ourselves, ready for interrogation.

"I think we should take them out of JD's bag," Liz said, as we approached the security kiosk, bristling with cameras and armed guards.

"Just leave them there," I dissented, "they probably won't bother looking."

"Well, I'd rather not take any chances," she said, "it would look bad if they found them when we could have declared them."

"But we don't even know if Marmite is a banned substance," I protested.

"All the more reason to show them," she said firmly and rummaged inside. She extracted a batch of wholemeal bread sandwiches, generously slathered with the yeasty black paste, cut neatly into quarters, crust-less and wrapped in cling-film. I had to admit they looked dodgy.

Smiling nervously, Liz offered them to the Security

Officer and began to explain, "these are my son's Marmite sandwiches – he needs them for his medication."

His eyes flicked from sandwich to JD and back while JD sat in his wheelchair, fingers in mouth, studying the ceiling – a stylish combination of steel and glass.

"Marmite?" he said, raising an eyebrow, "is that a medicine?"

This could all go horribly wrong - he had probably never heard of the peculiarly British condiment. "No," I explained, "it's a strong yeast-flavoured spread."

He studied the sandwiches in Liz's hand for a while before inquiring, "is it alcoholic?"

"No, but it packs a powerful flavour," I replied, "so it disguises the taste of the tablets he takes to control his fits."

Liz quipped, "yes, you either love it or hate it."

"And he *loves* it!" I added, pointing at JD.

The Officer smiled, "I'll have to give it a try," and waved us through.

Now late afternoon by our body-clocks, we yearned to get on the road for the one-hundred-and-twenty-mile drive to our first log cabin. But a two-hour wait to pick up the hire car and a three-hour detour through New York city centre scuppered all hopes of reaching it before nightfall. For thirty minutes, we sat in gridlock among several hundred blaring car horns while a traffic cop blew her whistle and waved her arms fruitlessly. Like driving through a film set, we passed iconic buildings and bridges, basket-ball yards, the Manhattan skyline and dodged school-bus yellow cabs. The GPS guided us over Brooklyn Bridge, through China Town and under the Hudson River before we hit the rolling hills and open roads west of the Big Apple.

The sun dropped over the horizon and eyelids drooped. Crossing time zones extended our day by five hours and JD needed his night dose of Epilim, before he drifted to sleep. Miss it and a seizure was guaranteed.

Dinner at a road-side restaurant, with bright lights, pretty waitresses and noisy diners provided enough stimulation to keep him awake a little longer. I pressed two tablets into a tube of fusilli, swamped in "to-may-to and bay-zil" and popped it into his mouth. He swallowed without chewing.

"Two tablets down and two to go," I announced.

I prepared a second tube with more tablets, dragged it through some red sauce and waited in anticipation for JD's mouth to open, signalling his readiness. After years of handfeeding him, Liz and I knew that any attempt to hurry would be met with resistance.

For a minute, he studied the ceiling and glanced at passing waitresses, then he looked at me and opened his mouth. I reacted swiftly and pushed in the soggy fusilli-wrapped tablets.

"Success!" I cried out, slapping the table in triumph, "job done, medicine administered."

"Well done," Liz said.

"Well done Dad," Georgina added.

"Well done JD," Victoria complimented.

Our campsite nestled in a forest clearing beside the Appalachian Trail, in the heart of Amish country. No alcohol permitted on site and lights off by eleven. We arrived late, to no sign of life, except for the firefly flashes of orange and green in the air, dancing to a chorus of crickets and croaking frogs. Our log cabin was equipped with a bunk bed for Victoria and Georgina, a double bed for Liz and me and a large mattress for JD. He dozed in the car, so we unloaded and set up inside, dragging his bedding to a corner and walling it in with suitcases and nappy bags. As the girls crashed out, I carried him indoors still asleep, head on my shoulder, changed and tucked him under the sheets, exhausted after twenty-four hours on the road.

***

A week later, we swapped our log cabin in Pennsylvania for another near Niagara Falls and pondered over the problem of giving JD the fullest experience. Everything must be 'in his face', overloading as many senses as possible. An obvious solution popped into my head.

"Let's take him to the bottom of the Bridal Veil Falls," I suggested to Liz, "he'll love it, especially on such a sticky day."

Liz nodded her approval. His trip to the US would be as memorable for him as for his sisters. We headed for the Cave of the Winds and the lift down to the base of the falls.

After collecting a fistful of bright yellow capes at the entrance, we descended to a series of ramps leading across the rocks a few feet from the roaring torrent. Immediately, JD chuckled and screamed with joy as a cool spray doused him and the cascading water thundered by. Rolling along the first ramp with a firm grip on the handles, I dropped the wheels one step at a time down to the next ramp, edging closer to the fall. A queue of caped tourists formed behind, unable to pass along the narrow walkway.

"We'd better not go too far," Liz shouted, barely audible above the cacophony, "you've got to get him back up."

"Too late," I yelled, "besides, he's enjoying it too much."

We crossed several ramps to the foot of the falls on to a viewing platform. I tilted the wheelchair to face the crest, one-hundred-and-eighty-feet above.

"Well, you made it JD," I shouted, "this is where your great-great-grand-uncle met his fate in 1883."

Captain Matthew Webb, the first man to swim the English Channel, was crushed when he attempted to swim across the Whirlpool Rapids, a short distance from where we stood. The revelation that he was a distant relative of the legendary Victorian hero was swamped, literally, by the sight before him.

A Marmite sandwich picnic on Goat Island, followed by a Maid of the Mist boat trip to the base of the Horseshoe Falls completed his action-packed day.

\*\*\*

The following week we drove to Danbury in Connecticut to re-unite with our repatriated friends, Alan and Nili. They sacrificed the basement of their new home for us, a beautiful log cabin beside a lake in a forest, for our final week. On a warm and muggy morning, after Liz and Nili left for a day's excursion to Long Island, Alan turned up in a golf buggy, with Tally the Collie in the back seat.

"C'mon," he announced, "let's go for a dip in the pond."

I studied the buggy and considered logistics – would it seat five and dog with room for a folded wheelchair, towels and JD's emergency bag? It would be a squeeze, but Alan had planned the venture well.

"JD can sit up front between you and me, Victoria and Georgina in the back with Tally, and the wheelchair can go in place of the golf clubs," he insisted.

"No problem," I said, shakily.

"No problem," he said, confidently.

A ride in a golf buggy followed by a swim in a lake would be a unique experience, and another once-in-a-lifetime opportunity for JD, to add to his trip through New York and the base of Niagara Falls. We bundled aboard and set off.

Alan twisted the open buggy through the quiet residential streets while JD sat engrossed, fingers in mouth, watching the trees and houses flash by. No one batted an eye as the contraption whirred past, over-loaded with a disabled teenager sandwiched between two middle-aged men, two young ladies and a dog buried under a pile of beach towels and a wheelchair poking out the golf-club cage. Alan seemed unconcerned hurtling down the hill at breakneck speed, waving and singing out cheery "Hi"s to neighbours in their gardens. It was all a perfectly normal occurrence for the residents of Candlewood Lake.

We parked by a jetty that stretched ten yards over the lake. All was still and clear with no one around. I undressed JD, leaving him in only a nappy, strapped in his wheelchair and wrapped in a towel, before testing the water temperature. Anything cooler than warm would not be tolerated. Alan and I considered how best to lower him down a set of wooden rungs into the lake. More importantly, we considered how to extract him after, and quickly in case of an emergency. He needed both of us while in the lake, one to hold him while treading water furiously, and the other to take over when necessary. I had taken him into water many times before, but freshwater lacked the buoyancy of seawater, and it would take more effort to keep his head above the surface.

Alan and the dog threw themselves in the lake and swam over to the steps while I descended one-handed with an arm wrapped round JD's waist and his chin hooked over my shoulder. The final step hung a foot below the surface. The only way into the water would be to plunge, potentially submerging JD. Who knows what deadly bacteria he could swallow? He would not understand any advice to close his mouth, so we were stuck.

"Pass JD to me," Alan raised his arms, "then you lower yourself in and I'll pass him back."

"Good plan!"

Grabbing the ladder with one hand, I leaned out and swung JD around, who was promptly plucked from me.

Once safely in the water and re-assured by its warmth, his face creased into a grin. He wrapped his arms around my neck, and shook his head from side to side, chuckling and crying out in delight. He must live his life fully, undiminished by his disability, and seize every opportunity to do the things that everyone else can, no matter how unusual.

If anyone ever asks, "has JD swum in a lake?"

I could answer happily, "yes! *And* he's ridden in a golf buggy! On the *same day*!"

\*\*\*

On our last day in the US, Alan chaperoned us on a whirlwind tour of the Big Apple. We headed for the bright lights of Times Square. An hour later, we stood beneath the clock inside Grand Central Station, reputedly the world's most expensive timepiece, and scene of many blockbuster movies. The Empire State Building came next on our to-do list, taking the VIP disabled lift to the eighty-sixth floor and the viewing platform. From a thousand feet up, we plummeted below ground into the Subway, via a street lift a block away, with the intention of taking a train to Ground Zero and a ferry to the Statue of Liberty. The large and grubby lift was daubed with graffiti - a prelude to the scene below street level. Sweltering, dusty, littered, over-crowded, dimly lit and menacing, a stark contrast to the glitz and glass of Manhattan only feet above our heads. Having mis-read the directions, we caught the wrong train and alighted at the Flatiron Building. As consolation for missing our tight deadline, we re-planned and hailed a yellow cab to Little Italy for 'caw-fee' and cakes.

The excessive heat and high humidity were our main concerns for JD throughout the day. Skin rashes from soggy nappies and dehydration are two immediate effects. So, our visits to the many iconic sites were punctuated by short breaks in air-conditioned cafes where we could use the disabled facilities and encourage him to drink. Perversely, he will only co-operate if conditions are cool and dry.

Later in the afternoon, we wandered through Central Park and visited the John Lennon Memorial, just a few hundred yards from where the former Beatle was gunned down. Not wanting to be locked the wrong side of the park gates after nightfall, we retired to a restaurant opposite Trump Tower where we set JD's Marmite sandwiches at the table as an appetiser for his meal and medication. For a second time in three weeks, we explained the provenance of JD's favourite foodstuff to a native New Yorker.

Our adventure ended at midnight at Alan and Nili's house in Connecticut. JD slept in the car for the two-hour journey back, snoozed deeply as I carried him from the car, washed, changed and put him to bed. Such was the effect of the city that never sleeps.

With sadness, we said goodbye to our friends the next day. After skirting around the east side of New York, we returned the car and caught the shuttle to our terminal. Like many airports, JFK provided a special vehicle for transporting and on-boarding disabled passengers. We shared it with JD to advise the stewards and assistants on lifting him, all the while looking out for signs of impending fits.

The return flight offered little time for rest. Just like all our holidays, Liz and I were exhausted from carrying, washing, changing and feeding JD, the broken sleep and from the emotional strain of medicating, rehydrating and reducing the possibility of seizure. We joked that we needed another holiday so soon after finishing one. But we always want him with us despite the effort. He will do everything we do, no debate, and we must make up the rules for him – what he can do, what he cannot. It is what New Yorkers call an 'empire state of mind'. With every challenge, lies opportunity.

TWO JOURNEYS-Undiminished and Unforgotten

Jeremy (aged seventeen) in Grand Central Station

# CHARLIE THE MUTT

December 2009.

We have a mutt - a four-legged gift for Georgina's fourteenth birthday present.

"It's either we have a dog and me, or no dog and not me," she warned a few weeks earlier.

"A bichon frise," she insisted, "like Monty."

Monty was Julie's dog, who Georgina and JD grew up with, so her choice came as no surprise. But a bichon frise was an expensive breed, so we persuaded her to pop into our local Animal Rescue Centre, where there was an excellent selection of mutts.

After several visits, she eventually fell in love with Charlie, a three-year-old Staffordshire Terrier-Alsatian-Collie bitch. Charlie arrived today and met JD for the first time. He watched her, and she was curious about the human who moved on four legs, just like her.

JD is still chronically underweight for a seventeen-year-old boy. He weighs only forty-eight pounds, about the same as an average six to seven-year-old, but heavy enough when lifting him in and out of the bath, car, and wheelchair. Liz and I accept that he must move into full-time care eventually. We have been told that this means finding a placement in a care home of Surrey Council's choosing and one that meets their sufficiency criteria. A cheaper option would be a team of live-in carers, with strangers sleeping in our house, eating and watching telly with us, competing for the bathroom, and so on. A bloody nightmare. Even then, we would not be able to lie in our bed and do nothing when we hear JD self-harming at night. It would be too traumatic.

Caring for JD is so difficult now, physically and emotionally. He is heavier and stronger, yet still behaves like a newborn. All is fine when I put him to bed at around ten o'clock, after reading him a story. He plants his thumb in his mouth, buries himself under the quilt and drifts off to sleep. Then I turn on the baby monitor and go to bed a couple of hours later. At midnight, a blanket of calm and quiet descends over our house, and if we are lucky, may stay unruffled for an hour or two. But without fail, he will wake once, twice, thrice, and chaos will erupt.

The hissing monitor crackles into life, rousing us from sleep.

*Thunk, thunk, thunk,* the sound of JD hitting himself in frustration, rage or fear, fills our senses.

Minutes later, the monitor broadcasts a loud wail. Sometimes he hits himself so hard that he splits a lip, blacks an eye or bloodies his nose. By morning, he could have been three rounds with Mike Tyson. There is no way on Earth we can adopt the same attitude as parents of small children do and dismiss his antics as attention-seeking. They may well be, but we must respond every time to prevent him seriously damaging himself.

His sleep pattern has always been unpredictable. We should have adapted to broken sleep after seventeen years and nine months, but we have not. By now, we should understand why he does not sleep, but we do not. Despite consultations with the paediatrician, neurologist and behavioural psychologist, no explanation is forthcoming. We can only guess. Maybe hunger, thirst or soiled nappy was to blame in his early years. Seizures could have been the culprits throughout childhood and pre-adolescence. Now, we think it is because he is bored and wants attention. We cope with his and our sleep deprivation because there is no choice.

Over the years, we have accumulated a mountain of special equipment for JD. A sturdy feeding chair rests in the kitchen, a massive standing frame occupies a large chunk of our lounge and toys are scattered in every room. In 2005, we modified the downstairs extension, and made him a bedroom that houses a huge pneumatically powered bed with side grill to stop him falling out, and a beautiful multi-sensory corner donated by his friends at synagogue on his bar mitzvah. There is a wet room adjacent to his bedroom, into which we squeeze an adult wheelchair, wheelchair covers and hoist for lifting him in and out of the bath. There are signs of JD's presence everywhere, except for his sisters' bedrooms. There are other signs around the house, such as lumps gouged out of walls by his wheelchair and carpet stains from the food he regurgitated or ejected. We tried to remove the stains and even cleaned them professionally, but they are too stubborn. My advice to house-proud parents of children with similar conditions is to paint your walls dark and buy even darker carpets.

So, we must accept the fact that JD cannot be in our care permanently. That is a painful admission to make about our dearly loved son. But we cannot go on for much longer, we need help. Charlie provides a small modicum of help by just *being around*. Our latest addition to the family does not realise the impact she is making. When we are tired or upset by JD's shenanigans, she comes to see what the fuss is about and does her utmost to console us. She plants herself before Liz or me, demanding attention. Her dark eyes search ours for answers we do not have. She nudges us with her nose when we are agitated by JD's behaviour, reminding us to stop and think instead of wallow in pity and fatigue. She is our emotional sponge.

Charlie the mutt

# BUCKETS 'N' SPADES

February 2010.

Social Services agreed to fund twenty-one days of respite care over the year, and we plan to make the most of it. JD is spending a weekend at a Norwood home in London called Buckets 'n' Spades that has capacity for a dozen children with learning and physical disabilities. He stayed there four times last year, when Social Services were less generous with their respite care allowance. Unusually for them, they increased the allowance. Maybe the message that we are exhausted reached the people with the purse strings who decided to take preventative measures before we break down completely.

The extra respite will give Liz and me a break from a routine of feeding, medicating, bathing, carrying, changing and entertaining JD for seven days every week. We have never measured the time and energy we dedicate to him. But we know that we are drained, our buckets are empty. But our devotion to him and his siblings is absolute, just as it is for most parents. So, I feel guilty admitting I need time away from my son – I have given up and handed him to someone else.

But I understand why a break is necessary. We need healing time and a chance to give some attention to his sisters. Roxanne and Victoria left home for university already, and we can never reclaim lost time with them. Georgina is at school and at a difficult teen-age, when she does not want to be seen with her parents, let alone hang-out with them. We hope it is not too little, too late.

Liz dropped JD off at Buckets 'n' Spades this afternoon, in time for the evening Sabbath service, and we arranged to collect him two days later. The home is run by young adults with buckets of energy, which they need in spades. The place buzzes with activity and JD brightens when he arrives. Maybe my assumption that he always wants his parents around is wrong. He is almost eighteen years old. When I was his age, my parents were the last people I wanted to be with. So, a weekend away from us must be good for him and may be something he wants. If it was unwanted, he would let us know in no uncertain terms. He broadcasts his feelings by vocalising, by the looks he gives, gestures and body language. Thankfully, he makes only happy noises when he is at Buckets 'n' Spades.

# A NIGHT OUT WITH THE BOYS

It was JD's eighteenth birthday on March 30$^{th}$ and time for his inaugural beer and curry with 'the boys'. By boys, I mean a group of my forty, fifty and sixty-something friends who have known JD since his birth. I booked a table for twenty at an Indian restaurant in West Byfleet, ten miles away. The staff were told about his special needs and catered for his unique culinary requirements but fell short of providing Marmite sandwiches. They prepared a long table, so he could sit in the middle with me on his feeding side.

Instead of poppadums, he started with naan bread and polished off an entire bowl of nibbles with his medicines, including a deadly hot chilli and lime pickle that is usually left behind. Impressive. He washed it down with a couple of mouthfuls of Cobra beer. The lamb biryani was tender and perfect, melting in his mouth. All the time, the conversation flowed, and JD chipped in with the occasional "aaaahh," "eeerrrr" and "er-her-her," when he was not too busy stuffing his face. The evening concluded with a rousing rendition of "happy birthday" before he was lifted into his waiting chariot.

# PARENTS GET LOST

May 2010.

"JD is going on a camping trip," Liz announced over breakfast.

"I didn't know anything about this," I said, "when are we taking him?"

"Not us," she replied, "parents aren't allowed."

"Errrr," chimed JD, as if to support our exclusion.

"His school has organised a 'Parents Get Lost' activity week in Exmoor," Liz continued, "through an organisation called the Calvert Trust."

She handed me a small leaflet. Their mission was to *'enable people with disabilities to achieve their potential through the challenge of adventurous activities in the countryside'*, just the kind of mission JD would be interested in.

"Wow! What will we do while he's away?"

"Not spend our mornings, evenings and nights looking after him," she replied swiftly. For the first time since JD's birth, in 1992, we would be without him for more than two nights. For five days, I would not need to give him his breakfast, get him ready for school, change his nappy six times every day, rush back from work to bath him and put him to bed. Liz would not need to hurry home from work to feed him or get up to him several times in the night. It would be welcome respite.

We dropped JD off at school on Monday morning, with a suitcase full of clothes, two large bags of adult diapers, a jar of Marmite and his medicine for the week ahead. Stephen, JD's best mate from school, and eight other children with special needs also boarded the bus for the four-hour drive to Exmoor National Park.

Georgina was at school, so we did absolutely *nothing* apart from re-charge our batteries. The house was eerily quiet in the evenings and at night. The baby-alarm stayed off and I did not need to tip-toe to bed in case I woke JD up. We slept undisturbed for four whole nights. We read, watched TV, listened to the radio in the mornings undisturbed, talked about our day when we came home from work and school, and ate together. "Why are you bolting your food?" we accused each other, more than once in the week. It is a tough habit to break, after years of being eating opportunists.

On Friday evening JD came home supercharged with excitement. Prolonged vocalisations, squeals of delight and chuckles. During the week, e-mailed photos taken at the Calvert Trust Exmoor Centre revealed the highlights of his outdoor adventures. He sailed on a pontoon with Stephen, specially adapted for two wheelchair passengers, and felt the breeze across the Wistlandpound Reservoir, bordered by spruces and pines. He practiced archery by sticking an arrow in a target, aided by a helper. He abseiled up and down a forty-foot rock face in a special harness while wearing a hard hat. The photos recorded him beaming from ear to ear during the ascent. Clearly, he has not inherited my fear of heights, because I would have been a gibbering wreck.

They took him horse-riding, as he does every Thursday at home, first in a saddle and in a two-person chariot through the grounds of the Centre. After such an exciting week, packed with adventure, I was surprised he was so pleased to see us.

# CHANGES

June 2010.

JD is changing. Reminders of his disappearing childhood are everywhere - the wispy hairs on his body, the deepening voice, and the wiry muscles like steel cords in his limbs. The latter is due to his regular physiotherapy sessions at school. I must accept that he is no longer the precious little boy I can carry around like a toddler - he is an eighteen-year-old young man. But he will never be able to do the same things his peers can unaided. He will forever depend on someone to feed, wash, clothe and medicate him. Liz and I accepted that fact years ago, but it makes it impossible for me to treat him as if he did not have his condition. His dependence makes the bond between us so strong.

Next year, he will leave his special needs school, Portesbery in Camberley for ever. Who knows what will happen after? One thing is certain – if we leave the decision to Surrey's Transition Team, then we must bow to their definition of 'sufficient' care, which will be well below the standard we expect and by other parents of loved ones. The 'sufficiency bar' rises and falls to suit the political agenda. When central Government cuts the spending budget in times of austerity, it reduces hand-outs to local Government, who then lower the bar.

Things are moving though, mainly due to the appointment of a dynamic County Transition Team Care

Manager, June. She is an ex-State Registered Nurse who sank her teeth into JD's case and badgered Surrey Heath to fund full-time care in a home in North London, managed by Norwood. We know Norwood well. We visited the Annie Lawson School in Ravenswood Village sixteen years ago, when we sought a special needs school placement for JD. I take the Friday evening sabbath services there every month and have grown fond of the wonderfully caring and characterful disabled adults who attend. Norwood manages Buckets 'n' Spades, where JD goes for occasional weekend breaks. We like what we see of Norwood, which will help to soften the blow when we let JD go.

The Care Home Manager at Woodcock Dell, one of Norwood's homes, and their Funding Manager visited JD when he stayed at Buckets 'n' Spades a few days ago. They conducted a preliminary assessment to see if Norwood could fulfil his complex care needs. Thankfully, they reported to June that he passed their tests with flying colours. Things are changing unusually quickly.

## WOODCOCK DELL

Four weeks after Norwood gave JD the 'thumbs up', Liz and I visited Woodcock Dell, his possible new home. Vicky, the Care Home Manager, and Philma, his potential Primary Carer, showed us around. They introduced us to five of the seven adult residents, who could be his future family if funding is approved. The residents' concern for each other is so strong. Perhaps caring so deeply for someone 'rubs off' onto others, like a 'caring infection'? The vibe in Woodcock Dell as at least as strong as in Ravenswood village. I was reminded of our first visit to a Norwood home years earlier and the palpable happiness, love and warmth. The instinct on crossing the threshold is to smile.

The Woodcock Dell residents have learning and physical disabilities with needs as complex as JD's. We sat in the dining room over a pot of tea and biscuits and talked about life in the home, while rich and varied sounds from the residents drifted around the house. Melvin, the most senior, aged over seventy sat in his wheelchair singing, "a bee bop bop".

"Melvin is making his happy noises," Vicky informed us, "he sings like that when all is well."

Barbara, one of two residents who could walk, approached our table.

"Hello Barbara," Philma looked up, "have you come to say hello to our guests?"

Barbara sighed and took my hand.

"She wants to show you around the house," Vicky laughed, "she is the mother figure of the home, after all."

Holding my hand, Barbara led me from the dining room and into the lounge. Robin, a man in his thirties, sat in a wheelchair with his back to the long front window. His carer paraded in front of him and pretended to trip over an imaginary obstacle. Robin threw his head back and his face creased with silent laughter. The ritual repeated with the same effect.

His carer explained, "Robin has a slapstick sense of humour – he roared out loud a few weeks ago when he saw someone fall flat on their face."

Philma interrupted my guided tour of the home, "I'm sorry Barbara, but I must take Laurence so we can talk about Jeremy, the young man who might be coming to stay with us."

Another carer took her hand from mine, "come on Babs, you can show me around the house."

"Besides," Philma added, "we have opened our best biscuits."

A large man in a wheelchair on the far side of the room yelled, "don't eat them or you'll get fat like me!"

"Thank you, Allan," said Philma, between bouts of laughter.

A minute later, a woman in her mid-twenties shuffled into the room and stood before JD. His eyes locked on to her. She stared at him for a few seconds before turning and leaving the room, and JD's eyes followed.

"I think he likes her," I said.

"Jeremy, she is Raquel," Vicky said, pointing at her as she stopped and turned to regard him again from the hallway.

With fingers in his mouth, he murmured, "mmm".

"He definitely likes her," Liz agreed.

We left Woodcock Dell reassured for JD's future. He would be happy in such a delightfully crazy and chaotic place. But letting him go would still be a struggle for me.

# LETTING GO

Vicky and Philma visited JD at Portesbery School during lunchtime, a week after our trip to Woodcock Dell.

"Mealtimes are always the best time to see how someone with complex needs interacts with their carer," Vicky explained, "so we have arranged to see him in his school and then see him with you at supper, if that's OK."

A few minutes before five o'clock, Liz opened the front door to Vicky and Philma. Charlie went berserk when two strangers intruded on her territory, much to JD's amusement. Liz invited them into the kitchen where JD sat waiting for his customary starter of Marmite sandwich and Epilim tablets. With a grumble, Charlie abandoned her attempt to repel the infiltrators and slumped in her basket.

"Our turn to bring out the biscuits," Liz announced and placed a selection of figgy rolls and chocolate digestives on the table.

I tore off a bite-sized chunk of sandwich and pressed four tablets into the brown goo. JD opened his mouth in anticipation.

"Aaahhh," he said, as if he were at a Dentist's.

"Aaahhh," Liz and I repeated.

"It's always good to talk, isn't it JD?" Liz said.

Philma and Vicky watched in silence, as we proceeded from starter to mains – tomato and tuna pasta.

"I will miss this," I said suddenly, picturing a time when he would no longer be sat waiting for me to give him his supper, "I can't help feeling like I'm abandoning him."

"That's normal," Vicky replied, "every parent we've met felt the same way about letting their child go."

She continued, "you cannot look after him for the rest of your life."

"Probably not," I admitted, "we're getting weaker and smaller as we age, while JD will only get stronger and bigger."

Everything she said made sense, but the emotional tie was still too strong.

"There are parents I know of who continued to care for their child until they became so frail, they had to stop," she explained, "by then, handing over had become a necessity, and even harder for them to let go."

We must let him go now, while we have the chance, or never. Liz is burned out from fighting continuously, without respite. She clings to a thin rope. She fought an eighteen-year war for JD, armed with telephone battle-axe and slashing e-mail, to give him the best quality of life. I did the heavy work - the physical stuff, like bathing him, lifting him in and out of the car, pushing his wheelchair over sand and through mud, carrying him while dancing at friends' and family celebrations. During that time, my love for him grew stronger than I could ever imagine. I remember those dark days when he was my "doll son" because he was floppy, unresponsive, "a shell", a bitter disappointment, and not the son I expected or wanted. If only I could tell myself then about what he would become, and the journey he would take us on.

Even after Vicky's and Philma's convincing reasons to let JD go, and had departed for Woodcock Dell, the guilt remained. I worry that he will be forgotten. I must never let that happen! Wherever he goes and whoever ends up caring for him, he will be unforgotten. The positive impact he made on people must be remembered. Liz knows that letting JD go as soon as possible is a necessity for her. Either JD stays with us, and she breaks down completely, or JD leaves. There is also the possibility, small though it may be, that we are sentencing him to a life in the wrong place.

# NEW HOME, NEW FAMILY

October 2010.

June persuaded her management to fund JD's full-time care in Woodcock Dell. Woodcock Dell and Norwood confirmed that they can meet his care needs and we agreed to proceed. JD will leave home in four months. There are a few details to sort out, such as whether to take his standing frame and massive cot-bed with him and what to do with his multi-sensory equipment that our friends bought him for his bar mitzvah.

He will have a few weekend stayovers in Woodcock Dell between now and his last day at home, so he can adjust to his new home and new family.

# LAST DAY IN SCHOOL

February 18th 2011.

Portesbery school threw a leaving party for JD, on his last day. His classmates, teachers and therapists popped in for one last cuddle. Perhaps JD would have been upset if he understood the significance of the event. He has spent over sixteen happy years there.

For years, we fought for a placement in a Jewish school and lost and he stayed where he was. We never had anything against Portesbery - they met his physical and learning disability needs, but could not meet his cultural needs, although they tried their best. Keeping kosher was one thing they struggled with. What to do with him during the big Christian festivals like Christmas and Easter was another. But JD loved his time at Portesbery and I saw why - the school was filled with so many characterful students. He built strong friendships with his classmates, like his best pal Stephen, who popped around for birthday parties, tea, games and a chat.

No more shall I dress and ready him for the school bus at a quarter past eight and never again will he arrive at our door at four, expecting Marmite sandwiches.

# LEAVING

February 20th 2011.

JD leaves home today forever. He enjoyed his weekends at Woodcock Dell. He slept through the night without waking, ate everything on offer and regarded the ladies with interest.

We reached our limit after caring for JD for so long. How can I describe what it is like looking after a severely disabled child? Imagine being a parent of a newborn. When your baby cries, you drop whatever you are doing, no matter how important, and rush to attend. Baby takes absolute priority over anything, everything, and everyone. You cannot help yourself. A baby's cry triggers our fight-or-flight instinct, according to neuroscientists, even if the baby is unrelated. If you have ever sat on public transport near a screaming baby, you will know the effect its cry has on your system.

Now suppose that a parent continued the newborn baby routine for *nineteen years*, instead of for a few weeks until baby settled into a sleeping rhythm. Because JD *never* settled. Now imagine that baby weighs over four stones, is five feet tall, has epilepsy, reflux, scoliosis, is doubly incontinent, and self-harms if left unattended for more than a few minutes. That is what it was like. JD leaving home will affect the whole family. We will regain hours of time every day, hours spent feeding, bathing, medicating, reading him bed-time stories, taking him on walks and listening out for him at nights. Our fight-or-flight responses will lie dormant.

We acquired so much stuff for JD over the years. A massive standing frame takes up a large chunk of our lounge, there is a heavy feeding chair in the kitchen, an enormous bed with a pneumatic device for raising and lowering, a commode, a winch to lift him in and out of the bath which I never used because JD hates it. Our synagogue friends donated a superb multi-sensory corner in his bedroom. When JD leaves, our house will be a lot emptier, not just because of his absence.

On one hand, I am looking forward to the free time and space. God knows what we will do with it. On the other hand, I will miss him *so* much. My precious son has been my constant buddy, walking companion, confidante, even though he may not have understood what I confided. We were inseparable. Wherever he went, I went and vice-versa. He may not walk or talk, but he is a mountain of personality and has a strong sense for big occasions. I worry about whether he will think I have deserted him. I also worry about whether Woodcock Dell can care for him as much as we do.

So, we will drive him thirty-five miles to Woodcock Dell, just as we have done for the past few weekends, drop him off and then drive home. We will visit every Sunday and take him out to a local park. Once a month, he will come home for a weekend - correction, stay in *our house* for a weekend. I must accept that our house will no longer be his home.

This morning, we loaded the car with his clothes, toys, books and possessions, as if we were driving him to college for his first year as an undergraduate. He was leaving home for good this time, but he probably did not know - it was just another trip in the car to him, a treat. He always loved travelling.

He sat on the back seat while we cruised on the M3 listening to the radio.

I turned to him and said, "well JD, this is it, today is the first day of the rest of your life."

He reached out with his left hand, and we held hands until the car pulled into the driveway at Woodcock Dell.

We dropped him and his luggage off, hung around awkwardly for a few minutes and then drove home in silence. Home is so quiet, eerie, and empty without him. Suddenly, there is nothing to do. No bath-time, no story to read to him, no one to play my guitar to. The signs of JD are everywhere. I did not expect his leaving to be so painful. Neither did I expect so much guilt for sending him away forever, for abandoning him. I laid on the floor in his room and cried for an hour. Then I told myself that I had to let him go. We could not be full-time carers for much longer. He left for our sakes, his sisters' and, of course, for his own sake.

I needed to get out of the house, so Charlie the mutt took me for a walk in the woods.

# THEY WANT TO OPERATE ON HIM!

JD's honeymoon period with his new home in Woodcock Dell is over. Six months after moving out, he returned to his old ways of self-harming. It happens mostly at night when his housemates are asleep, out of sight and all is quiet. When he lived with us, we used a baby alarm to listen for the murmurs of discontent that would turn to self-harm if left unchecked. Even then, we never got to him before he thumped himself a few times. The only way to prevent him from damaging himself was to be with him continuously throughout the night. It is no consolation knowing that his challenging behaviour is as difficult to deal with for his carers as it was for us.

Woodcock Dell phoned me while I was working at home. JD was admitted to Northwick Park Hospital in north London because he beat himself up during the night. His ear was so badly swollen that his GP referred him to A&E, where a consultant urged a surgical procedure to reduce the swelling. They intended to operate at six o'clock that evening. Both Woodcock Dell and I knew that there would be major complications with anaesthesia and recovery, because of his epilepsy, scoliosis and other conditions. I must voice my concerns. So, I dropped everything and prepared to hack through the afternoon rush-hour traffic to the hospital. Georgina insisted on coming with me.

"He's my brother!" she reminded me, tearfully.

We arrived at the hospital ninety minutes later and rushed to his ward. The unbearable midsummer heat lingered in the small ward, even with the windows wide open. For four hours, JD and Christina, his carer, waited to be seen. He lay on a bed without sides, shaking his head, uncomfortably hot, frustrated and in pain from the beating he gave himself. His left ear glowed crimson red, with tinges of blue on a large swelling at the tip and back. Christina looked more exhausted than JD, from fighting to stop him self-harming and rolling off the bed on to the hard floor, inflicting more serious damage than he ever could by hitting himself.

"He's been here for hours, and he hasn't had a drink, a pad change or anything!" she protested, "and they want to operate on him!"

Flushed from suffocating heat and exertion preventing JD hurting himself, her only concern was for him. She *could* have said, "I've been here for four hours, and I'm knackered." But she did not. Not a thought for her own well-being crossed her mind. My concern for JD's welfare in Woodcock Dell's hands evaporated. I could trust them to care for him.

I offered to take over from Christina while she grabbed a drink in the hospital cafe. She explained that he arrived in Woodcock Dell's bus which returned home for change pads, feeding and drinking equipment, Marmite, cartons of juice, spare clothes – all the essential caboodle. There is no such thing as a quick drop-off with JD. She checked him over again, then explained to him what was happening, hovered about, and left.

I sat on the bed and put JD on my lap, "it's OK JD, we're here."

He rested his head on my chest, sighed and put his fingers in his mouth.

"He looks," began Georgina, struggling to stop tears running down her cheeks, "he looks…" She could not get the words out. With one arm wrapped around my son, I reached out the other to my youngest daughter.

"What is it sweetie?"

She sat beside me.

"He looks so frail," she stammered and sobbed, "it's so unfair," then rested her head on my shoulder.

So absorbed had I been in JD's condition, I completely overlooked Georgina's love for him. I recalled how she fought for her older brother more than once. JD would be OK, not only would Woodcock Dell be there for him when Liz and I are gone – his sisters would be too.

Philma arrived with several overnight bags stuffed with clothes, change pads, medicines, creams, cups, paper towels, food, drinks - nothing had been overlooked. She pulled the curtains around his bed, and we changed him. Thirty minutes later, the consultant arrived to inspect JD and administer his pre-op anaesthetic.

Immediately, I unloaded my worries, "is it really necessary to operate?"

The consultant looked up, "there is some bad bruising and a risk of permanent cosmetic damage, although there may be risks in operating too."

"He has epilepsy and takes a cocktail of medicines," I pressed on, "will that complicate anaesthesia and recovery?"

"Probably," he paused for a moment, "but I think the risk of reviving him outweighs the risk of not operating."

With bated breath, I waited to hear the announcement that Philma, Georgina and I wanted.

"If he was a supermodel, then the operation to prevent a cauliflower ear would be beneficial but, given his medical condition, I am going to advise against it."

They discharged JD thirty minutes later and he returned to Woodcock Dell, tired, hot and hungry. Georgina and I met him there with his new family. We always suspected that JD would return to his old ways of self-harming eventually. Even after countless discussions with his psychologist, we never knew what upsets him. We could only speculate and vary his night-time routine by laying him down on the bedroom floor, singing to him, carrying him to other rooms, turning on his bubble tube and, on a few occasions, taking him for a drive in the car.

JD's challenging behaviour ultimately convinced Liz and I that we could not care for him indefinitely. As he grows larger, heavier and stronger, he would inflict more serious damage to himself and, quite possibly, to us as well. Today was the first and, hopefully, the last confirmation.

# SIR ANDREW WILL SEE THE YOUNG MAN NOW

November 17th 2012.

JD and his family were invited to the annual Norwood fundraising dinner in the Grosvenor House Hotel in Mayfair. Norwood's main fundraising event pulls out all the stops to convince some very generous people to contribute to the charity. A thousand guests and a galaxy of stars attended including Sir Andrew Lloyd-Webber, Myleene Klass, the Rt Hon Ed Milliband (Leader of the Labour Party) and several other luminaries. The girls were disappointed not to see Simon Cowell, who recorded a special appeal, with JD featuring in the video.

JD and Philma were waiting for us when we arrived at six o'clock. Dapper in his posh suit and another four inches taller since he left home, he looks more like a young man than a boy. The relationship between him and Philma was so strong after twenty-one months of living in Woodcock Dell. He would glance at her, and their eyes would lock for a half-second. Then they would carry on, reassured by each other's presence. Seeing the brief glances reminded me of when he lived with us. JD and I used our eyes to communicate too. One look asks, "are you there?" and the other answers, "I'm here."

We wandered for thirty minutes around the grand banqueting suite before a photographer ushered us on to a photo stand, alongside the celebrities. Pushing a heavy wheelchair, a forest of famous people stood between me and our allocated spot, centre stage. The celebrities were busy manoeuvring themselves into position and not guarding their rears, unaware of the lumbering JD-tank approaching from behind. Partly blinded by the lights and deafened by the noise of laughter and chitter-chatter, serious damage would be inflicted if I did not take great care and exercise tact. I wheeled him on to the stand and shouted, "gangway please, we don't want to run over anyone famous!"

The conversation stopped, and several heads turned. Myleene Klass waved us on, "go for it!"

Like the Sea of Reeds parting, JD and I waded through a corridor of showbiz personalities to our designated place. I stood beside him and next to Ed Milliband, who turned to me, and offered his hand.

"Thank you for turning up," he said quietly.

I shook his hand and replied, "I wouldn't have missed it for the world."

Myleene Klass presented herself to JD, crouched down and peered into his eyes.

"Hello Jeremy," she said, "I'm Myleene."

"Errrrr," JD replied. His eyes locked on hers.

She stood behind holding his wheelchair, while Liz, Roxanne, Victoria and Georgina readied themselves for the photo-shoot.

Seated at one of fifty dinner tables each set for twenty, I was given the honour of feeding JD. I wanted to "for old times' sake," I said to Philma. Nearly two years had passed since he left home, and I sorely missed our mealtimes together. JD was effusive, vocal and ate everything offered. His sense of good taste was untouched by the virus that devastated him as he lay inside the womb. He relished every mouthful and continued eating well after the other guests at our table finished. He ate during Ed Milliband's speech, Sir Andrew Lloyd-Webber's piano recital, and during an interview by Myleene Klass. Our waiters hovered anxiously nearby.

Finally, JD finished his mains, and his plate and cutlery were whisked away. The MC gave an order to open the mysterious brown envelopes on the dinner tables. A hush fell on the room, as chequebooks and pens were extracted from pockets and handbags, cheques torn from stubs, and envelopes rustled. Norwood raised three million pounds from previous fundraising dinners, a quarter of the annual target required to sustain the level of care they provide. We shared the room with some seriously generous people.

JD's favourite dessert arrived - chocolate mousse with fruity trimmings. He leaned forward, opened his mouth and pawed. His eyes locked on to his pudding. I scooped a spoonful up and delivered it with haste. After the third mouthful, a waiter tapped me on the shoulder, "Sir Andrew will see the young man now."

Liz was aghast at the proposal to interrupt his pudding. She replied politely, "please tell Sir Andrew that the young man is having his pudding and will be ready in ten minutes."

JD polished off his and half of my dessert in a record time of fifteen minutes. After a brisk wipe-down, I wheeled him to our delayed audience and photo-shoot with Sir Andrew.

We waited on the photo-stand. JD sat in front, I stood behind, with Liz and the girls on either side. A cheer announced the arrival of Sir Andrew, the crowd parted, he emerged beaming and pressed on to the stand. He bent down and introduced himself to JD. It was a one-sided tête à tête. JD's eyes fastened on Myleene Klass, a few feet away, ignoring Sir Andrew, who inquired if he enjoyed his evening then moved closer and repeated his question. He is certainly seeing the young man now, I thought, while panicking over the peril Sir Andrew now faced. Being so close to JD, he was in imminent danger of receiving a hand in the face, especially if he continued obstructing JD's view of Ms Klass. His proximity also raised the embarrassing prospect of receiving a messy spraying. At any moment, JD could shake his head and eject a glob of chocolate mousse and dribble over a Knight of the realm's expensive attire. I prayed that he did not move closer.

Fortunately, Sir Andrew abandoned his attempt to elicit a response from JD and stood to one side. Thus, we avoided a serious breach of etiquette and the photo-shoot passed without incident.

*Jeremy and family at the Norwood fundraising event in 2012*

# THE PROMISE

Sunday December 23rd, 2012.

Promises must be kept, especially when made to a loved one. In 2006 I promised to 'walk the whole road' for JD. The 'road' in question was the GR10, a network of mountain paths along the Pyrenees that stretches from the Atlantic to Mediterranean coasts. Back then, I knew nothing about its extent apart from two miles we walked five thousand feet up near Mont Louis, fifty miles from Perpignan. But JD loved our little trip, and we would have gone further if the terrain was suitable for his wheelchair. Little did I know how much angst that day would create, ruminating over the pros and cons of walking the whole road. Well now I have a stack of good reasons.

First, there is my promise. I could easily forget but then I would never forgive myself. How do I know what JD understands or feels? That is still an unanswered question, even after nineteen years of living and caring for him. Did he understand my promise? I must assume he did, otherwise I am being selective about what *I think* he understands. So, if he understood, how would he feel as years rolled by without me making any attempt to keep it?

Second, the walk would be a sign of gratitude to and respect for JD's carers. Since JD moved into Woodcock Dell's care nearly two years ago, we have come to know his new family, their relatives and their carers. We celebrated at their birthday parties, sang along at pantomimes and musical evenings at the home and attended fundraising events. The carers work so tirelessly, selflessly, and resolutely. Their dedication and attachment to the people they care for is conspicuous. They make sure that less able and dependent adults and children live the best lives they can. They are unsung heroes and I want them to know what their effort means to me.

Third, I would dedicate the walk to everyone in Norwood. I have seen the same strong relationships in other Norwood homes. The Friday evening synagogue services at Ravenswood village are organised chaos. Adults of all shapes and sizes, with different disabilities wander around the synagogue, or 'help me' by changing the page in my service book or tell me something important. There are random outbursts of noise - laughter, screams, shouts and tantrums. Anything can and does happen while leading a (dis)ordered Sabbath service. I have been given an insight into their lives, their relationships with each other and with their carers. But what impresses me most is how they look after each other. Adults in the village who can talk will speak for those that cannot. They tell me who is unwell and, more tragically, who died in the past week. They feel the pain of losing someone dear to them but often do not know how to express it. If only everyone could behave with such concern for each other, then the world would be a happier place. I suspect that people with a learning disability inherit a 'caring gene' that imbues them with a stronger sense of altruism than us unfortunate normal people. Perhaps we are the disabled ones?

My confidence and trust in the carers in Woodcock Dell and in other Norwood homes has soared. If I could step into a time machine and return to those dark days in 1992, when JD was condemned on the cruel evidence of blood samples, CT scans and EEGs, when I thought that nothing would ever get better, I would say to my younger self, "*everything will be OK.*" He is safe and happy in his new family and that is all that matters.

Fourth, walking a mountain range would be like taking a trip to Mars. I have never done anything like it or tackled anything as arduous. But everyone should test themselves and do something memorable at least once in their lives. My life has been an unextraordinary roll along a production line - school, University and straight into a steady job that never involved much physical work.

Fifth, I would be forced to face my fear of heights, and that would make the walk an ordeal of mountainous proportions. I cannot even climb a ladder, yet I will need to traverse deep gorges, precipices and cliff faces. Could I climb a mountain or negotiate a narrow path along an exposed ridge? Would I run away or fight my fear? It would be a (monu)mental and physical trial.

A sixth reason to keep my promise to JD is that it presents an opportunity to do something constructive. An IT consultant's job is not constructive. It does little to improve peoples' lives. Instead, it boosts my employer's, directors' and stockholders' personal wealth. Their sole focus is on improving the bottom line by increasing revenue, cutting costs, and maximising dividends. Profit and money are the only drivers. Quality of life has no tangible benefit to the corporation because happiness, love and kindness cannot be measured or traded. Only work that improves someone else's quality of life is constructive. Care-workers, doctors, nurses, paramedics, and firefighters make positive differences to peoples' lives. So, it is time for me to pay back society. Walking the whole road will help improve the quality of life for JD, his new family and his carers in Woodcock Dell.

My walk would raise money for Norwood, the charity who manage Woodcock Dell, Ravenswood Village and other homes. They need at least twelve million pounds every year in donations to survive. Caring for people with physical or learning disabilities, the elderly or terminally ill, need such organisations. If it were possible to translate their effort into monetary value, it would dwarf the UK's

Gross Domestic Product, the fifth wealthiest nation on the planet. There is an unseen and unrecognised army of carers, who fight the battles for those who cannot fight for themselves. And they do not get the recognition they deserve.

So, I built a compelling case to walk the GR10. I promised to do it for JD and there are strong reasons. It would not be just for JD, but for his carers too. It is a chance to give something back to the carers at Woodcock Dell and Norwood, for what they do for him. I want the walk to demonstrate what their commitment means to me and, at the same time, raise some desperately needed cash for the home.

But such a long march will take between eight and twelve weeks and I am still working. My company would not let me take off all that time in one go. So, I must do the walk after retiring which will not be until 2021, when I will be sixty-six. By then, I will be slower, and harder to stay fit. These are not excuses - I will keep my promise to JD no matter how long it takes to pluck up courage and find time.

Until that time comes, I will research the GR10 and the science of long-distance walking. '*Stuff I Know About Walking*' by L.R. Smith is the smallest book in the world. It advises the reader to,

"put one foot in front of the other, then repeat until the end"

and "don't do anything stupid."

The last note is based on my only experience of walking in mountains, in the Lake District in 1974, when I was a spritely nineteen-year-old.

One of my friends organised a week's camping and hike near Scafell Pike. For late August, the English weather was unusually kind - warm, still and overcast, so we decided to climb two thousand feet from our camp site, near Eskdale Green, to the summit. Our group of eight teenagers set off on a quiet country road bordered by dry-stone walls, resisting the tempting pubs. We turned left at Boot and picked up a stony path that led gently upwards and alongside Burnmoor Tarn. So far, we had done it by the book, and made healthy progress, with many laughs on the way, and our spirits were high. Scafell Pike summit was four miles further if we stayed on the path. However, one of my more daring friends, Martin, persuaded me that we could "get there more quickly if we took the direct route," pointing up a steep slope on our right. His idea seemed simple; it was over a mile shorter if we took a straight line to the summit. I agreed, and our party split into two, the 'sensibles' and the 'stupids', with Martin and I the sole members of the latter.

We bid farewell and began our climb, while the sensibles ambled on the longer route. A scramble on loose scree took us on to a ridge, from where I saw a sharp descent into a deep ravine. My heart pounded, and my legs shook with fear, when Martin exhorted, "We must take the most direct path," and pointed down into the ravine and up a vertiginous rock face on the other side. Without any chance to object, he clambered down, and I followed, unwilling to fail him or show my fear. The descent was not too bad, but the ascent of the rock face on the other side is filed in my memory as the most terrifying minutes of my life. We scaled half-way up the face on to a narrow ledge, no more than six inches wide, with a hundred-foot drop behind us. Martin edged along, reaching out for finger-holds and toeholds, whistling and humming tunelessly. I struggled to suppress panic and mulled over how ill-equipped I was for hiking on rocks, cursing my cheap and badly worn pumps.

The ledge ended abruptly before a gap in the rock face. A second ledge beyond the gap faced us six feet away. Without hesitation, Martin launched himself at a root protruding from a rock face and landed safely on the second ledge. He turned to me, eyes sparkling with exhilaration, but I hesitated.

"Jump!" he yelled again, "aim for the root." He shook the thick grey lifeline, encouragingly.

Then he added, "and mind the gap," but I was not in the mood for laughing at his topical joke about London Underground's recently introduced passenger announcement.

I flew for minutes across the gap. During that time, when I held nothing and my body trod on air, my heart stopped beating. I wondered about death. Would I feel anything? I thought about the sensibles, where they were and if they were having a good time, my mum and dad, my brother Terry in Australia, my sisters, and my other brothers. I longed to be in the cosy tent. My collection of heavy rock records - who will inherit them when I am gone? Clear thoughts popped into my head, with my life suspended a couple of hundred feet above waiting rocks.

Relief, joy and exultation blew morbidity away when my feet touched rock and my hands grasped the precious root. Without pausing, Martin continued shuffling along the ledge, and I followed. There was no turning back. Shortly after, the ledge broadened, and we climbed to less dangerous terrain. Scafell Pike lay directly ahead, and we jogged towards it, then scrambled up another steep slope on to a proper path, a few yards from the summit. Victory was so important to Martin. The stupids beat the sensibles to the top. But I would *never* climb mountains again.

As I contemplate fulfilling my promise to JD, that traumatic memory holds me back. What would walking a mountain range be like? Would there be *weeks* of the same terror I faced in 1974? My heart tells me I *must* do it, but my memory says, "don't!"

# THE BIG WHEEL OF TERROR

June 2013.

The memory of my Scafell Pike ascent still haunts me, so I tried DIY psychoanalysis. If I understood my fear, then I could better manage it. During my introspection, I uncovered a long-forgotten memory and a possible cause.

Can a fear of heights gene pass from generation to generation? I do not think so, because my parents do not have one, and neither do my siblings – it is only me. So, I must have *caught* my fear, like a disease or a virus, possibly from some terrifying incident that occurred in my past. I was born without a fear of heights and now I have one - *quod erat demonstrandum*.

When I was five years old, I loved to climb a tall conifer tree in our back garden. I clambered on to its lowest branch and picked my way through the branches and needles to the top, about twenty feet above the ground. Once there, I swayed from side-to-side singing, "bring back, bring back, O bring back my bonny to me." Why that song, I will never know, but I was not afraid, even though the entire trunk swayed perilously across our garden and over the fence into next door's garden as well. For months, if not years, I enjoyed my little ritual. Why did my parents let me indulge in something so dangerous? Nowadays, the local authority would whisk a small child away from such irresponsible parenting.

Sometime between then and nineteen years, my age

when I ascended Scafell Pike, I was traumatised by an incident that gave me a fear of heights. I wracked my brains. Then I remembered, although I could not be precise about when it occurred. My parents entrusted my older brother, Terry, to escort me to a local fun fair. Terry is three years older than me, and the deadliest of enemies back then, always fighting and arguing.

Terry persuaded me to accompany him on a 'big wheel' ride at a local fair in London. I must have been about ten years old because we moved forty miles away from the area before my eleventh birthday. In the 1960s, with no Health and Safety Executive, fairground rides were far more hazardous. Nowadays, passengers are strapped in and sealed before the wheel begins spinning, but no such precautions were taken then. There were no nimby-wimby harnesses or seat belts to hold me securely. The big wheel was twelve sofas made of shiny slippery plastic, and flimsy bars in front for passengers to cling to. Our bar rested against its latch. I remember well because Terry demonstrated how easily it could be removed shortly after the ride started. To make the ride more challenging on a windy day, my beloved brother rocked our bench so that it arced forward and backward. One moment I stared up at the sky and the next stared down at the ground fifty feet below. I wrapped my arms around the back of the bench in terror, desperately trying to stay on the seat and pleading, "stop! Stop!"

The big wheel controller reluctantly brought the ride to an end to let me off, while other passengers watched me tremble and walk, white-faced with fear, to safety by the exit. After my 'big wheel of terror' experience, I never climbed the tree in our back garden again.

# PANTS ALL THE WAY DOWN

November 2013.

A hole appeared in our daily routine after JD moved to Woodcock Dell. Time we spent tending to him became available. With nothing to do for hours, we were suddenly free from constant anxiety. Is he having a fit? Why is he not drinking? Does his pad need changing? Why is he hitting himself? Norwood and Woodcock Dell cut the high-tension wire, so we could spring back to our three daughters. Liz started laughing again. She laughs now with more conviction and release than she has for over twenty years. Tiredness, stress and anxiety no longer restrain us or dampen our enthusiasm. When we go out as a family, we are gone in a minute, instead of twenty with JD.

Liz and I visit JD every Sunday and take him out for a few hours. Canons Park, Bentley Priory, Hampstead Heath, Fryant Park, Welsh Harp and Golder's Hill Park are his favourite places. The latter is the archetypal English park with everything one would expect. Soft rolling hills, criss-crossed by footpaths, lead into woods and onto Hampstead Heath. Entering through the wrought-iron gates, we pass tennis courts to music playing at the top of the hill. Sunday afternoons in spring and summer are the best times to visit. We have been treated to afternoons of klezmer, jazz, folk and flamenco, lying on a picnic rug under the shade of a large oak tree close to the bandstand. If the weather is bad, then we visit the small zoo, deer enclosure or butterfly house, a large greenhouse filled with orchids and other spectacular flowers. Sometimes we spend hours inside the café feasting on home-made cakes while the British weather unleashes its worst on the public.

JD stays with us for a weekend every month. We kept his pneumatic bed and the multi-sensory corner donated by his friends, so he could always visit. His bedroom will always be *his*. We do the same things he enjoyed when he lived with us. He sees family and friends, goes for walks in the forest, rides on his special bike, goes shopping and to synagogue. His absence helps us notice the small changes in him. His communication has improved, so he will look someone in the eyes when they attract his attention, smile at them, or treat them to a toothy grin more frequently. Yesterday, one of our friends cried out joyously, "he smiled at me!"

Eight months after JD left home, I joined a choir to take up some of the time I spent with JD when he lived at home. We meet in Woking once every week for three hours, the same amount of time bathing JD, putting him to bed, reading him a story. Singing is just as enjoyable as being with him and keeps my mind from dwelling on happy times lost. How strange that I did not realise how happy I was when he was with me. Joining a choir is an opportunity to build new friendships and develop what meagre singing ability I have. Little did my fellow choristers know that they would receive regular verbal poundings about walking the GR10 at every rehearsal.

I also joined a three-piece band as wannabe rhythm and bass guitarist and harmony singer, with Melanie as our lead singer, and Bev as lead guitarist. We started off by just jamming together until Bev convinced us to become an 'official' band and play in public, without understanding the full ramifications. One is less exposed in a choir because individual mistakes are lost among a greater and in theory, more pleasant, sound. But we are each a vital component in a three-piece, so even the simplest mistake will crash the machine. Despite the exposure, we perform with a 'you only live once' attitude and a shared determination to 'give it a go'. Performing before a potential avalanche of rotten tomatoes is strangely exhilarating. Before every gig, I remind myself "if you don't try, then you'll never know what will happen," even when the possibility of pants-falling embarrassment is high. The same is true every time I tell someone about walking the GR10 - I increase the pressure on myself and set my pants up for a fall for my family and friends to see.

The 'whole road' I promised to walk is far longer and tougher than I thought it was on that gloriously sunny summer's day in 2006. Since then, I have rooted out facts and read many accounts from GR10 'trekkers', as they call themselves. Reputable authorities on popular walking routes classify the GR10 as 'arduous', tougher than 'easy', 'moderate', 'hard', and 'very hard'.

An easy trek is a stroll in a park for a few miles on flat ground, or a long stagger home from the pub. 'Moderate' is like an eight-mile walk up and down a few hills. 'Hard' is where things get tough on knees and legs - the equivalent of climbing a small mountain, or a range of hills, climbing up and down over a thousand feet in a day. One category up from there is 'very hard', like climbing and descending Mount Snowdon in a day. The Three Peaks Challenge involves scuttling up and down Mount Snowdon, Ben Nevis and Scafell Pike in twenty-four hours. That is arduous. The GR10 will be like that *every day* for *between eight and ten weeks*. It is the category just below 'impossible'.

'Arduous' says nothing about organic dangers and difficulties. There are tales of trekkers meeting wild dogs called 'patou' on the GR10. Brown bears roam the Pyrenees too. They are concentrated mostly in the middle of the range, in the Parc National des Pyrenees, where I must walk in my third, fourth and fifth weeks. The Pyrenean bear is related to and shares the same eating habits as its American cousin, the grizzly, so one will happily chew on a passing trekker if it feels peckish. They eat some of the thousands of sheep that graze on juicy mountain grass. In fact, the estimated number of sheep killed by Pyrenean bears varies from one hundred to three hundred every year. That is a whole lotta sheep, and it is only a matter of time before a bear catches a weary human. I hope it will not be me.

Some sections of the GR10 are dangerous, especially for inexperienced trekkers. Occasionally, a few fall off a path and meet a rocky doom. The 'Cicerone Guide to the GR10', written by a trekker who survived it six times, delivers the hard facts. The route is five hundred and fifty miles long and the total altitude gain, the amount of 'upping' and 'downing', is equivalent to climbing and descending Mount Everest from sea level five times. It starts in Hendaye, on the Atlantic coast and close to the border with Spain. From there, the path climbs mountain peaks, plunges into valleys, curls around deep gorges, scales cliff faces, before descending into the popular town of Banyuls-sur-mer on the Mediterranean coast.

An average day entails a thirteen-mile trek and over three thousand feet of climbing and descending. Some days are harder and only a few are easier. The toughest day comes in the third week, with a climb of six thousand feet over seventeen miles. That is arduous for someone who rarely walks more than two or three miles in a day.

So, the trek will be arduous, shared by patou and wild bears, with terrifying ascents to test my fear of heights to the limit. Every day could include one or more 'big wheel of terror' moments. I will carry enough stuff on my back to survive a nuclear winter, making it even more arduous. I could have chosen something easy and safe, like a one-hundred-and-thirty mile walk along the Grand Union Canal, flat and bear-free. I could have walked a comfortable ten miles every day, six days a week, finished every day with a pie and a pint, and been back home two weeks later. JD could have done some of it with me. But the easy trek would not be a big enough sign of respect for his carers - I want my sign to be a massive flashing one, with blaring horns and sirens that bellow, "this is what your efforts mean to me." Besides, I promised JD I would walk *that* road, not another much easier road.

My decision is made. I dismiss the negatives and *will* walk the Pyrenees from the Atlantic to the Mediterranean Sea and keep my promise to JD and honour his carers. Apart from a complete lack of fitness, having no trekking equipment, relevant experience or walking companions, my job is the only thing stopping me from leaving for Hendaye tomorrow. I need to either walk or work - I cannot do both.

Speaking of my job, I like the work and my work colleagues, but dislike the company I work for. They are mean and do not care for their employees. They invented a new language to hide their avarice. 'To sack' has become 'to right-size', a 'person' is now a 'resource', a 'salary freeze' is referred to as a 'benefits adjustment', and 'mass redundancy' is called 'optimise the workforce'. Euphemisms abound in the new corporate-speak. Their world is supported on plinths of pants, all the way down. But throughout the unsettled times, my area of expertise, Artificial Intelligence, kept me in demand and I enjoyed working on many interesting projects, developing smart computer systems for steel plants, oil platforms, ships and large call centres. And I grew up with colleagues who were around when I was wet behind the ears thirty years ago. Together, we have battled through the rightsizing, benefits adjustments, and workforce optimisations. I bump into them occasionally, and we greet like long-lost brothers in arms - we fought and survived.

The promise to JD is far more important than work, which means that I must retire. Since the Great Crash of 2008, my company has constantly re-organised, cut and tightened its employees' belts. They are offering an 'Expression of Wish programme', a euphemism for voluntary redundancies, to all their resources – I mean, employees. I will express my wish to leave their flat, colourless, featureless void and join the rounded, bright, and colourful world of the retired. Then there will be no reason to delay.

# A STEP NEARER

October 2014.

I expressed my wish to leave the corporate world and it came true. The company fairy waved her right-sized wand and decreed, "you shall go." I submitted my retirement request in June, a day before scarpering off on holiday. My boss phoned a few days later, while Liz and I were en route to Canet-Plage on the Mediterranean coast. After a feeble attempt at convincing me to stay, he succumbed to my persuasive case for voluntary self-dismissal. To be fair, he was sympathetic and understood why I wished to leave when I gave my reasons, one of them being, "I must do this thing for my son."

So, I worked for another three months in a limbo state of excitement, trepidation and sadness. I questioned and analysed what I had achieved in thirty years of diligent service to my employer. After ten minutes of deep thought with no end product, I gave up and wrote a 'List of Things to do When I Retire'. 'Walk the Pyrenees for JD' was at the top, followed by 'spend more time with the girls', 'see the Northern Lights', 'visit my brother Terry in Australia', 'make pasta', 'write an AI application to help the learning disabled', 'do more music' and 'write a book'. A hit parade of things I wanted to do but was always too busy looking after a family of four and working.

Today was my last day at work. Never again will I hack through diabolical traffic for meetings, get suited and booted, drink the awful machine coffee, listen to global meetings where the Executive asks, "any questions?" and no one asks any because they are too afraid. On the other hand, never again will I be told I am a 'guru' in Artificial Intelligence, a title reserved for an "influential teacher or popular expert," according to the Oxford Dictionary, or feel that sense of companionship when a client invites me to their fortieth birthday party.

To mark my departure, my team leader sidled up and presented me with a sealed envelope. She stood back and waited while I opened it, and six people seated nearby swivelled their office chairs around to witness the momentous occasion. I thanked her for the unexpected card, containing about a dozen signatures and assorted witticisms, like "I thought you'd already gone," "so long, and thanks for all the fish" and "put the cat out before you leave." A short round of applause later, everyone swivelled back round to their computer screens and the moment was forgotten.

Although saddened by my silent whimper of a departure from a company I worked for since 1985, a weight has been lifted. I am a step closer towards the trek. Now I must talk to people who can help me plan and prepare for it and I can set a date.

# TALKING AND DOING

December 2014.

Talking about doing something is easy, doing it is hard. For eight years, I talked about trekking 'that road' for JD but did nothing, except read about it. I have not set a date, trained, bought equipment, or thought about how to show my appreciation for his carers. Should I give them donations directly? If I did, then twenty-five percent would go to the taxman, which would be like walking a quarter of the way, or 135 miles, for the Inland Revenue. What about buying something for the home to make it easier for the carers? Would Norwood, Woodcock Dell's parent charity, permit that? Or will they want donations to go to them, and then distributed to all their care homes?

Last week, on my weekly visit to JD, I told him about my plan to walk the GR10.

"I'm going to walk that road for you JD. We walked a little part of it in 2006, do you remember?"

"Errrr," he murmured, from the passenger seat, meaning a surprised "really?" a sceptical "yeah, right," a resigned "about time too," or just "cheers dad."

I continued, "but I must speak to Vicky about it when we get back to Woodcock Dell."

Vicky is JD's care home manager, who Liz and I see regularly to discuss his well-being, medication and progress. She would be exactly the right person to talk to about the plan to raise funds for the home.

We spent the morning walking through the trees in Canons Park, as I gave JD facts about 'that road'.

"It's a bit further than we thought JD," I explained, "five hundred and forty miles, from the Atlantic to the Mediterranean."

At this news, he put his thumb in his mouth, and leaned to one side, pondering.

"*And*," I gave the word emphasis for dramatic effect, "there are bears – yes, bears!"

"Mmmm," he said, as the wheelchair came to a sudden stop, arrested by a tree root.

"And it looks like I'll be walking it on my own," lifting the wheels over the obstruction and continuing along the muddy path.

"But I'm sorry JD, you can't come with me," I admitted, with more than a trace of regret. There was little hope I could take him with me. The more I researched the GR10, the less likely it seemed.

"Besides, it would be dangerous with all those bears and patou around."

Someone passed by as I spoke, and I wondered what conclusion they drew from the snippet of our conversation.

"And God knows where I'll stay, or where I'll get food."

Later that day, after giving JD his lunch, we took the lift upstairs to Vicky's office for our meeting. I told her about my unplanned journey along the Pyrenees. She leaned forward to make sure she had heard correctly, struggling to hide a look of incredulity at the thought of a sixty-year-old walking five hundred and forty miles along a mountain range for her care home. I continued, without allowing her time to raise any doubts.

"Maybe the donations could go towards something that would make it easier to care for Jeremy and his housemates?" I suggested.

Vicky thought for a moment, "a larger dining area

would be useful – then we could eat together in one sitting."

I was delighted to hear her suggestion. It vindicated the idea of the trek and provided me with a clear target. Although I did not realise it at the time, it was a green light moment. Now there was a financial target as well as an emotional one, set when I made my promise to JD. We agreed I would need to raise thirty-five thousand pounds for an extension, but I should discuss the intricacies of finance with Norwood as soon as possible. Vicky explained that the fundraising team, who are tasked with raising twelve million pounds every year via organised events, publicity and support, would be "only too pleased to help."

Today, a week after announcing my intention to JD and Vicky, I met Norwood's finance and fundraising teams. As Vicky predicted, they reacted enthusiastically.

"So, when are you going?" asked Stephanie, leaning forward eagerly.

With no answer, I voiced my thoughts, "Well, I'll need at least six months to train, and I can only walk between June and September, according to the Cicerone Guide to the GR10."

"Why's that?"

"There will be snow outside those months, and many refuges are closed as well."

"So, it's unlikely to be this year," Stephanie concluded, sitting back in her chair again.

"Regretfully yes, the earliest will be next year."

"Well, let me know some definite dates and I can help you with publicity," she offered, "and I'll try to find some volunteers to walk with you."

That was an offer I could not refuse. Finding someone, or some two, or more, to walk with would be a Godsend.

I left Norwood HQ having finally done *something*. I know now how to show my appreciation to the carers. I will raise thirty-five-thousand pounds for Woodcock Dell *and* fulfil my promise to JD. The way ahead was much clearer now, except for knowing *when*.

# BIRTHRIGHT

March 2015.

In one of my favourite films, the main character Papillon cries, "Guilty as charged! I'm guilty of a wasted life." The film is a factual account of the author's years incarcerated in a penal colony in French Guyana, sentenced to life for murdering a pimp. The realisation spurs Papillon to attempt a dangerous and successful escape and return to lead a full life.

A full life is what I always wanted for JD. I want his life to be undiminished by his disability. I want more than basic or adequate care for the rest of his life, where he is fed, medicated, washed and kept safe. Although more than Papillon had for his crime, basic care is less than an average pet dog gets. At least dogs are taken out for walks, given the occasional treat, and are sometimes taken on holiday with their owners. Yet basic is the best that many people in care can expect. I want JD's care to be more than basic – so he can lead a fuller life, be taken out for walks, interact with people outside his home and, ideally, have a holiday like he used to do with us every year. His life would be diminished by basic care.

Of course, Woodcock Dell's level of care is far more than basic, otherwise we would still be caring for him now. He is taken out frequently, goes shopping, visits other homes and is treated to wonderful birthday parties with home-made cakes. But I still feel 'guilty as charged' when

Liz and I leave him behind for our annual holiday.

Two weeks ago, JD *was* taken on a holiday, although officially, it was a 'Birthright' tour of Israel. Norwood assembled a team of volunteers and carers, and seven other young disabled adults in their care and organised a tour of the places that are central to the Jewish faith and help them strengthen their sense of Jewish identity. It was his second visit to Israel, his first was with us in 2008, but this visit was different. Instead of being with his biological family, he was surrounded by his Norwood family of youngsters and carers with unbounded energy and enthusiasm. Liz and I were told firmly by Vicky and Philma that we were banned from contacting him while he was immersed in his full-on Israel experience.

Yesterday, I wrote an article for our synagogue's newsletter on JD's behalf, and with his voice.

*"I'm knackered, but in a good way. All the things that are important to me, namely food, girls and music are there in Israel. If you've never been there, then you should go. It's got all that and more besides. Like God for instance. If you fancy a hefty dose of God, then Israel's your venue.*

*I left the UK with three carers from Woodcock Dell and seven other dudes from various Norwood homes on Monday. They brought their carers too, so there were more carer dudes than cared-for dudes. We flew to Ben Gurion and caught a special wheelchair-friendly bus to our first hotel. That was our main means of transport for the rest of our Birthright tour.*

*We were all pretty wasted the next morning after our late night, but we perked up after our first Israeli breakfast. Then we got more grub, in the form of pita which we had to make first, followed by riding on donkeys. I felt like I'd arrived in the Bible.*

*The next day we went cycling on some specially adapted bikes. Then we visited these cool caves in Rosh Hannikrah on the Lebanese border and took the cable car to the top so we could see the sea and beautiful countryside. Afterwards, we visited a goat farm and milked a few goats and made some cheese.*

*On Thursday we walked in a forest in north Galilee and planted an acorn, so maybe if I go back and visit in a few years, they will have sprouted into mighty oaks. In the afternoon, we all had a go at pressing olives and grinding spices. That was pretty hard work, but we didn't mind, because we all got to eat the fruits of our labours afterwards. Then we headed off to another hotel in Jerusalem for the main feature of our tour.*

*It was cold in Jerusalem on Friday. So cold in fact, I had to put away my cutaways and string vest and wear long sleeves and respectable trousers. Although that might have been because I was visiting the Old City and it's not cool to wander around half naked like your average sun-seeking Brit in Malaga. So, we visited the Kotel (Western Wall) and I posted a message in the wall, as is the custom. Sorry I can't tell you what my message was because it's between me and 'Him Upstairs'. After that, we returned to the hotel for Shabbat, nosh, music and singing.*

*Everything closes on Shabbat in Israel. The place is so quiet, you can hear the birds tweeting - I'm surprised they're allowed to on Shabbat - and that's about all. So, we chilled out by the pool, then in the evening, we watched some films, ate popcorn and stuff.*

*Sunday was an energetic day and made up for the previous day's relative inactivity. Honestly, I can't understand why all the carers still look so pooped out. We started the day with a trip to the Biblical Zoo where we got to see some interesting animals. This was a surprise to me because I thought that I was going to see Moses and Aaron in a cage or maybe Adam and Eve up a tree, as the word 'Biblical' implies. "I demand a refund," I wanted to yell but couldn't because I had my fingers in my mouth at the time. The high point was seeing the Ark at the zoo, so it did live up to its name after all. The pizza there was excellent. In the afternoon, we visited Yad Vashem (the Holocaust Museum) where we each lit a candle during a service in the memory of the Holocaust victims. Then we sojourned back to downtown Jerusalem city for some serious shopping, dinner at the hotel and more musical entertainment.*

*Monday was another brilliant day. We got hot by driving down into the Dead Sea valley and ascending Masada by cable car. Then we went for a dip in the Dead Sea and watched in amusement as one of our carers drifted helplessly over the briny water towards Jordan. I counted them all out and I counted them all back, so I assume that they were rescued. Or maybe there's a distant shore on the banks of the Dead Sea where they wash up eventually? Then we all got plastered, literally, in mud. To round off the day of excellence, we were treated to a light and sound show in Jerusalem.*

*Day Nine, Tuesday, was our penultimate day and I decided I want to be a sailor. We drove to Tel Aviv where we went out in a boat in the sea and watched a turtle. The boat trip was fantastic, and I couldn't stop chuckling as it bounced on the waves. Oh, put a parrot on my shoulder and cast me adrift matey.*

*Wednesday was our last day in Israel and we spent the morning in Mini Israel, took lunch and then boarded our flight home in the afternoon. I was worn out when I got back to Woodcock Dell, but happy to see all my housemates again. It was a whirlwind tour and something I will always remember fondly.*

*I've been sleeping and eating better since I had my Birthright - or 'holiday of a lifetime' as my dad calls it - and am truly thankful for those that made it possible. My three carers took the rest of the week off, some say it was for another holiday but that doesn't make much sense because they've just had one."*

Jeremy, aged twenty-two, on Birthright tour in Israel

# SOME MANLY SHOPPING

April 2015.

A good friend of mine, Paul, offered to take me shopping for essential trekking gear. He has been hiking on mountains for years, leading Duke of Edinburgh's award participants on rigorous expeditions to toughen them up and knock some sense into them. Of course, the DofE award does not really share those aspirations – for many parents, it is an opportunity for their young adults to discover and develop their potential.

Paul's snappy advice was, "feet, sleep and back." In other words, never scrimp on gear for your feet, for sleeping or carrying stuff. It was never going to be a cheap day out. But I jumped at his offer and drove us to Guildford to buy some sturdy walking boots, look at sleeping bags, rucksacks and some 'layers'. For the uninitiated, clothing for the long-distance trekker is worn in layers. The base layer is a thin, lightweight and permeable vest or T-shirt and underpants, a middle layer over that for warmth and, if it gets very cold, a top layer such as a fleece. The trekker also requires good heavy-duty socks that will survive being marinated in sweaty feet and stewed inside boots for ten hours or more, six days every week for several weeks. Merino wool socks are "definitely the best," according to Paul. I bought six pairs, one for each walking day, on the assumption that I would wash them all on my one rest day every week.

It is perfectly acceptable for a trekker to wear the same underpants for six days, provided they are of high quality. Paul argued this point convincingly and backed it up with specific examples. Underpants became the main topic of our conversation as we strode briskly through the busy streets of Guildford, oscillating between hiking and camping shops. Every store was occupied by people who knew what they wanted, whereas I had no clue, which was why Paul was with me. No one batted an eyelid at the sight of two men rifling through racks of underpants for a pair that would stand up to the vigorous workout they would soon receive. In the end, Paul advised me to purchase the finest, and most expensive Merino boxers, reversible and lightweight. They were the last pair left on the rack, so I supplemented them with long johns, made of the same material, which I planned to wear as pyjama bottoms or during the day if the weather was nippy. The purchase, with two lightweight high-tech vests, completed my base layer. I made a note to remove seven pairs of Captain Underpants briefs and seven thick cotton t-shirts off my equipment list.

My daughter Roxanne lent me her Leki poles that saw action in the Himalayas, so I saved some money. Although I could not avoid other big money items on my list, like boots. Paul lectured me on the options.

"Trainers for evening wear only, *never* for walking the distances you'll be doing," he advised, somewhat ominously, "I would strongly advise lightweight, waterproof trekking boots to give you the ankle support you'll need."

"That sounds expensive," I said.

"You don't get 'owt for nowt'," he retorted.

"I didn't know you came from up north," I scanned his face for signs of northern-ness.

"I'm not, but you'll have to pay more for the most reputable makes, like Brasher, Merrell and Karrimor."

"Aha, Karrimor - I've got their trainers!" I exclaimed,

pleased that my choice of evening footwear, made months earlier, had been vindicated by my knowledgeable chaperone.

So, I splashed out a hundred pounds on a pair of Merrell boots, with excellent ankle support, confident that they would bear my feet safely for five hundred and forty miles.

Later that day, I ordered a light-weight solar panel to charge my mobile phone and primary navigation aid. It will also charge my iPod, so I can listen to soothing music while inching nervously along narrow mountain paths.

With the right clothing and equipment for a long trek, I must start training soon if I am going next year, as I suggested to Norwood three months ago. I raised their hopes as well as JD's. There is no turning back.

# OUR FRIENDS IN THE FOOTHILLS

Three days trekking in the Pyrenees in June will be a perfect opportunity for serious training with my new gear. Liz and I are flying to France to stay with Liz's cousin, Jonathan, and his wife Sarah, in Bouriège, a small village seventy miles south of Toulouse, in the foothills. Jonathan and I have planned a walk in the mountains together, while Liz accompanies Sarah on their expeditions to the shops, cafes and galleries.

Jonathan is a retired lift control engineer, so he should have all the skills needed to carry us up and down the mountains. We also share a desire to spend the rest of our lives being physically and mentally active, instead of being chained to a computer screen or watching telly in slippers and cardigans. He is more active than me, converting the bakery opposite their house to an artist's studio, digging vegetable plots and re-tiling roofs. Sarah is a retired GP and master-chef who likes socialising with neighbours and rustling up exotic recipes from whatever Jonathan brings back from the fields. A symbiotic relationship, and complete change from their disparate career lives.

We bought our apartment in Canet-Plage shortly after they decided to split their time between living in their new-build sea-side apartment on the busy English south coast and their rustic three-storied house in Bouriège, in the tranquil Languedoc countryside. Even though we were only sixty miles away in Canet-Plage, we never visited until after JD left home six years later. We were always too busy tending to him and his sisters, doing things that would keep them happy.

Now I must start training immediately. I cannot just turn up in two months and expect to complete three consecutive days of tough upping and downing on the rocks.

# SOME VIGOROUS EXERCISE

May 2015.

"I've started training," I informed JD today. Liz and I took him to Golder's Hill Park, where he enjoyed an abundance of trees while I subjected myself to vigorous exercise. One of his favourite routes requires me to push his wheelchair through a forest at the back of the park, where ash, oak and maples rise over a soft bed of fallen leaves, earth and twigs.

He chuckled at the trees and erratic motion as his wheelchair bumped and bounced over the uneven surface, occasionally grinding to a full stop in muddy patches. I wondered what he found so funny. Maybe it was the huffing and puffing as I pushed, almost horizontal, with my arms out straight and locked on the handles. The soft surface made the going tough, but I needed to get into shape for my expedition in six weeks.

"I've had three long walks this week, JD," I reported, between gasps.

On Monday, eager to try out my new walking gear, I took Charlie the mutt for a three-mile scamper up and down hills. Boots, Merino wool socks and matching underpants passed the test with flying colours. Two days later, we completed a four-mile round-trip on a flat track beside Bisley Rifle Range. I stepped up to six miles on Friday. Everything was progressing nicely for the forthcoming expedition.

"I'm increasing by one mile every week, until I'm managing twelve miles a day for five consecutive days," I announced, "that should be enough to get me into shape."

JD sighed, put his thumb in his mouth, tilted his head to listen to the rustling leaves. Like his sisters, he is more interested in what is happening now than in what I might be doing later.

# EXPEDITION TO THE PYRENEES

June 2015.

"What on Earth have you got in there?" exclaimed Sarah, as I hobbled into arrivals at Toulouse airport, doubled over with a bulky rucksack.

"I tried telling him," Liz answered, "but at least he left the kitchen sink at home."

"You're only going for three days!" Sarah said, as a look of concern grew on Jonathan's face.

We hugged and shook hands, shying from the customary 'triple cheek peck' greetings on display. Jonathan pointed at the lump on my back and said wryly, "I hope you're not planning to lug all that about the whole time."

"Of course," I said, "that's the point!"

Jonathan and I planned an expedition to the mountains as a test for next year, when I hoped to walk the whole range. It would be a full-dress rehearsal, wearing and carrying the trekking gear I bought earlier in the year. *So what* if it was a tad heavy? I needed to know my physical limits. One day of strenuous walking seemed possible, but how would I feel the morning after? Could I do another day if my muscles screamed "enough already!"? I am physically fit for my age, eat healthily, not overweight and exercised to compensate for my physical inactivity at work. But I never exercised strenuously for consecutive days over several weeks. Three days of tough walking in the mountains would be a glimpse at what the full trek would be like.

I could test the technology too. How much trust could I place in my phone? How effective would the solar panel be? And how useful would the phone apps be? Would they help me backtrack if I took a wrong turn? One app could record my distance travelled, average speed, altitude and calories burned, but would that be useful or interesting after a hard walk?

Everything for next year's trek was stuffed in my rucksack. Nothing was excluded. But did I have the right equipment for a long trek? My multi-purpose knife has a small blade for making sandwiches out of a baguette, scissors for cutting tape and ropes, a corkscrew, bottle opener and twenty other hooks, blades and instruments whose purposes were a deep mystery to me. Maybe I would find out on the expedition? Ten yards of cord were stowed in an easy-to-reach pocket, next to my knife, just in case I needed to scale any rock faces. My experienced trekking friend, Paul, advised me to buy clear bottles, so I could check the contents for signs of life before drinking. I brought four, each with a one-litre capacity. Paul also recommended wrapping four yards of gaffer tape around a bottle, so I did not need to carry an entire roll. "Take only what you need," he advised, "and no more."

Three phone cables and a spare battery would sustain my phone while on the move, so I could navigate and keep in contact. The head torch and batteries would save me if I ever needed to walk in the dark or get up in the night. My medicine kit was well-stocked with compeed anti-blister plasters, antiseptic cream, gauze for more serious cuts, water purifying tablets, aspirin, plasters, surgical tape and antihistamine for insect bites and stings.

My washbag was stuffed with a full bottle of shampoo, bar of soap, tube of toothpaste, razors, toothbrush, flannel, sun-cream and two small packs of washing powder. That was encased in a dry sack, in case of leakage.

I even packed a portable washing machine, called a 'scrubba bag', shipped over from Australia. Resembling a dry sack, I could toss in my dirty socks, T-shirt, trekking trousers and pants, add washing powder and water, then seal and twirl it about my head like a bushman with billy-can at a billabong. To complete the image, I could use didgeridoos as walking poles and wear a corked hat to keep the flies off.

While Sarah and Liz caught up on family news, Jonathan gave me the low-down on our three-day walk.

"I'm not sure if the weather will be good enough for a trip to the mountains," he said, "tomorrow's forecast is heavy rain and thunder."

"You mean I packed this lot for nothing?" I joked, gesturing to my rucksack.

"We'll still do some walking, no matter what the weather, but I urge you to leave some of that load behind."

"I won't have that choice next year - whatever I start the trek with must finish with me."

After much persuasion from Jonathan, Liz and Sarah, I consented to remove most of my clothes, trainers and toiletries and shed twenty pounds of weight.

"You'll feel better for it," Jonathan said.

# THE MAD DOG OF BOURIÈGE

A grey start to the expedition. Jonathan pointed at the dark clouds mustering over the mountains and proposed a local walk, a "twelve-miler or thereabouts."

"I think the weather's brightening up tomorrow, so we can try Pic Carlit," he added, "as a consolation prize."

Carlit is one of the highest peaks in the French Pyrenees, standing at nine-and-a-half thousand feet. The ascent would be a stiff head-for-heights test. Exposure on peaks was something I would face many times on the full trek. The sooner I learned to cope, the better.

We left Bourière beneath an overcast sky. Despite the absence of mountains, there was still plenty of climbing and descending on long rolling slopes along narrow farm roads and tracks. For thirty minutes we placed our trust in a path through some woods, until it disappeared under tall ferns and brambles. We thrashed and hacked through the undergrowth using walking poles as machetes, collecting a few cuts and scratches along the way.

"I knew the poles would come in handy," I said, as we emerged from the woods.

"They have many uses," Jonathan agreed, "warding off bears for example."

"And patous, man plus stick versus semi-feral dog would be a close contest."

"You'd probably stand a better chance if you threw it," he suggested, "in any case, you might be able to test the idea soon."

I was alarmed at the revelation, "You mean we're going to meet a real patou?"

"Don't know if it qualifies as a patou, it lives on a farm we're passing, slavering jaws, barks a lot and it attacked me recently."

"Did it bite you?"

"It didn't have the chance, I barked back - loudly."

"So, walking poles at the ready," I thrust forward with an extended pole, "*en garde* Monsieur chien!"

"That won't work," Jonathan said, "it doesn't understand Franglais and, besides, it's probably mad, so any attempt to communicate or reason with it will be wasted."

As we approached 'Mad Mutt Farm' a few miles further on, I wrapped the ribbons at the ends of my walking poles around my wrists, ready for combat.

"Let me go first," Jonathan volunteered, "just in case it's in for business – I'll create a diversion so you can slip past."

"Well," I said, "that's mighty heroic of you! And in return for your bravery, I will lend you my medicine-kit."

With bated breath, we passed through the farm as noiselessly as possible. We heard not a sound, not a single moo, grunt, bleat, cluck or bark. A hundred yards beyond, we finally relaxed.

"Hmm," I uttered, "it must have been on its lunch break."

"Gorging itself on a bear, I suspect," responded Jonathan.

Apart from the damage inflicted by a few brambles, we completed the day unscathed, with appendages intact. We had not made it to the mountains, but we still climbed a thousand-six-hundred feet, half as much as I could expect in an average day next year.

# A FULL-ON DAY

We rose at seven for a sixty-mile drive to Lac Bouillouses and the trail up Pic Carlit. A lonely sun hung in a cloudless sky. We bid farewell to Liz and Sarah, wished them "bonne chance" for their alternative trek around the shops and cafés of Limoux, climbed into Jonathan's metal horse and headed south towards the mountains.

Two hours later, we parked by a long four-storey refuge near the Lac. A dozen trekkers, looking purposeful and confident, began their daily routine. They hoisted heavy rucksacks, double-tied boot laces and adjusted walking poles effortlessly. A few raised their heads to glance at the newbie who struggled to stand up with a bulky rucksack and twist Leki poles to the right length. Some smiled when the end of one pole sprung out completely, after rough treatment.

"Schoolboy error," I confessed, obliterating my credibility among the local trekking community.

Five minutes after re-assembling my walking pole, we set off on the Carlit trail, a wide stony path that became rougher and rockier. Drawing nearer to Carlit, I recalled my only experience of mountain hiking, a terrifying short-cut up Scafell Pike forty years earlier. Had time healed the trauma of that trip? From a three-mile distance, Carlit loomed over the surrounding peaks, but no fear came, just worry about disgracing myself. There must be a good reason why fear is the only emotion that is not regenerated. When I recall a happy occasion, a residue of that happiness washes over. The same is true of sad moments or times when I was angry. But fear seems different - only its memory remains.

The path cut between a mountain lake and a boulder field draped in snow.

"Snow? In June?", I exclaimed.

Jonathan looked unsurprised, "well, we are over six thousand feet up."

Snow on the mountains is nothing like it is in cosy Surrey, where one knows that feet will meet solid ground. But in the mountains, snow is painted over rocks, crevices and crevasses. We passed a cavern with a white-crusted roof. What was once packed with snow had melted from underneath, leaving a fragile layer above a void. An unsuspecting trekker taking a short-cut would have an unpleasant surprise when they plummeted to a rocky doom. Mountain snow must be treated with caution, it is not what it seems.

Two hours of steady climbing later, we paused for a break. Ten missed calls and texts from Roxanne demanded immediate attention. Her final voicemail urged, "Dad! Pick up the phone!" I fumbled for my phone and tapped in her number, while Jonathan looked worried.

She picked up immediately.

"Er … dad," code for "I need something," or a cue for good news.

"I'm having a baby!"

My daughter is going to be a mum? So that would make me a grandfather, Liz a grandmother and JD an uncle. How can that be possible? Only yesterday I was spoon-feeding, bathing and reading her bed-time stories. Time slips by so quickly.

I sputtered, "how?"

"You don't really want the details do you dad?"

"No, no, definitely not. I mean, when's the little one due?"

Jonathan removed his rucksack and plonked down on a rock. I forgot about my eaves-dropping companion.

"In March," she answered, and launched into technical medical details while my mind raced ahead. She will need help. She is a junior doctor *and* pregnant. Peter is a junior doctor too, so how will they cope? What if she is assigned consecutive twelve-hour night shifts in the later stage of pregnancy, while trying to save lives? My paternal, and new grand-paternal worries were dazzled by Roxanne's glowing delight. Such calls are rare and even rarer while on a mountain.

After hanging up, Jonathan extended his hand, "congratulations, and welcome to the grandpa club."

For the next hour, I followed him over rocks, planning for the coming months without paying attention to the approaching peak.

The climb became steeper, and the drop grew on both sides, bringing a dreadful feeling of vulnerability and shaking me from my daze. I trembled uncontrollably. My fear of heights woke from a forty-year slumber. We scrambled up loose grey scree towards the summit.

*One foot higher, one foot further to fall, another foot and even higher, don't look, don't look!*

I sucked air in gasps. Jonathan suggested a lunch-stop on a ridge near the top, after ascending two-and-a-half thousand feet in four miles. Exhaustion, overtaken by elation at Roxanne's news, then fear, the eventual victor. A boulder rested on the slope ahead, a haven of solidity and security. I raced up the slope to claim it.

Jonathan observed, "it's been a full-on day, hasn't it?"

"I couldn't have put it better."

"You have Josh to thank for that," he added, "'full-on day' is a young person's phrase." Josh is Jonathan's son.

"My kids have used it too," I said.

"I've been wanting to use it for a while now," he admitted with satisfaction, "so thank you for giving me the opportunity."

We munched on baguette, molten cheese and tomato while I mulled over the tornado of emotions stirred up by Roxanne's news, the re-awakened fear of heights and the awesome beauty of the view from our picnic spot.

"Everything looks so crystal clear," I remarked, staring at icing sugar-coated mountains silhouetted against a cloudless sky.

"No pollution and thinner air."

"And the colours seem so much richer," I added, admiring the chromatic blues of numerous mountain lakes and greens illuminating the valley floor two thousand feet below, "it's like an oil painting."

"It makes you glad to be alive, doesn't it?" he said, sucking in a lungful of air.

I thought of JD and his only experience on a mountain top. In 2006, we took him by telecabine from Font Romeu, only a few miles from Carlit. I recalled his puzzlement as he tried to touch the snow through the plexiglass window. But getting him to this viewing spot would be beyond my ability and far too dangerous. With regret, I conceded that there were some places he would never see, no matter how determined his parents were.

Jonathan glanced at his watch. "We should be getting back. Are you going to be alright going down?"

I stood up and began shaking instantly, not from the chilly wind. "I'll have to be, otherwise I'll be stuck here and never see my first grandchild."

"You could use your walking poles," he suggested, "it might help."

The downward journey is supposedly worse than the upward one, according to experienced mountaineers. That is when most accidents happen. A long steep slope of loose rock stretched five hundred feet to safety below.

"I doubt it, but I have nothing to lose," I said.

I stabbed a pole into the ground and took a nervous step down. The fear evaporated. Armed with two high-tech sticks, I transformed into a mountain gazelle.

"This is incredible! How can two poles make such a difference?"

"I wouldn't analyse it too closely if I were you," Jonathan replied, "it might stop working."

"Ain't psychology blooming marvellous?"

We descended to secure ground at the foot of the scree slope in minutes. From there, conversation slowed as fatigue grew, until we became too knackered to utter more than a grunt. We staggered to the car hot, hungry and exhausted.

At our overnight cabin in the deserted ski resort of Les Angles, Jonathan struggled with confusing hot water tank instructions while I rustled up something massive to eat. A whole bear would have been well-received, but we made do with basic food, bought especially to simulate the conditions I would experience on the full trek. We devoured tins of mackerel, bread, fruit, tomatoes and Sarah's home-made delights speedily and silently. After washing down a bottle of local wine, we crashed out. Normally I am a night owl who reads and listens to music until the small hours, but the lamp was out seconds before slipping into oblivion. A fitting end to a full-on day.

# FOOD

The day began with a rousing rendition of the 'Muppet's Theme'. I must change the wake-up call if I share a bunk in a refuge or cabane. Fellow backpackers would not appreciate such a raucous awakening.

Our log cabin sat above a forest of evergreens with the ice-blue Lac Matemale, like a sheet of stained glass just beyond. Set among a group of a dozen log cabins, each with capacity for a large group of keen skiers, the area would buzz with human activity in the winter. But the ski lift that passed a hundred yards in front of our balcony was dormant, its cable swinging in a light breeze. No one came here in the summer, apart from trekkers like us, so birdsong and buzzing and chirping insects filled the airwaves.

Jonathan planned a thirteen-mile circular walk from the commune of Puyvalador, with a climb on to a ridge overlooked by the Pic de Madrès, at eight thousand two hundred feet. We parked in the village square and headed toward the Pic at a brisk pace. Jonathan promoted me to Chief Navigator, a huge sacrifice for him, knowing his love for maps. I led us across a barrage at the northern end of Lac de Puyvalador onto a track and up a steep slope through a forest, shielded from the full gaze of the sun.

Walking does strange things to body and mind. The rhythmic movement of trekking poles and limbs synchronised with breathing induced a meditative state.

The world outside ceased to exist, my mind wandered while my body maintained a constant pulse, like a Buddhist mantra, even as the gradient increased.

From twenty yards behind, Jonathan called, "you won't enjoy it if you go so fast!"

Snatched from one world into the real one by Jonathan's intervention, I stared at the rough holes under my feet, dug by wild boar searching for grubs. The dense pine forest muffled the sharp crack of a bough straining in a warm breeze. Nectarine insects, hoverflies and butterflies hummed through the air. Maybe slipping into my own world would be a common occurrence on the long and lonely trek next year? Which would be better? A *mindless* state with a fast and steady pace, or *mindful* state and slower, absorbing the experience with every sense? The first would help me complete the mission for JD swifter than the second, but joylessly.

The path meandered through the forest for a couple of miles up to a plateau. A cabane stood a few yards off, a striking contrast to the one we passed near Pic Carlit the day before that was no more than a corrugated tin hut over bare earth, dingy and windowless.

"Worth a look," Jonathan said, wandering over grass and through the open door.

"Wow!" I said, "I'd be more than happy to stay here."

About the size of an average lounge, the cabane boasted pastel painted walls, a pine table, hung pictures and a sturdy one-up-one-down bunk. A stack of logs outside, with instructions to replace what was used, compensated for the lack of heating and power.

"Possible, although I'd need a sleeping bag, mat, torch, toilet paper."

"Glad to hear you're making an inventory," Jonathan mused, "as if you've not got enough in that sack already."

"And maybe a tent and burner as well."

"Burner, yes. But why would you need a tent if you're staying in a cabane?"

"In case it was occupied."

The full strength of the sun bore down when we stepped outside. By mid-day, three out of my four litres of water were gone. Apart from the drinking well in Puyvalador, we had passed no water sources. Where could I refill on a much longer trek? I would need at least four litres each day, especially in heat like this.

A gently declining and well-maintained path led us into a scattered village called Real, a hundred feet above the eastern bank of Lac de Puyvalador.

"You can put the map and phone away now I think," Jonathan said, pointing out the Lac and the barrage we crossed that morning, two miles away.

His was the first remark made by either of us for an hour as the heat, intensity of the sun and lack of shade dried up conversation.

On the journey to re-unite with Liz and Sarah in Bourière, I obsessed over Eccles cakes and croissants smothered in fig jam, forgetting loved ones and what they had done since leaving two days earlier. Thoughts of food swept aside far more important matters, like Roxanne's news of our first grandchild. How would my mind be affected on a longer journey?

# MORE QUESTIONS THAN ANSWERS

With no blisters, strains or sprains, except for a few scratches from hacking through prickly undergrowth, I should survive the punishment meted out by eight weeks on the GR10. But I carried only a half-load in my rucksack, another twenty-six pounds would have made the expedition far tougher. So, am I being a tad over-confident? Not one day was as arduous as a typical GR10 day of three-thousand-three-hundred feet climbing over thirteen miles. Not enough upping and downing on day one, a paltry eight miles on the second, and easier terrain on the third. Doubt over my fitness lingers.

We climbed the same amount on the last two days, which was a surprise, given that we ascended Carlit, one of the great Pyrenean peaks, on the second day. On day three, there were no boulders to clamber over or scree to scramble. The path took us on comfortable forest tracks, through grassy fields and along tarmac roads. Eight miles of rocks and boulders is more exhausting than thirteen miles of forest tracks. The type of terrain strains the body more than upping and downing, and both drain stamina more quickly than distance.

Walking poles will be crucial. My fear of heights returned with vengeance on Pic Carlit, but a pair of sticks provided a psychological crutch to lean on, as well as a physical one. I hope there are no places on the GR10 where poles are useless, like vertical rock faces or narrow ledges.

How will I cope by myself for eight weeks of arduous trekking? Jonathan deflected my fear of heights and shortened the miles with his companionship. Without a partner, I will rely on self-motivation. The promise to JD and what his carers do for him will give me that, but will it be enough to counter the fear that will surely surface on exposed heights? And suppose I fall down a ravine, slide down a snowfield or break an ankle in a remote place, who will ever know? That possibility really scares me.

The technology worked perfectly. The solar panel kept my phone charged, GPS reception was excellent, and my phone map was accurate. The MapMyWalk app collected all kinds of interesting statistics for planning the full route, like my average pace and calories burned. I have a better idea of timings because of three days on a variety of different terrains. But what if I lose reception and cannot access my phone map? I will need a backup, probably paper maps, so I must learn how to use a compass properly.

I will need four litres of water each day. The last two days were unbearably hot, and I rationed my last drops. Four litres add nine pounds to my burgeoning rucksack. I could take three litres and purification tablets, if I can find water en route. But if I cannot, then there is a risk of dehydration.

On our second day, we drove for twenty minutes before finding a shop with provisions. How did travellers manage in bygone days? Either they carried food to last weeks or they hunted and foraged. The Pyrenees teem with marmots, wild boar, bears and birds, but nothing edible, apart from sheep and cows who are protected by fierce dogs. Hunting is not a serious option, so I must stock up for weeks and forage for high calorie snacks in shops, whenever I find any. The three-day adventure has raised more questions than answers.

# CLOSING WINDOW

October 2015.

After returning from France, I lapsed into my old habit of walking Charlie the mutt around the local park. Four months passed before I dusted down my rucksack and began training again. But six miles on easy terrain three times every week with a light rucksack is pathetically inadequate.

Next year is approaching quickly and I must start publicising the trek. More time prevaricating means less time fundraising. And I must meet Norwood's fundraising team again because the last time we met, I could not give them a departure date, so there was little they could do to help. But the window of opportunity is closing fast. I must go next year because our first grandchild is due in five months and Liz's and my baby-sitting services will be required. The next generation is on its way, and I want to be there for them.

# WHEN DAD JOKES GO WRONG

New Year's Day 2016.

My training programme cannot be interrupted by anything as trivial as the weather. That would be a bold statement if I lived somewhere with a harsher climate than outer London's commuter belt, where the worst we experience is a light dusting of snow that freezes traffic to a standstill. So, mutt and I ramped up the distance and trampled local pathways in wind, hail and rain, in search of more challenging terrain.

Amidst the all-consuming training regime, when I am out of the house for three hours, four days every week, I have a family to tend to. I transformed from a consultant in Artificial Intelligence to househusband. Liz, Victoria and Georgina go to work, while I squeeze training between regular duties like cleaning, shopping for food and cooking. And I dedicate Tuesdays to visiting JD in his home at Woodcock Dell. There is little time left for anything else.

But the routine will change after the arrival of our first grandchild in two months, when I will apply my househusbandry skills to help Roxanne and Peter. Then Victoria announced some news, while on the receiving end of one of my dad jokes. She was in the kitchen having a cup of tea when she said, cautiously, "err,...dad?"

"Wassup? Are you pregnant?" I joked, my back turned to her while washing my hands at the sink.

A pregnant silence followed. My dad jokes are normally swatted aside by my daughters, but not on this occasion. With the tap still running, I turned to see her eyes sparkle and smiling.

Her baby is due in late August. After a celebratory cup of tea and cracking open our finest chocolate biscuits, I realised that the trek must finish before September, so I can be around to help. Allowing ten weeks for the trek, I must start before mid-June. Delaying another year is not an option - who knows what will happen? More babies and grandchildren? I am no spring chicken and not getting younger.

Ian at Norwood contacted me about the trek. He is their Challenges Programme Manager, responsible for organising fundraising events, such as walks along the Great Wall in China, the London to Brighton cycle ride and the cycle ride through Israel. He suggested meeting to investigate specific ways his team can help. I need help with my donations page, finding volunteers to walk with and publicity, publicity and more publicity. Time for the trek is running out, and I must get a wiggle on.

# NOCTURNAL ACTIVITIES

January 10th 2016.

In daylight I train and in darkness I suck up GR10 facts. The Internet is a fabulous source. There are blogs, Wikipedia articles and YouTube clips of the Great French Walks (Grand Randonnée) and, best of all, Google Maps. I am a junkie who gets a fix by zooming in on the Pyrenees and inhaling satellite images and photos. My ultimate high was a three-mile 'street view' trip along the GR10 from its start at the beach in Hendaye, through busy streets towards the mountains, until it ended abruptly at a footpath and disappeared behind bushes.

But there are things I would rather not see, like vertigo-inducing images taken from the GR10, YouTube clips of trekkers scaling cliff walls and running fearlessly with head-torches along rocky tracks in the dark. Too much information can be a bad thing.

Only a few complete the GR10. About one hundred trekkers leave Hendaye each day between June and August. So, I was jubilant to find out that another ninety-nine will set off from Hendaye with me, then crushed to discover that ninety turn off after five days for the Camino, the ancient pilgrim's route, at St-Jean-Pied-de-Port. But for the first five days I should enjoy the company of pilgrims destined for Santiago de Compostela and Finisterre, the 'End of the World'.

"Never mind," I muttered, "there will be nine other

trekkers in my vicinity."

But that consoling thought evaporated when I learned that most give up after one or two weeks and only a hardy handful struggle on to the end at Banyuls-sur-mer. I will be on my own for most of the trek unless I find companions.

I also learned that most people embarking on the GR10 are experienced hikers who shun modern navigation aids like mobile phones in favour of maps, compasses and signposts. They have a confidence and an instinct I lack. They can study a map and compass, survey the landscape and know exactly where they are. Therein lies the difficulty with maps – they are only effective if the person carrying them knows how to read the land and establish a precise location.

"Never mind," I muttered again, "I will have my trusty Cicerone Guide to the GR10," a small and weighty book that breaks the route up into fifty day-long treks, with a little map for each day's journey, directions and photos. Written in 2006, the book is becoming more and more out-dated as route changes and deviations are discovered by bloggers. The directions are unclear, telling the reader where not to go, rather than where to go. So, perhaps the book is not as trustworthy as I think.

On my three-day expedition with Jonathan to the Pyrenees, I could pinpoint our location to within a few metres, with a strong GPS signal. The technology worked so well that I never tested my ability to read a paper map or look at signposts. Dependence on my phone is so great that I will be helpless without it. The organic methods used for centuries – paper maps, compass and orienteering skills - are my backup but I have had no practice. One wrong turn could mean spending a lonely night on a bald mountain.

I must be able to see the route on my phone to know if I am on the right track. But the GR10 is not marked on Google Maps, so I have wiled away night hours checking it against the Cicerone guidebook. Sometimes, the route is obvious – a section of a mountain road, a village street, a track meandering up a mountain, or a forest path beside a lake. But often, there are no clues.

The culmination of many nights' activities resulted in a list of three hundred Google Maps links that illustrate short sections of the GR10, created painstakingly from the Cicerone guidebook. I can see each section marked in luminous green on my phone, so I know exactly where I am in relation to it. Currently, I am six hundred miles from the start in Hendaye. The list includes distances, altitude gain and descent and journey times. I added contingency because I will be slower than the times suggested by the Cicerone guidebook. Now I can estimate *when* and *where* I will be, which will be crucial If Norwood finds volunteers to walk with.

I must prepare for walking the whole road for JD on my own. I will probably wander off the path occasionally and navigate without the benefit of a second opinion. Somehow, I must overcome my dreadful fear of heights. There *will* be sheer drops, vertical climbs and exposed places. The trek will be physically and psychologically demanding, but that is no reason to give up. My confidence wanes, and I doubt my strength to fulfil my promise. Quiet moments, such as before sleep, are when the worries and fears wake.

# RETURN TO NORWOOD

Norwood now know that I will start my fundraising walk for JD, his carers and Woodcock Dell in early June. Allowing three months to finish, I should be home by September, in time for the birth of our second grandchild. Ian and Diana from the Fundraising team offered to create my donations page. Annoyingly, two percent of whatever I raise will be lost on commission charges. In the unlikely event I meet the thirty-five-thousand pounds target needed for Woodcock Dell's dining room extension, the donations company will receive seven hundred pounds. So, I need to raise thirty-six thousand pounds.

Diana advised me to create a Facebook account for uploading photos and as an online diary of events. Facebook has never been my thing, despite working in IT all my life. Too many people spend too much time telling everyone what they are doing, what they have just done, their opinions, instead of being *with* friends and family. But she convinced me that it will be useful for the trek, so I will step into the world of blogging.

*"Rounding a hairpin on a cliff edge, I was confronted by a hungry bear, slavering jaws open, teeth bared and ready. I must capture this moment for my eager public on Facebook - my followers want drama, and they shall not be disappointed.*

*Facing my assailant, I asked, "Excuse me Monsieur Bear, can I take a selfie with you?"*

*The bear paused to oblige. Who could refuse such a request, after all? Being an avid Facebook user itself, it friended me so that it could savour our time together. We posed for the camera, cheek to furry cheek. The bear waited politely while I uploaded the image and tapped in an account of our brief and final encounter."*

Ian offered to help with publicity but warned that the press offered only limited support for Norwood's fundraising events. They occasionally print an article a few weeks after each event, he explained.

"What's the point in that? It's too late for readers to donate, isn't it?" I asked.

"We're just grateful for whatever they print about us," he replied tactfully.

My hopes are not high for publicity from the press.

Norwood will look for companions to walk with me, but it is a huge commitment for someone to make. Few people can spare the time. Even if a volunteer steps forward, I will not know them, they will not know me, and we will not meet until we are at our rendezvous. How will we recognise each other? They might expect me to pay for their accommodation and food. The trek will cost over five thousand pounds for equipment, flights, accommodation and food, just for me. If I am expected to pay for volunteers as well, then I may as well take out a loan.

If this trek was a business, it would be insolvent if revenue never covered costs. The Chief Finance Officer of 'Walk the Pyrenees for Jeremy and Norwood' plc would advise me to, "give the money you spend on expenses directly to Woodcock Dell and stay at home." But their advice ignores two motives whose value cannot be measured – my promise to JD to 'walk the whole road' and the sign of respect and gratitude to his carers. Maybe I should not get so hung up about the money and just focus on them instead. Even if I raise zero pounds for JD's home, the value remains.

# THE LAND DOWN UNDER

I flew away from the cold wet gloom of an English winter and stepped into the hot arid brilliance of an Australian summer a day later. My older brother Terry convinced me that Australia was the right place for heat training, something I could never get in England. He is the same brother who introduced me to the 'big wheel of terror' in my childhood and my nemesis for so many years. It was not until after he emigrated in 1971, when he was eighteen, that I forgave him and missed him being around. Unlike me, he has a strong sense of adventure. A few months after emigrating, he found his dream job as a park worker and bushfire-fighter in Kuringai Chase national park, twenty miles north of Sydney. Later, he graduated in Geology at Monash University and was entrusted to lead parties of undergrads into the bush to take rock samples. His knowledge of the flora, fauna, climate and geology of the country is encyclopaedic.

The difficult part of the visit was not the long-haul flight, or the training walks in the heat, but not seeing JD for over three weeks. On the Tuesday before I left England, I told him the news.

"JD, daddy is going to Australia to see Uncle Terry."

"Mmmm," he replied as I spooned a mouthful of fried fish smothered in mayonnaise into his waiting mouth. It could have meant, "Mmmm, tasty" or "Mmmm, oh right."

"I won't be able to see you again until the Sunday after

I get back," I announced regretfully.

He pondered, pushing the fish around his mouth with his tongue, occasionally digging it out the roof of his mouth with his thumb.

I continued, "so, I won't be coming to see you on Sunday, or next Tuesday, but mummy will see you on Sunday."

It is painful telling JD that I cannot visit. There are others with conditions like his who are never visited. That is so tragic. One of my greatest fears for my son is that he will be forgotten, like some adults in care appear to be. I hope that my walk for him will mean he is never forgotten. After all, I would not be doing it if it were not for him.

With a heavy heart, I left Woodcock Dell and reflected on our conversation on the hour-long drive home. Still brooding, I packed for my flight the next morning. If I feel like this before a three-week absence from JD, how will I feel when I say goodbye for a ten-week trek along the Pyrenees?

Early on Wednesday morning, I said goodbye to Liz at Heathrow airport. My first experience of a long-haul flight was every bit as uncomfortable as expected. Restless legs, over-eating, and insomnia for twenty-six hours. For another hour I battled with the intelligent passport control system at Melbourne airport that stubbornly refused to verify that I wore *my* face and not someone else's. My brother had no such difficulty when I emerged from arrivals. We had not seen one another since my sister's funeral three years earlier, but recognition was immediate.

Terry introduced me to his Australian muscle car, called affectionately 'The Balrog' in honour of the 'denizen of the deep' from 'The Lord of the Rings', an HSV six-point-two-litre supercharged V8 saloon with Walkinshaw modifications that boosted output to a mighty seven hundred and fifty horsepower, as much va-va-voom as a Ferrari supercar. The irony was that there is virtually nowhere in the state of Victoria where he could apply more than a tenth of that power, owing to the stringent speed regulations.

"Bastards they are," said Terry, crawling sedately at sixty kilometres per hour on the ring-road around Melbourne towards his apartment in Malvern, five miles south-east of the city centre.

"I agree," I said, for the sake of argument and without knowing who or what he referred to.

"At least in England, they call these bastard 'safety enforcement cameras' what they are!"

"What?" I queried, "bastard speed enforcement cameras?"

"They should be honest and just call 'em money grabbing bastard cameras."

Terry had a fair point. One moment, the speed signs said one hundred, then a mile further fell to sixty, then rose to eighty and down to sixty again. It was a full-time job concentrating on the speed signs, to the obvious detriment of road safety. The Australian authorities seemed to be fishing for unaware motorists.

"I've already been caught by these bastards before, for doing fifty-six in a fifty zone, and got a one-hundred-and-forty-dollar bill!"

"That's a bit steep," I said.

"Then the bastards suspend your license if you get caught again!"

Over the next ten days, I was treated to Terry's exceptional hospitality and generosity. Despite the lack of space, he sacrificed his only bedroom for me while he slept on the lounge floor. Every room in his apartment was lined with books on a broad range of subjects, mostly Geology, Geography, Meteorology, Mathematics, Astronomy and Botany. Apart from the complete works of J.R. Tolkien, there were no fiction books.

"Have you read *all* of these?" I asked.

"Yeh," came the short reply, and I believed him.

"So, you're walking the Pyrenees?" he asked, "are you

taking Jeremy with you?"

"Good gracious no," I replied, "it would be far too difficult, and I'd have to carry him on my back for most of the way."

"So how is the young man?" he inquired, "and how are the carers I met when we went to the Santana concert?" When Terry last visited England, we took JD to Wembley Arena to experience a rock concert.

"Oh, you mean Helen and Philma," I replied, "they're fine, still there, dedicating themselves to looking after JD and his housemates."

"Yeh, I know just how difficult the job is," and he pressed on to remind me about his time working in a care home when he was seventeen, "I used to have to wash and dress them, cook and entertain them."

Those were troubled times, I recollected, just after Terry dropped out of school and took on a series of jobs. He was a hard worker, and gained experience in the local Forestry Commission, a woodyard, farms and a care home a few miles from our parent's home in a Hampshire village. But his mind was always set on moving to the last great frontier of Australia, at a time when it was possible to buy a one-way ticket for ten pounds and settle there. He found his spiritual home and made a new life for himself, re-started his education and became an Australian citizen through-and-through.

"So, with the jetlag, I thought we could go walkabout the streets of Melbourne today," he proposed, "then tomorrow, you, Wendy and me can all go for a proper walk in the Dandenongs, a few miles away."

"Sounds like an excellent idea," I did not feel tired, although it would catch up eventually.

Terry set out our agenda for the next two weeks. It would be alternating between a day of medium to long distance walking and a day of light walking, typically visiting the local sights in Melbourne, or shopping in interesting places, like the huge Chinese food market in

Box Hill, a nearby suburb. There would be opportunity to train in temperatures that would "easily exceed" those of a Pyrenean summer.

# BLOODY MAN!

We were in the middle of an Australian summer, yet it was abnormally cool.

"I brought the English weather with me," I ventured. Warm and comfortable enough for me, but to most Aussies, twenty-five degrees Celsius felt like a Siberian winter.

"Nah, it's the bastard cold front hanging over the Tasman Sea," Terry contradicted. I rarely disagreed with him because he was often right. I waited for the lecture on isobars, cyclones and La Nina, but it did not come.

"Typical," he continued, "last week, it hit forty on two days. I think I'm gonna take you up north, somewhere inland like Echuca, where it's *always* hot."

"Sounds good," I said, "I have experienced temperatures over forty Celsius before, but never walked far in them." I was referring to my trip with the family to the Dead Sea valley in April 2008, when the heat was intolerable, and I spent all my time forcing water into JD with an oral syringe.

So, we agreed it would be beneficial to drive one hundred and fifty miles north to the border of New South Wales, to Echuca on Tuesday, for heat training. To prepare for the excursion, Terry suggested "somewhere more local, like the Dandenong Ranges, where I scattered Mum's and Dad's ashes."

Family funerals were the only times I saw Terry since

his emigration. First at my father's in 2003, then my mother's in 2008, and my eldest sister's in 2013. The Dandenong trip was an unexpected opportunity to pay my respects to my parents, as well as continue with my training programme.

On a hot and sunny Sunday, we picked up Terry's girlfriend, Wendy, in The Balrog and headed east for the Dandenong Ranges, thirty miles away. Wendy emigrated from China six years earlier and was still learning the subtleties of the English language, and the novelties of the Australian dialect. She struggled with a few consonants, notably 's', 'z' and 'k'.

"You like China food, Lauren?" she inquired from the back seat.

"Chinese food, not China food, you silly woman!" interjected Terry.

"You bloody man," Wendy retorted, her favourite term of endearment.

"And it's Laurence, not Lauren!" he responded.

The exchange between Terry and Wendy was normal. There was no malice behind the words, just gentle vocal jousting with a healthy mutual respect. Wendy was the only person I knew who could squash Terry's occasional angry outbursts.

"Look at this dickhead," he exclaimed, jabbing a finger at the car in front, "he's too close – stupid bastard!"

"You bloody man," Wendy said, "*you* have di' head."

When the laughter subsided, the reason for the outburst was forgotten.

The apartment blocks, colonial houses and bungalows of the Melbourne suburbs gave way to yellow-green open plains stretching to the horizon, with lines of Acacias and gum trees in the foreground and at the roadsides. The uniqueness of the scene told the observer where they were, "you're in Australia," it cried. A mob of kangaroos would complete the picture perfectly.

We turned on to a single-lane road that climbed and

wound through a forest of tall mountain ash, wattles and giant ferns to a picnic-area set among the trees. Terry parked away from a group of cars and coaches near the café and souvenir shop. "I don't want any bastard scratching my car," he explained.

Terry and Wendy held hands as I lifted my rucksack on to my back. The humidity had risen considerably since we left, and the strength of the sun was more intense than I could remember.

"Don't forget to put on your sun-cream," Terry advised, "in Melbourne, the sun's as strong as it is in Cairo." I lathered a handful on my neck, arms and face and kept my trekking trousers rolled down, as a protection from the sun and attack from the deadly spiders, snakes and other insects that lurked in the undergrowth. I tucked my trousers into my thick Merino wool socks to prevent creepy-crawlies from ravaging my legs and migrating upwards.

"You know, Australia has the most venomous snakes and spiders in the world," Terry added. It was at such times I would be lost without such information, I thought, as my eyes swept the ground before my feet. Terry and Wendy led me to a wide track, flanked on both sides by two-hundred-foot mountain ash and stringy bark trees. Five hundred yards further, he dived into the bush and shouted, "this way, and don't touch any branches and watch where you put your feet."

I followed nervously, conjuring up images of myriads of giant webs and fat juicy leeches hanging from the ferns. Terry stopped and pointed at the base of a particularly tall tree.

"This is it, this is where mum's and dad's ashes are," he said, "I scattered them here when I came back from England in 2003 and 2008, so they'll be a part of this tree now."

Like both of us, and JD, my parents loved trees. Theirs was a noble specimen, and worthy of absorbing their ashes, measuring eight feet across and a hundred-and-eighty feet tall. We stood in silence, paying our respects, while Wendy waited on the track.

"You and dad had some spectacular arguments," I reminded Terry.

"Yeh, he was stubborn," he replied, "just like all of us."

After a few seconds of silence, he added, "but I was more stubborn and often wrong."

The heat intensified as we followed the tree-lined path, high branches offered shade but no respite from the steamy humidity. The forest track continued for another two miles before joining a narrow road and descending steeply into a small town. Without shade, my head fried, even with 'dad hat' secured. Sun-cream trickled down my nose and cheeks, on to my neck and down my chest. But the heat did not bother Terry, who enthused over the native flora and fauna.

On the ascent back into the forest, there was a brief flurry of words in English and Chinese between Terry and Wendy. She climbed onto his back.

"Wendy's tired - she doesn't like the heat," he explained, "so I'll carry her, she weighs about the same as your rucksack I reckon."

Six miles and six hundred feet of climbing in extreme heat was a good test. The visit to the tree that thrived on our parents' ashes was an unexpected bonus.

# HEAT

"Get up yer lazy bastard," Terry said, cup of tea in hand, "we've got a long journey ahead."

My head swam after a night spent waking, anxious and with chest thumping. At three in the morning, I searched the Internet for causes. Some Websites advised, "seek medical advice – IMMEDIATELY." They were too dramatic, so I ignored them and concluded that I was having an anxiety attack, something I am not normally prone to. I missed JD and the rest of my family. In six months, I would be stepping into the unknown, and my mind was telling me, "You're not ready!" Those two reasons were reasonable explanations for my nighttime panic.

When I told Terry, he scolded me, "you should have woken me!"

Despite all our childhood fights and arguments, he still played the role of the big brother, protecting his younger sibling. I saw the same behaviour in his care for Wendy.

We hit the road in The Balrog, heading for Echuca and extreme heat training. Our destination lay one hundred and fifty miles north of Melbourne, on the border with New South Wales. Heavy commuter traffic slowed our progress to a crawl through the suburbs. Just like our road trip with Wendy to the Dandenong Ranges two days earlier, Terry loved showing off his passive driving skills.

"Now, take this bastard here," he pointed at the car

alongside at a junction, "you wait and see. He'll try and cut me up where the road narrows on the other side of the lights."

"What are you going to do?" I asked. With that amount of power at my feet, it would not happen.

"I'm just gonna let him," he replied to my surprise. This was not the Terry I used to know.

"The bastard speed sign over there means I'll get a ticket if I burn him up, so I'm gonna let him get a ticket if he wants one," he explained.

"That's smart thinking – lure him into your trap."

We left the suburbs and joined the freeway north. Even with little traffic, continuously changing speed limits denied us all chance of unleashing The Balrog. The miles drifted past, and we talked on a wide range of subjects – Cosmology, Geology, rock music, the forthcoming trek, JD, the girls, Liz, Wendy and Charlie the mutt.

Three hours later, we arrived at the Echuca Visitor Centre, situated on a broad dusty street lined with painted wooden buildings and sheltered walkways. Beyond the street, the Murray, part of Australia's longest river system, slithered by on its long journey to the Southern Ocean, forty miles south-east of Adelaide. A paddle-steamer chugged past rows of yachts moored on the near bank, completing an American deep south scene.

A blast-furnace of heat and soggy humidity socked me in the face as I stepped out of the air-conditioned car. "Strewth!" I uttered, like a true Aussie.

"Yeh," Terry beamed, "this is more like it - proper heat."

"Let's go to the Visitor Centre," he proposed, "see what walks there are around here."

He bounded ahead, while I applied sun-cream, tucked trousers into socks, checked the medicine kit and head-net were on hand. Everything that moved in Australia wanted to eat, bite, sting or kill me, so the head-net-and-trousers ritual was a necessary act of self-preservation.

Inside a cool office, a stout lady dressed in khaki shorts and green T-shirt with a 'Echuca-Moama Visitor Centre' logo greeted us.

"Hi gents," she said. I was disappointed it was not "G'day". Perhaps the cliché had served its time?

Terry got straight to the point, "Hello, are there any good walks around here?"

"Yeh," she answered, "you can follow the bank of the river, through the trees and round back through town."

"Only, my brother here," Terry gestured, "has come all the way from England for some heat training, in preparation for his trek along the Pyrenees this year."

The lady looked me up and down before advising, "well, you fellas had better stick to the path then."

"Why?" I asked.

"The brown snakes are out today. We've had a few incidents because some drongos wandered into the bush."

I gulped and Terry smirked, then thanked her politely.

"Rubbish," he said, when we stepped out into the forty-three-degree heat, "what a load of bollocks! Brown snakes are more likely to run, unless they feel threatened."

"They'd need legs for that," I added.

But the damage was done. I watched the ground with every step. In England, I could look ahead, but here, one's life depended on accurate feet placement. Constant vigilance was essential. We followed a path into a forest.

"Ah, river red gums," Terry began his morning symposium early. He lectured on the variants of each tree species, their differences, and the soil they preferred, while my eyes watched every footfall. Dry compacted mud, as hard as rock, red and coated with a thin layer of dust. I sweated profusely, even when still, in the intolerable heat and humidity. Meanwhile, Terry bounded through the forest recounting tales of trips into the Australian bush, where "temperatures were *much* higher."

Suddenly I spotted several finger-sized holes in the ground.

"Are these bull-ant holes?"

The Australian bull-ant is legendary, growing to prehistoric proportions. It could administer an astonishingly painful bite from one end and an even more painful sting from the other. Years before, Terry had posted one back home, shrivelled but preserved in a bottle of after-shave lotion, after a week-long journey. In his letter, he claimed it was as "big as my thumb," and I wanted to see for myself.

"Could be," answered Terry, "why don't you poke it and see?"

I picked up a stick, after inspecting it for killer spiders, snakes and hornets, and gently prodded a hole. Instantly, a large black ant emerged, antennae waving angrily. An inch long, far larger than the common British ant.

"That's huge!" I exclaimed, "is it a bull-ant?"

"Nah, just a wood-ant, a tiddler."

Disappointed, but I was not on a bull-ant safari. After five miles of energy-sapping heat, my pace slowed to a shuffle along smooth flat ground, even with a paltry thirteen pounds on my back. If the Pyrenees ever got as hot, I would *never* make it.

# OLD BULL ANT

Terry had been my chauffeur and chaperone for five days, escorting me around the most popular walking spots near Melbourne. On Thursday, we visited Hanging Rock, forty-five miles north-west of the city and the site of Joan Lindsay's novel 'Picnic at Hanging Rock', published in 1967. The book is written as though it were a factual account of the disappearance of three schoolgirls in 1900, and the myth was re-enforced by the theatre at the Discovery Centre.

Hanging Rock is the only significant feature in an otherwise flat landscape, that rises several hundred feet above the plain. The streaky textured rock is an unusual reddish-brown in colour and the air around about is completely still, creating an aura of mystery.

Terry wasted no time explaining its provenance, "about seven million years ago, this area was a massive volcanic plane, and the Rock was an active volcano. It's what's known as a *mamelon*, or magma that congealed as it was forced up the vent, forming a seal."

He went on to explain the column-like rock formations, "the magma cooled, contracted and split to make these shapes."

We encountered no one on a soundless ascent to the summit, not even birds or animals. From the top, we were treated to a panoramic view of Melbourne city centre, with its distinctive Eureka and Rialto Towers, nearby Mount

Macedon, the Dandenongs and, about fifty miles south, the You Yangs Regional Park, where we were headed on Thursday.

Two days later, we jumped into The Balrog for more strenuous training at the You Yangs Regional Park, forty miles west of Melbourne.

"This is one of the driest areas in Victoria," Terry announced, "you can tell from the vegetation and presence of red, yellow and blue gum trees, or *eucalyptus camaldulensis*, *leucoxylon* and *pseudoglobulus*, to give them their proper names."

"Gawd help me," I uttered in despair.

Impressed with his profound knowledge, I wished I could identify trees and rattle off their Latin names. Still looking down at my feet for fear of stepping on a death sentence, I spotted something large and red, moving slowly.

Terry declared, "at last, a bull-ant!"

A monster ant, a thumb in length, moved slowly over a rock as if lost or sick.

"Poor bastard, it's probably about to kick the bucket," Terry said, "but don't get too close, you'll be in agony if it stings."

The poor beast lumbered clumsily into undergrowth.

"Where do bull-ants go to die?" I asked, not expecting an answer, but I should have known better.

"They're carried away from the nest and buried," Terry answered, "it's a behaviour called *necrophoresis*, evolved to prevent infection."

"Fascinating," I said, "and highly logical."

## BAD MANORS

"Fancy a cuppa coffee?" Terry asked, as we headed towards the site of Australia's second-worst bush fire, on 'Black Saturday' in 2009, around Marysville, sixty miles north-east of Melbourne.

"Good idea," I agreed.

We stopped at a town called Narbethong at the end of the Black Spur Drive, destroyed in the 2009 fire and famous for the Narbethong Hotel that featured in the 1959 post-apocalyptic science fiction film 'On the Beach' with Gregory Peck, Ava Gardner and Fred Astaire. We pulled into a ranch-house, set back off the road opposite a dense forest of mountain ash.

A sign over the entrance read 'King Henry VIII Manor House Eatery'. Someone sat in a rocking-chair on the veranda.

"This is unusual," Terry said.

"It's like no Costa I've ever seen," I added.

We approached the entrance, and the rocker, a lady in her late fifties, stood up and ambled towards us, "G'day gents, can I help?"

"We'd just like a coffee or tea, if that's OK," Terry answered.

"Sure, gents, come on in and sit down," she ushered us inside.

The interior was a jumble of museum, bric-a-brac shop and posh restaurant. Crystal chandeliers hung from the ceiling, and the room was adorned with stuffed animals and random collections of paintings, pottery and trinkets. Amidst the cornucopia stood six perfectly set circular dining tables with silver knives, forks, spoons and napkins arranged for royalty. While I admired the décor, Terry conversed with our hostess, who introduced herself as Shirley.

There was a shuffling sound from behind, "Jeez! What the fuck's that? I dunno whether to shoot it or shag it."

The owner of the voice was an old man, about my height, silver-haired with thick bushy eyebrows. His remark was directed at Terry's shock of thick curly white hair, my brother's most distinctive feature. Terry turned around, unsure whether to laugh or take offence.

"I'm Dennis," said the man, "and this is Shirley, my bit on the side."

We laughed, and the tension lifted.

"Come on gents, sit yerselves down," Dennis said, pulling a chair out for me, while Shirley showed Terry to a seat opposite.

"What can we get yer?" Dennis asked, pulling a chair up to the table and sitting between us, "my missus will get yer whatever you want. I'm too old to be a waiter, never had the fuckin' patience for it anyway, eighty-three years is enough of a fuckin' stint."

As Shirley went to make tea, Dennis entertained us with colourful banter decorated liberally with four-letter words. He was direct and rude at times, but likeable and someone who would not, or could not, hide his feelings and views. He talked uninterrupted for ten minutes about his formative years as the owner of a restaurant of the same name in the Dandenong Ranges. His previous property was burned to a cinder in the terrible fire of February 2009, along with one thousand seven hundred square miles of forest and the loss of a hundred and seventy-three lives. He recounted the tale of a neighbour who survived the inferno by swimming to the middle of a lake as a wall of six-hundred-foot-high flame closed in. Dennis and Shirley very narrowly escaped with their lives.

"The trouble was," said Dennis, "the poor bastard didn't know that all the fuckin' snakes in the forest had the same idea," and guffawed with laughter.

"He was lucky they were there just to get outta the furnace, otherwise he woulda been fucked," he added.

Terry watched him intently, and then exclaimed, "I know you, you were voted the rudest hotel proprietor in Victoria!"

Dennis beamed proudly, shuffled over to a cabinet, rifled around and produced a crumpled newspaper cutting from 1987 with his photo and a half-page report on his antics. "Yeh, that's me! Australia's answer to Basil Fawlty."

We talked and drank tea for an hour before leaving, with Dennis and Shirley waving from the veranda.

"You know," I said as we drove off, "it's encounters like that that make lasting memories."

"Yeh," Terry said, "and the tea wasn't bad either."

The road climbed, and the forest closed in. Evidence of the great fire was all about – blackened and leafless trees, tall and grey, ghost-like, with shattered branches, dwarfing many young saplings. Suddenly, Terry pulled the car into a lookout bay and stopped, "this'll do," he said, "you'll get an idea of its scale from here."

We stood about a thousand feet up, overlooking tree-covered mountains as far as the eye could see.

"If you look over there," Terry pointed right, "that thick band of lighter green are the young mountain ash that grew sixty feet in seven years." The landscape was mottled green, with thinner patches of younger trees here and there. The wide tracks left by the Black Saturday fireball as it devastated everything in its path were slowly disappearing.

"The flames would have been three times as tall as the trees themselves," Terry said, "and, being eucalyptus and full of oil, there's no gentle flicker that builds up gradually

– they explode in flame, with no warning."

I peered up at a two-hundred-foot tree and tried to imagine what it must have been like. One tree ablaze would be terrifying enough, one million of them was unimaginable. The fire obliterated several towns in the area, including Marysville, nestling in the valley ahead. We parked by one of the four buildings left in the town, the Crossways Country Inn. A short line of London plane trees nearby, were the only survivors of the inferno. Many homes were re-built, but the town was quiet, deserted, as if the land grieved the loss of trees, animals and people who perished.

"JD likes trees, doesn't he?" Terry broke the silence. I nodded.

"Well, he'll love this one," and clambered back into the car.

We drove ten miles east towards the Yarra Ranges. Many of the trees on both sides of the road were victims of the bush fire, no more than blackened trunks with splintered branches. But from death comes life. Sunlight illuminated the ground, and young saplings sprung up in the spaces vacated by their two-hundred-foot-tall ancestors.

We pulled off-road onto a forest track. I tucked my trouser bottoms into socks, to defend against creatures waiting for unsuspecting 'poms'. We clambered over a wooden gate on to a narrow forest path with overhanging branches and tall ferns.

"Does this count as bushwalking?" I asked.

"Nah, this is nothing," Terry replied before repeating his warning, "just don't put your hands on anything."

I joked nervously, "so, when does the velociraptor appear?"

"It's not man-eating raptors you should worry about," Terry replied, "it's leeches. They drop down on to you and attach themselves to your neck and face. There are six-inch-long tiger leeches that suck from both ends."

"Bloody typical!" I said, "Australia always has something worse than imagination." I pulled my 'dad-hat' down firmly, securing it against infiltration.

The path twisted through the dense jungle, over a small stream, before we came face-to-face with the largest tree in the world, before its tip was lopped off on 26$^{th}$ October 2011. Unimaginatively named 'The Big Tree', it stood at just over two-hundred-and-eighty-eight feet, according to the plaque bashed into the ground at its feet.

"Loads of even taller trees were crisped on Black Saturday," Terry said, "including a couple of three-hundred-footers."

"Better not tell JD," I said, "he'd be upset to hear that, he has a special relationship with trees."

"Do you think you'll ever bring him out here?" Terry asked. The question put me on the spot. Logic answered, "no, probably not," then indignation, "but his able-bodied peers have, so why shouldn't he?"

"Yeh," agreed Terry, "why not? He'd love it!"

How could someone with JD's condition get from England to a place like this, the middle of the Australian bush? The long-haul flight would be the first challenge, the next would be carrying him a mile into a jungle. A wheelchair would be impractical. He would need a specially adapted chair, with tracks instead of wheels to negotiate the bumps and ruts. A papoose might suffice, except he is as tall as me and weighs five stones, so it would need to be a heavy-duty one. A crazy thought popped into my head, "I could carry him in my rucksack!"

JD would love the Australian jungle, hacking through the giant ferns and bushes, staring three-hundred feet up at the canopy. I wondered if he ever thought about such places. When he sees a picture of a forest, does he recognise it, or does he see random patterns and swirls of colours? Other twenty-somethings can study brochures of exotic faraway places and visit them, does JD have the same yearning? I *could* have brought him with me, I just did not *try*.

# LONG JOURNEYS

What did I learn from three weeks in Australia? Look down in case you step on a brown snake with enough venom to kill eighty men. Watch out where you sit lest you inadvertently put your bum on a nest of bull-ants. Beware of your hands because there are deadly spiders out to get you. Keep your arms, legs, neck and head covered as protection against blood-sucking leeches. The list goes on. But there are no such dangers for me to worry about in the Pyrenees and I must unlearn all that I learned and start looking ahead instead of down at my feet.

But I also learned that extreme heat, like the kind I felt in Echuca, saps energy more quickly than rugged terrain and extreme gradients. I hoped it would not get as hot on the Pyrenees in mid-Summer.

Terry insisted on driving me to Melbourne airport for my return flight. I patted the car bonnet, "Thank you, Balrog, for the memorable road trips" and heaved on my rucksack.

"We mustn't leave it so long next time," I said, inside the terminal.

"Let's hope no one kicks the bucket," he replied, "I wouldn't want that to be the reason for visiting."

"I'll send you photos of my trek on the mountains."

"Yeh, I'd like that, and Wendy says she will cook you some real Chinese dumplings next time you're over."

We both felt awkward at saying goodbyes, so we

embraced and then I plunged into the queue for security checks. I did not know when I would see Terry again. It could be at the next family funeral in England, or perhaps in Australia, with Liz.

I struggled to sleep on the return flight, flitting between watching films, tackling Killer Sudoku puzzles with eyelids drooping, and listening to music, interrupted by trays of food with impossible-to-unwrap tin foil cartons. Terry's question at the foot of 'The Big Tree' still played on my mind. Could JD ever go to Australia? Our family trip to New York in 2009 was difficult enough. To give him a safe space, we booked a business class seat and an adjacent seat for me. But it took two to toilet him, mealtimes were three times longer than normal and he never slept. Could JD cope on a flight three times longer?

Somewhere over the Himalayas, I concluded that the only solution would be to break the trip into shorter flights with overnight stops. Two or three full-time carers would be needed – one person could not manage his complex needs on their own. They would need to operate a shift system, so that one could rest while the other two supported JD.

Three-hundred-and-fifty passengers boarded my flight from Melbourne, and not one baby or disabled passenger was among them. Although, there were some exhausted parents with small children, who they kept occupied by playing cartoons on iPads, and colouring books and crayons. But no one like JD. I guessed that it is considered just too difficult to take someone like him on long journeys. We shall see about that.

# THE BEST LAID PLANS

The Ariège region is the wildest section of the Pyrenees. Sandwiched by Andorra to the south, and Toulouse in the north, it takes a week to traverse. I will enter from the west, three miles east of the mountain village of Labach, and emerge in the east, a couple of miles west of Pic Carlit. The trouble is, there are no refuges, shops and only a few cabanes. The Cicerone guidebook advises trekkers to carry a tent, sleeping bag, cooking equipment and food and not walk alone. But all that extra stuff adds weight, and my load is great enough already.

The Ariège also happens to be the Pyrenean bear's preferred habitat, probably because there are so few humans stopping them from indulging in their favourite pastime harassing sheep. I assume that bears are a good reason for not trekking solo, because they are more likely to 'have a go' at a feeble human than at a gang of two or more.

Thankfully, I found a 'gang' of two walking companions. Jonathan, my companion on the three-day expedition last June, was so inspired by the incomparable scenery and wholesome living, that he wants more and agreed to accompany me for the first three days of the trek. My friend Avi announced his intention to join me for the last four days, if I make it that far. Like me, he has no experience of mountains, but he carries a fearlessness and confidence to counter my trepidation. The trouble is they will be nowhere near the Ariège when they are with me, so will not suffice as a natural bear repellent.

I have no choice but to spend more nights poring over Google Maps and the Cicerone guide re-planning for the Ariège. I cannot take food or camping equipment with me and must avoid encounters with bears.

I could exit the GR10 at Eylie d'en Haut, in the south-western corner of the Ariège and drop down the mountain to a remote village called Sentein, then head north-east through a wooded valley to the ancient town of St-Girons. From there, turn south-east to Aulus-les-Bains and pick up an unmarked path to Niaux that climbs steeply and cuts across the hairpins of a mountain road. But does the steep sixteen-mile path from Aulus-les-bains to Niaux actually exist? Even if I made it there, an unpleasant main road walk from Niaux to the popular holiday resort of Ax-les-Thermes awaits. A busy road connects Ax to Merens-les-Vals on the eastern end of the Ariège, where I could re-join the GR10. The diversion could be done in a week assuming that my hand-crafted route exists. I know that the mountain road from Eylie to Sentein, and the routes from Sentein to St-Girons and Ax to Merens exist because I walked them in 'street view'.

Even if the diversion is possible, is it part of 'the whole road' I promised to walk for JD? I asked him while on a trip to the park on a breezy Tuesday morning.

"I have a dilemma JD", I began, wheels rolling over mulched leaves.

He appeared more interested in the branches swaying in the wind than the noise from behind.

"That road I promised to walk for you has nowhere to buy food."

"No bread, cheese, fruit or Marmite," I hoped the last item in the shopping list would get his attention. He responded with a sigh. Perhaps he refused to accept that there was somewhere on Planet Earth where Marmite was not in plentiful supply.

"There's nowhere to stay either and I have no tent, so I must divert."

We stopped by our favourite park bench. I turned his wheelchair to face me.

"This walk is for you JD, so this is important," I gazed into his eyes.

"Are you alright if I take a different path for a little bit, then re-join?"

His eyes locked onto mine and then he grinned.

"That's good enough JD, I'll take that as a yes."

Trundling around Welsh Harp, I realised how far out of my depth I was. Three days of walking in the Pyrenees is my only experience. At least I did not need to wrestle with a tent at the top of a mountain now that JD gave his blessing for a diversion. I turned to help from an Internet blog called the 'Pyrenean Way'.

*"Hi. I am planning to walk the GR10 for my profoundly disabled son's care home (link to my donations page here). I have been on a three-day trial trek along the Pyrenees with my rucksack with forty-four pounds weight of essentials to test my physical capabilities and identify other difficulties I may have.*

*I do not know how to get food and water and there seems to be little advice about this in guidebooks and Websites. I had to drive ten miles before finding an open shop. I'm worried that, having completed a day's walk, I must walk many miles to buy provisions, or to find a cashpoint. Please can you advise? How did you manage on your trek along the GR10?"*

The next day, the blog's author replied *"Can you give me an idea of how much mountain experience you have please. For example, which part of the Pyrenees did you do and how many hours did it take?"*

His response confirmed what I already knew – my lack of experience shone like a beacon.

I answered, *"Thanks for the reply. I have had little mountain walking experience although I have been training in the UK rigorously for the past few months. I walked for three days on the Pyrenees, although not on the GR10. On the first day, I walked twelve miles on hills around Bouriège. The second day I walked up Pic Carlit from Lac Bouillouses, which the GR10 skirts around. The third day I climbed about three thousand feet from Puyvalador towards Madres, thirteen miles in total.*

*I averaged 1½mph, including stops for food and drink, over the three days. Not fast I know, but as an experiment, I convinced myself that I can do it provided I maintain my training regime. I would be extremely grateful for your advice."*

A week later, he replied again, "*Hi Laurence. The climb up Carlit is the equivalent of what you might expect each day on the GR10. What concerns me most is the weight you have in your rucksack. Forty-four pounds is much more than you need to carry, even if it includes a tent. My kit list (above), which includes everything I wear and everything in my rucksack, weighs in at twenty-three pounds (though I admit walking from hostel to hostel reduces weight). There are loads of sites about ultra-light walking; a real inspiration for me.*

*If you are intending to camp you will need sometimes to carry three days food but no more than that. With planning you shouldn't need to leave the trail to re-supply. Though there are few villages and fewer shops you can eat at refuges and get them to provide picnics (phone in advance). As for water, take purifying tablets.*"

The author gave me more than I asked. Logistics should not be a problem – food can be bought at refuges. But he raised a concern about the weight in my rucksack. His kit-list, intended for a six-day trek along a section of the GR10, weighed only half of mine. There was no sleeping bag, spare socks, pants, phone battery or enough toiletries for two months – that lot bumped up the kit-list to thirty pounds. The eleven paper maps I needed for the whole GR10 would add another pound and three litres of water would push it up another seven.

The point about weight must be taken seriously, so I replied, *"Thanks again. I am thinking of walking from mid-June onwards. I expect it will take me about two months, if I walk six days every week. Forty-four pounds includes three litres of water. It does not include a tent but does include a sleeping bag and mat (very lightweight). I will re-examine my kit list."*

# POINT OF NO RETURN

February 9th 2016.

Tuesday mornings are my JD-visiting times, our quality time together. Then home by mid-afternoon for quality time with the mutt and to cook dinner for Liz, Victoria and Georgina. Training on Tuesdays is not possible because it is dark outside well before the chores are done. But preparing for the trek is not just about training for the physical hardships to come, there are plenty of other things to do, like planning the route, brushing up on French and raising publicity to encourage donations. The non-physical things are as important yet more time-consuming.

All is quiet now. The mutt has been walked and fed and is crashed out in her basket, the family has eaten, Georgina is out with her friends, and Victoria is in bed. Liz is asleep on the sofa with the TV on and I am at the computer screen again. Diana from Norwood's Fundraising Team created my donations page for me while I was in Australia, which was a huge help. I added some words about JD, his condition, his carers at Woodcock Dell and what they do for him, the trek and why I am doing it. It is ready to be unleashed on the public.

I put the finishing touches to my Facebook page, uploaded some photos, added a link to the donations page and invited my family and friends to join. Social media tools are undoubtedly powerful ways of publicising the trek, and Facebook is a tool with a global reach. Within seconds, my eldest daughter Roxanne posted, "Facebook just got a whole lot uglier." I expect mischievous comments like that to inspire me during the trek.

My fingers are poised over the keyboard, hovering over the 'Donate' button, while I stare at my donations page. I was advised to be the first donor because "no one likes to be first," according to Diana. Pressing the button will take me past the point of no return - I *must* do the trek, otherwise return all donations. When someone donates, it is a contract, I must do what they expect.

Motionless, hesitant, prevaricating between going and staying, the doubts creep into my head again. Am I physically able? Last year's three-day expedition was a taster, a tiny morsel of what I could expect. Every day would be more gruelling than that second day ascending Pic Carlit. The trek will be tougher, longer and more arduous, with no one to spur me on. I will be accompanied for only seven out of fifty days. A 'big wheel of terror' could lie in wait, not just once or twice, but on every day for weeks. The uncontrollable trembling, panting, sweating hands and runaway anxiety on Pic Carlit was enough.

Charlie the mutt poked her head around the door. She was on her evening rounds, checking up on her humans, before she retired to her basket with a grumble. It wrenched me from thoughts of failure to the consequences of *not* doing it. If I do not go this year, then I will *never* go. Grandchildren will see to that, so my grandparent friends said. When they pass the weening stage, my time will disappear, and I would forever be 'granddad who never trekked'.

But in 2006, I promised JD that I would walk the whole road. I cannot break it. How could I tell him I was not going? The shame of telling my family and friends would be unbearable,

"I decided not to do it."

"Why not?" they will ask.

How would I answer them, having covered myself with false bravado? I should press 'Donate' and try. And if I fail, then at least I tried.

JD's picture sits on the bookcase facing me. Julie took it when he was four, wearing his yellow and blue Rugby top, sitting on the floor, happy. I thought about the things he had done since that photo was taken, and how he brought out the best in people without realising it. His image reminded me that this trek is not about *me*, it is about *him and his carers*. I am just an instrument. My pride can take the hit of failure, but I must try.

I pressed the 'Donate' button and watched the first donation go. "Daddy will be walking that road now, JD," I whispered to the picture on the bookcase, "there's no turning back."

A wave of grim determination washed away all negative thoughts. Whatever will be, will be, "que sera, sera." There was no one awake I could tell, apart from the mutt, my confidante.

Now for the hard part …

# ADDICTED

A Facebook user for one week and I am an addict already. Minutes after appealing for companions to join me on the trek, and posting an itinerary of my stops, dates, times and places to stay, it taunted me, "Psst! Maybe you've had a 'Like' already? Perhaps someone has posted a 'Comment' on your latest post?" I took a quick peek. An hour later, I checked again. I understood why many people are on-line permanently.

Every new donation had the same effect. The second came a few hours after I made the first. The high lasted for hours. Then I returned to my fundraising page to see if there were any more. One percent of the way towards the financial target after two days. My friends and family made a difference to JD's carers already. Facebook and donations are dealers in positive energy.

Publicity is a different ballgame, as unfamiliar to me as social media and trekking long distances. I thought Facebook would help me reach a world of potential donors. But it is limited to a tiny village of friends and family, about a hundred people and too few to hit my thirty-five-thousand-pound target. I must expand my borders to city-sized proportions. To help me, Norwood gave me contacts in three national newspapers to e-mail and telephone. My local newspaper is another source. I need three-and-a-half-thousand people to donate ten pounds each.

Self-doubt, rejection and disappointment are a trio of misery. What will I do if a reporter says the trek is of no interest to anyone except me? Who wants to read about a sixty-one-year-old fart walking a mountain range? Does the public *really* want to hear about his cause? Or about JD's condition? How about the sacrifices his carers make to keep him safe, healthy, happy? There are many more news-worthy stories waiting to be scooped.

When not seeking publicity or a fix on social media, I train with the mutt. Our regime has increased to six miles four times every week. I average three miles-per-hour on Surrey's pimple-hills. But I will be much slower in the mountains, over greater distances, when weighed down by a heavy rucksack. I should be able to average one mile-per-hour on ascents and two miles-per-hour on descents, based on my three-day expedition last year. Such useful data is crucial for planning journey times and avoiding walking in the dark. Numbers are addictive too.

Walking the mountains at night-time will increase the chance of bumping into bears or patous and bring a swift end to the trek. My only consolation – and I would not be around to see it – would be the publicity kick that would inevitably follow.

# A CARD FOR MISTER WILSON

Norwood's Publicity Team advised me to get some cards printed to hand out and leave in public places, so I ordered three hundred emblazoned with:
*'The Great Pyrenees Trek*
*Laurence Smith – Trekker*
*Walking the GR10 from June to August 2016 in aid of the carers at Norwood charity'*
and a link to my donations and Facebook pages. A picture of the view over Puyvalador, taken last year on my three-day expedition with Jonathan, added colour.

"Who are you going to give these to?" Liz asked, "everyone already knows about it."

"True," I answered, "but this is for people I meet and to hang in shop windows."

"Isn't that like begging?" she persisted.

She was uncomfortable with the idea of handing out cards asking for donations to strangers, and I did too, but it was for a good cause.

"Maybe, but I must do something to raise public awareness," I said.

I gave a stack of cards to Liz and my daughters for handing out to work colleagues. My plan was to distribute more to the dog-minders who JD sees on our Tuesday walks. One minder is responsible for the welfare of a Very Important Pooch called Mister Wilson, owned by an internationally acclaimed popular musician. The opportunity to publicise the trek via the upper echelons of the entertainments business was unmissable. So, I vowed to keep an eye out for the mutt's minder to whom I will dispense a card in the hope it will be passed on via Mister Wilson to its owner. Once in their hands, who knows where it will go? Maybe there will be an announcement at the musician's next gig before an adoring audience of thousands?

"This one's for JD's carers and all carers out there! Put your hands together Wembley!"

And the band starts playing.

# INTERNATIONAL RESCUE

The Austrian Alpine Club will rescue me by helicopter if I get lost, stranded or injured while roaming the Pyrenees. That is assured now I have paid my annual subscription. Experienced trekkers take the same precautions in case they ever need assistance while in remote places. There are horror stories of those who did not and sold their homes to pay for a fifty-thousand-pound helicopter ride of a lifetime. It is strange that there is no equivalent club for the Pyrenees, but the AAC's reach is wide, and the fee is only thirty pounds. If I need help while on a mountain, I must first call French emergency services on my phone. They then text a link to download an app on my phone and pinpoint my location for Scott, Virgil and Brains to come and fetch me in Thunderbird Two. Neat, if I have phone reception before I fall down a crevasse or Yogi Bear mistakes me for a picnic basket.

Having guaranteed my safe return, another "Errr, dad" moment occurred while in the kitchen with Victoria.

"Wassup?" I replied, "are you having another baby?"

"Not yet, but we've set a date for the wedding," she replied, "it's the last weekend in June."

"About time too!" I hugged her.

Liz bounced into the kitchen on hearing the news, "Wonderful, we can help organise it if you're too busy."

"No, it's OK thanks, we've chosen the venue already and put down a deposit," Victoria said, "you and Dad just need to turn up on the day."

How things have changed in one generation. Liz's mum and dad organised and paid for our wedding. We had no say - the venue, guests, entertainment, tablecloths and napkins were chosen for us. Liz's mum chose the colour scheme for our reception, the flowers, bridesmaids' dresses and her outfit. Nowadays, it is common for the bride and groom to organise it themselves while their parents hope for an invitation. Novelty weddings are also popular, where the marriage ceremony takes place on a remote beach, a mountain peak, or at the bottom of the sea, without the parents' knowledge. We are thankful that our children want us to be there with them to share their happy day.

My original plan was to start trekking in the middle of June. Now it must be delayed until after Victoria's wedding. So, the weekend after, I will fly to France and start the trek on Monday July 4th. But I must finish by the end of August, so I can return in time for the birth of the baby, and our second grandchild. Any delay, and I will be grounded indefinitely.

# TOUGH TRAINING

Three ten-mile walks on consecutive days in English midwinter, stress-testing my mountain gear made tough training. Trudging through persistent rain, wind and cold was a misery I never experienced in the Pyrenees last year. Even the poor mutt felt the effects of the continuous dousing. She is not the energetic pup she was. Aged nine, she is two years older than me in equivalent human years, and I hear her laboured panting at my side. But she sticks to me like glue, ball in mouth, hoping for her ball-throwing human to hurl it for her to chase.

How I wish I could take her with me! I would talk to her all the time, just as I do now. We would share our worries and carry our burdens together. I tell her about JD, convinced she understands what I am saying about the human who moves on four legs. But I suspect I would have to bear her extra weight over the more dangerous sections, or the effort would kill her.

Sometimes it is tough being a mutt.

# LET'S PARLEZ

Jonathan booked his flight to Biarritz and will meet me in Hendaye on Sunday 3$^{rd}$ July. His news nudged me into action. I will arrive the day before to allow time to recover from the journey, indulge in light training, acclimatise and buy provisions for the start of the trek.

Accommodation for the first five days needed to be found quickly, as beds would be grabbed by pilgrims destined for the Camino in St-Jean-Pied-de-Port. So immediately after booking my flight, I reserved a room for two in Hendaye. The hands on the clock whirred while searching for places to sleep over the three days we will walk together, all close to the route and offering meals. Thanks to an Internet booking site, I reserved our first and second nights in gites in the mountain villages of Olhette and Ainhoa, without having to test my poor French.

Then I hit a snag. I found a cheap hotel in the Basque village of Bidarray for our third night but could only make a reservation from a French website or by calling them. My French was too basic to phone and ask for a room, evening meal and breakfast for two. Inevitably, they would speak, and I would panic and fallback on the phrase used by any English-speaker with such a primitive French vocabulary, "je ne comprends pas" ("I don't understand"). Even worse, the hotel staff could respond in the local Basque dialect, rendering communication futile. They may as well come from the planet Tharg. So, I completed an on-line form and hoped for a confirmation. If they do not respond, then I must e-mail them in French, using Google Translate.

The irony is that we have holidayed in France so many times, yet I am still as nervous about speaking the language as before ever setting foot in the country. I must learn the lingo because French people will speak to me, and I must understand what they say. Basic communication, such as being able to ask, "can I stay here?" "where can I buy food?" and "are there any bears around here?" will be vital phrases for my repertoire.

Michel Thomas's 'Advanced French' plays on my iPod as I walk and helps breakdown my mental block with languages. As well as having a limited vocabulary, my grasp of tenses and comprehension is awful. But I must try while I am there, especially when seeking accommodation. I dare not book every night of the trek now in case I am delayed by bad weather or injury, it will knock out all my bookings for the remainder of the trek. So, I will reserve places for one week and, while in France, book ahead for the next week, and so on. I created a template French e-mail so I can insert the appropriate date before sending. Technology will compensate for my ineptitude at French, and at navigating.

Courtesy is another good reason to brush up on French – it is an important part of their culture. We have spent roughly a year living in France, accumulated over twenty-five years of holidays. In that time, I have picked up some essential customs and peculiarities. They kiss cheeks or shake hands when they greet and depart. They say "Bonjour" before launching into conversation. They call strangers "Monsieur" and "Madame." I recall an emergency appointment with a French GP after JD had caught an ear infection. Every patient entering the waiting room nodded and greeted others, "Bonjour Monsieur," "Bonjour Madame" and "Bonjour Madamoiselles." The same courtesy was offered on exit too.

The French respect attempts to speak their language, even if it is wrong. Whenever I mustered up courage to engage in conversation, they were always patient, albeit amused at my attempts. So, I must make every effort to speak to whoever I meet, and that means 'parlez-ing' French.

# DON'T FORGET THE KIBBLE!

February 29th 2016.

Mutt and I, in full trekking gear, completed three ten-mile walkies this week. I listened to the radio on my phone to relieve the boredom of treading the same path. "Woman's Hour," "Pop Master" and "The Jeremy Vine Show" helped the miles pass swiftly. But two earpieces can turn a normal person into someone with Tourette syndrome. Quiet for the first programme, I yelled out the wrong answers in the second and objected loudly to statements from callers in the third. On one occasion, I shouted "bollocks!" too loudly for the mutt's liking, who ran into the foliage and had to be coaxed out with kibble.

Al fresco radio had its pros and cons. Time and distance were swallowed up quickly by the distraction of quizzes and political chit-chat. Neither did I feel fatigue, until back at home. But all outside sounds were drowned and the phone battery drained quickly. In fact, all charge would have vanished without the solar panel. The greatest disincentive to flooding one's aural senses with conversation or music while trekking dangerous mountain paths is not hearing a thing. The unheard thing could be a hungry bear or angry patou stalking the wearer. Apart from that, it would be a missed opportunity to hear sounds that are rarely heard around where I live – birdsong, chirping insects, falling water, the sounds of nature.

Snacks are vital for longer walks, not only for

replenishment but also as a reward, something to look forward to, an incentive. This week I packed kibble and two tupperwares – the second for water. The mutt deserved an incentive too. She is a member of the team, although in truth, it was penance for my guilt. Too many times, she sat facing me, staring into my eyes as I munched, "Well? Where's mine? Have I not earned it?"

Mutt and I circumnavigated Bisley Rifle Ranges today by sticking to the perimeter fence as closely as possible. I attempted the circuit before but was forced to abort owing to houses obstructing the way, pushing me far from the fence until it disappeared. The last time I tried, I sank to my waist in a swamp after taking a short-cut over open ground, instead of taking the usual route along a gravel path. Mutt followed, observing my moves before proceeding cautiously. Mounds of coarse grass poking above murky water were deceptively secure. I stepped carefully from mound to mound, to keep my boots dry. After the first fifty yards, they became sparser and squishier. The mutt no longer followed behind, preferring to walk a parallel course on higher ground, making excellent progress. I thought the water was no more than six inches deep, but doubt crept in. I considered turning back and taking the longer route on firmer ground. The next instant, the small patch of ground I placed my trust in collapsed, and I plunged in water up to my waist. Shocked by the cold, my feet sank into the soft, muddy bed and began sucking me down. They squelched when I tried lifting them. Meanwhile, mutt sat on dry grass twenty yards away, watching with interest as her master struggled. She wondered if the kibble in my bag would float to the surface after I perished in the swamp. Fortunately for me and unhappily for the mutt, the tough mesh perimeter fence was within grasp, and I hauled myself out. We spent the next hour hiding behind a bush on higher ground, out of sight of any passing walkers, while I stripped, wrung out and hung my socks, trousers and shirt over the fence to dry.

There was an air of determination about mutt and me to find the elusive route around Bisley Ranges today. We gritted our teeth and proceeded, equipped with sandwiches (for human) and kibble (for mutt), flask of tea and Google Maps. Eleven miles and four hours later, we returned tired but triumphant. It was a pity that only next door's moggy was there to celebrate our return, and she did not look that impressed anyway.

# A REMINDER

"Well JD," I said as I pushed him along the path through Welsh Harp, "I've booked my flight and my first four nights in France."

He was too distracted by his surroundings to respond. He looked up at the trees instead, with his fingers in his mouth. I pressed on with my progress report.

"I'll be leaving in four months to walk that road for you, and I won't see you for a long time," and hastened to add, "but mummy will visit you every Sunday and I will phone you from the mountains."

We rumbled along the muddy path beside the reservoir, stopping every now and then to watch the rippling water, both equally lost in thought. What did he think? Maybe he understood what I said, or perhaps he was more interested in the antics of the ducks and geese at the water's edge. I looked for the signs in his face - the way his eyes moved, what he looked at, his expression, how he positioned his body – all revealed small clues. Was he upset in knowing that we would not see each other for eight weeks? It would be the first time we had been apart for so long.

A few weeks ago, Vicky, Woodcock Dell's Manager, suggested that we should start preparing JD for my departure by reducing the frequency of visits, so he could adapt to me not being around. Today I e-mailed her a shortened list of visit dates, starting in three weeks. It was a reminder that being away from JD for so long will be painful. I expected physical discomfort, but not emotional hardship.

# GRANDPARENTS AND UNCLE

March 2016.

"You are an uncle," I informed JD today, on our constitutional Tuesday trip around Welsh Harp, to see the pond life, the trees and dog-walkers with their packs of pooches.

"She's called Aryah," I continued, anticipating the question stuck in his head with no means of escape.

"Errr," he replied.

"When was she born? A good question JD," I interpreted.

"On Friday. Mummy and I drove to Great Yarmouth to see her, your big sister Roxanne, and brother-in-law Peter."

JD chuckled. I wanted to believe he found the news funny, "my sister! A mum? And me an uncle?"

"It's true JD," I assured him, "you may well titter at the thought, but you are indeed, an uncle."

His infectious laugh provided encouragement, "and she has pixie-ears, just like her mum."

A man sat on a park bench by the path must have wondered what we were laughing about as we rolled by, in our little bubble of mirth.

"And what's even funnier JD," I delivered the punchline, "is that mummy and I are now grandma and granddad."

# A WATERY TRUDGE

Paul, my trekking consultant, advised me to train on mountains instead of the gentle hills around Surrey.

"Walking on the flat is easy, walking up steep hills isn't," he said, "and don't underestimate the difficulty of walking down steep hills either."

Sadly, there are no mountains where I live. I looked out the window and checked. The nearest are over a hundred-and-twenty miles to the west, in Wales. But there is hope. A short walk away, a half-mile long path beside the Bisley Rifle Range fence climbs up and down four steep hills, each about forty feet high. Traversing them five times and back would be like climbing and descending one thousand-six-hundred feet over five miles, the same as a half-ascent of Mount Snowden. I would not need to drive to Wales and back, and waste petrol or time in traffic. In a gale and torrential rain, mutt and I set out to test our mettle.

Under normal conditions, rain falls vertically, runs down and over your boots. Ten minutes after leaving, we turned onto the Rifle Range path and into the face of the wind. Instantly, rain lashed my eyes and ran down my neck, like walking into a firehose. On the return leg, water invaded my waistband from behind and soaked my underpants. How mutt felt without protective clothing, I could only surmise. Each time we returned to the starting point, her eyes pleaded, "can we go home now?"

Despite the watery trudge, I declared our ordeal a

success. I was a little fitter and wiser, and mutt was wetter and well-rewarded for her faithfulness. I learned the pros and cons of waterproof trousers are. My trekking trousers could not cope with the constant dousing because they are 'water-resistant', entirely different to 'waterproof'. Only after the first mile did I step into proper protective clothing that repelled every droplet at the expense of dampness from sweat and condensation.

When we returned to base, mutt was in a sorry state, head bowed and soaked. I vowed never to take her out in such inclement conditions again.

# THE BLUE DOT AND THE GREEN LINE

The blue dot on my phone map is me and the green line is my route. Keep the blue dot on the green line and I will reach my destination. Simple. I have two mapping apps – Google Maps and MapMyWalk. The first app calculates a walking route from my starting location to my destination (a green line) and shows me where I am in relation to it. The second builds a track of where I have been (as a green line), which could be useful if I ever get lost and need to backtrack. But they can be wrong, as I found out on a training walk through Swinley Forest today.

Progress was good until I encountered a secure gate and fence protecting Ministry of Defence land from intruders, terrorists, zombies and other undesirables. The green line passed through the gate, blissfully unaware that it was for MoD personnel only. So I yomped around the fence, adding a mile and twenty minutes to my journey.

On unfamiliar territory for most of the way, I passed many forest tracks that were not shown on either of my phone maps. Some tracks appeared to lead the right way, but I was unsure, so I ignored them and stuck to the green line. How much detail is missing in digital maps and how critical will this be when I am in the mountains? Unlike paper maps, digital maps are constructed from satellite images, not by cartographers. My two precious mapping apps will lack detail and could be inaccurate in places. They cannot be trusted completely.

When GPS reception was poor, my map location drifted - the blue dot hovered to one side of the green line by as much as fifty yards, so I was unsure of where I was. That may not sound like much, but fifty yards near the summit of a mountain could be disastrous. My route along the Pyrenees follows the border with Spain for much of the way, so the blue dot could drift easily into another country.

Keeping the blue dot on the green line will not be so simple.

# THE ANOMALY

A second training day without the mutt, who was charged and found guilty of gross misconduct and confined to doggie-quarters. The night before, we left a raw chicken to de-frost on the cooker and forgot about it. Pity the mutt did not - she ate it while we slept. To make matters worse, she turned on the gas, presumably while pawing at the chicken. Or perhaps she was rustling up something tasty and forgot to turn it off before retiring to her basket stuffed with poulet rôti. The kitchen reeked of gas when Liz reached for the kettle in the morning.

Leaving the house, I set off in fresh air and sunshine for a twelve-mile walk around Swinley Forest. Two rucksacks are now necessary, a large one on my back and a small one over my chest for the stuff I need to access quickly, such as food, waterproofs, wallet, phone, map and compass. The chest rucksack will be crucial for speedily dispensing a 'Laurence Smith – Trekker' card to an inquisitive passer-by, should I encounter one.

Today, I carried twenty-two pounds weight behind and seven up front. On the Pyrenees, I will add another eighteen pounds of essentials to the back rucksack, bringing the total to a third of my bodyweight. Despite my underweight baggage, my legs were leaden, the rucksack straps pulled on my neck and shoulders and my pace slowed to two miles-per-hour.

To simulate conditions while walking 'the whole road'

for JD, I followed the green line on my phone, looking even more of an anomaly among dog-walkers, joggers, cyclists and gentlefolk of Surrey. While others were clad in jeans, tracksuits, woolly jumpers, T-shirts and trainers, I preferred mud-stained trousers, boots and wool socks, T-shirt and water-resistant coat, two rucksacks, emergency whistle around my neck, solar panel with cable dangling at my side, and eyes glued to phone.

A sense of separateness switches on whenever I don my trekking uniform and step outdoors. My dressing ritual reminds me why I am putting myself through the ordeal of trampling over the same mud-soaked hills and forests every day, through the best and worst of the English weather.

"I wear this unusual attire for my son," I want to tell people I pass, but they avoid eye contact, too nervous to engage with 'the anomaly'.

# MUSINGS OF A LONG-DISTANCE RAMBLER

March 29th 2016.

On long rambles, my mind rambles too. Whether the mutt's mind rambles also, I know not. A work colleague said that a third of a dog's brain is busy processing smells. This fact explains why it is impossible to lure her from some unseen ponging thing nestling in long grass, among a pile of fallen leaves or under a bush. So, I forgive Charlie the mutt for wandering into the undergrowth. It must be like window shopping to her.

Question. What can turn a normally docile mutt into a slavering hound of hell? Answer - a postman. Just before leaving today, the mutt went berserk at an audacious human popping letters through our letterbox. One second, she was snoozing peacefully. The next, she sprang up in outrage and bolted to the front door, teeth bared, prepared to inflict serious damage. She only reacts in this manner when postmen encroach on her territory. When the fish-man delivers, he is greeted with a sniff and a slobber.

Another question. According to dogs, how many species live on planet Earth and how should they be treated? Answer - three. Dogs, not dogs - also called humans - and postmen. Behaviour towards the first specie must be in accordance with General Etiquette Towards Fellow Mutts, as laid down in the Canine Code of Rover, circa 12AD ('After Dog'). The second specie must be treated with due deference and servility, with the occasional slurp across face, sharing of food while not being watched, and so on. The third specie must be bitten, preferably in a place where the great yellow ball in the sky doth not shine.

The questions were posed and answered in a four-hour march around Bisley Rifle Range today. Although, after Storm Katie left her droppings and detritus, we mulched – not marched -through fallen branches and leaves. Plenty of time to ramble, in more ways than one.

# HUMAN TORTOISE

I am a human tortoise. During day, I crawl slowly through the forests and heathland of Surrey with my home on my back. Everything I need is crammed into a bulging rucksack. From behind, an observer would see only a large blue hump for a shell and four appendages moving purposefully. I would struggle to upright myself if I fell onto my back. Maybe I would suffocate, just like an upturned tortoise. When I use walking poles, there would be six legs, so at such times, I become a human beetle.

But look inside the hump and you would find an assortment of vividly coloured sealable plastic sacks. Ask, and the human tortoise will tell you they are 'dry sacks'. The name is a giveaway. They keep the contents of my home dry. My rucksack shell is not entirely waterproof, you see, so the dry sacks are an essential commodity.

Like any responsible tortoise, I keep my house in order. A large green dry sack for my clothes, an orange one for repair kits and tools, lemon yellow with washing stuff, red with overnight clothes, a small green one containing toiletries, a medicine kit, and so on. Dry sacks serve the same purpose as a chest of drawers, except they are considerably lighter, malleable and waterproof.

Although I must confess to having a little bit of clutter, which is probably why I do not qualify for full tortoise-hood. Eleven GR10 maps, a pocket chess-set, Sudoku puzzle books, diary and pen, emergency blanket and walking poles litter my shell.

Inside my home, near the basement, I keep a sleeping bag, sleeping mat and bivvy bag. This is where I differ from an actual tortoise. I do not have the luxury of retreating inside my shell to sleep. Instead, I must pull everything out, unfurl the waterproof bivvy bag, insert the mat, sleeping bag and rucksack, and crawl in. In effect, I turn my house inside out. But refuges and gites will make this unnecessary provided they have a bed for me.

At thirty-three pounds, my home is heavier than it once was, and will be even heavier with food and water when I plod onto 'the whole road' in a few months' time.

# SAME BUT DIFFERENT

Three months until I set foot on the Pyrenees. Mutt and I were out every day this week, treading over the same ground. After six months of training, there is nowhere left to explore unless I drive. But that would entail loading rucksacks and Charlie in the car, hacking through traffic and finding somewhere to park. So again, we haunted the paths along Basingstoke Canal, around Bisley Range and through Lightwater Country Park, Swinley Forest and Mytchett Range.

Training is like commuting to work – there is nothing to think about because I always know where to go. My body has been programmed by repeated exposure to the same environment. Autopilot takes control, leaving my mind free for random thoughts to flit into my head.

*What kind of dog is Scooby-Doo – a greyhound, a labrador or a crossbreed?*

*Palindrome spelled backwards is 'emordnilap'.*

*What is the probability that any two people will cross paths at some time in their lives?*

*How do they repair telegraph wires and who are 'they'?*

Same territory, same routine, but different thoughts every day.

Monday. The human body is like a skyscraper – tall and thin and will topple over when too much lateral force is applied. This revelation explains why my neck and back hurt so much with a heavy rucksack. My muscles are working hard to counter the impulse to pull me backwards, just as a skyscraper's central column does in a gale. The trick to relieve stress must be to pack the heavy stuff, like sleeping bag and bivvy bag, close to my back with the lighter stuff furthest away.

Tuesday —I would normally take JD out, but for the schedule of reduced visits to prepare him for my eight-week-long disappearing act. Did he understand why I was not there? Morbid thoughts about what he could be thinking weighed me down,

"Where's dad?"

"He should be here by now!"

"Has he forgotten me?"

Cutting down visits is a necessary cruelty, for *both* our sakes not just JD's. I did not appreciate that fact when I e-mailed Vicky the schedule. I must toughen up emotionally as well as physically, which means not feeling guilty when I cannot see my son.

Wednesday was a bad head day. With nothing to keep me focussed, my brain became an empty house, a prime candidate for occupation. Before long, a cheesy pop tune took up residence like an unwanted squatter. The miles drifted by with a "Rockin' Robin" soundtrack playing on a never-ending loop. Somewhere along Basingstoke Canal I succumbed to the dangerously infectious hook "twiddy-diddly-dee, twiddly-diddly-dee" and whistled cheerfully. I even sung it out loud a few times.

On Thursday, I obsessed over the importance of companionship, and concluded that Charlie the mutt was an excellent human substitute. She never says anything profound, tells me where to go or warns me of impending storms, but she listens and is always by my side – except when she finds something tasty nearby. Such a pity I could not take her with me on the trek. Even if I could, she would need looking after, and require quarantining on her return to England. She must be stopped from chasing sheep and aggravating bears. She would also want to inspect every tuft of grass, tree, rock and object visited by the indigenous mountain inhabitants and undertake a rigorous chemical analysis of their deposits.

Of course, everywhere will be unfamiliar in the Pyrenees so my mind will be busy navigating, grappling with my fear of heights and watching out for bears. There will be no room for autopilot.

# LE PATOU

Too many worries for my liking. Will I fail in the first week? Will I go crazy walking solo for weeks on end? What fears await in them thar mountains? Narrow paths clinging to walls of rock and precipitous drops into deep gorges? Scrambles on narrow ridges with fingers clinging desperately to loose rocks? My worst nightmares are made of these images. Suppose I fall with no one around to hear my cries for help? What should I do if I meet a wild beast?

One such Pyrenean beast is the patou - a large dog that lives among grazing sheep. A patou protects its flock from bears, wolves and other predators. But because they have been brought up among sheep and have little human contact, they are unlike domesticated pooches. Approach one, pat its massive head and say, "good doggie" and one would return minus a few appendages, or in separate packages. An Internet article advised that if a patou bounds towards me with slavering jaws, I must keep calm, and refrain from running away, shouting or throwing anything at it. "Do *not* deter it with walking poles," the article said, "tempting though it may be." Instead, I should stand still and convince the beast that I am no threat to its flock. But how should I convince a feral canine of that? The advice is to "talk calmly" or "sing quietly". Maybe "you ain't nothin' but a hound-dog"?

With better weather, mutt and I scratched up some long-distance walks on our collar and belt. On Monday, the sun was in danger of coming out, so we packed suncream, water, lunch and kibble and headed on to Mytchett Ranges. But the Army got there before us, in the wee hours of the morning, and rutted the forest tracks. Despite their aversive tactics, we paraded through their training ground, fenced off to prevent civvies being shot or blown up by unexploded shells. Then we ventured through the remaining square miles of heath and forest shared by commuters, dog-walkers and trekkers-in-training.

A fourteen-mile excursion through Scots pines and lowland heath in Swinley Forest kept us busy for another day. The forest is my favourite place, a four-square mile oasis of peace bordered by busy roads that heave with traffic in the rush-hours. It is a Site of Special Scientific Interest, frequented by birdwatchers and twitchers, on the look-out for rare nesting birds. We passed the 'Queen of the Forest', an imposing oak tree that JD and I named on a cycle ride years ago, in memory of his fascination at its gnarled chunky branches. Ten minutes' walk away, we played fetch-the-stick in 'Charlie's Pond', named after the mutt's liking for its murky water. Fifteen minutes later, we crossed 'Spider Junction', or Lower Star Post, a union of eight forest tracks leading to Bagshot, Bracknell, Camberley, Sandhurst Military Academy, Crowthorne and the site of Cesar's Camp, an Iron Age fort constructed two-and-a-half-thousand years ago. There is plenty to see in the forest, but not for us because we are on a tight training schedule.

# WHAT CAN POSSIBLY GO RIGHT?

Half-full or half-empty? Which viewpoint comes more instinctively? Facing the immense challenge of walking a mountain range, I am a half-empty person. Why do I waste so much thinking time on long training walks imagining all the things that could go wrong? Falling off a mountain, mauled by a bear, savaged by a patou, injury, getting lost, losing my passport and money, sleeping rough. My mind probes every possibility. What if my rucksack tumbles down a gorge as I munch a baguette? How would I explain my failure to JD? The list of potential catastrophes keeps growing.

There are positives in every situation. Twenty-four years of caring for JD have shown me that. I must be more productive and re-train my mind to look for them. After four consecutive days of five-hour hikes with four litres of water and thirty-one pounds on my back, I set off on the fifth day determined to focus on what could go right instead of wrong.

Number one, suppose I kept my promise?

Treasure the moment when I could say, "JD, I walked the whole road for you. And you were with me all the way. Your journey through life is arduous, incomparably more so than a mere five-hundred-and-forty-mile trek. You kept me going. You were my inspiration."

Number two, helping his carers. A year from now, Woodcock Dell has a brand-new dining-room extension, financed by donations from the trek. I see JD and his new family eating together. No more shifts. Things are easier in his home.

There are so many positives that could come from leading a different life, even for a short while. If JD had no disability, then no way would I consider trekking a mountain range. I would stay at home and miss so many opportunities, like the chance to overcome my fear of heights. Fourteen percent of the UK suffer with acrophobia, some so badly that they cannot climb a flight of stairs. Exposure in small doses is a common treatment. If I over-dose, as I suspect I will, then maybe I will become de-sensitised.

I will meet other trekkers with stories to tell and hear their unique reasons for embarking on such a long journey. Inevitably, my French will improve, something I failed to do after twenty-five years of annual holidays. For two months or longer, I will be forced to speak, hear and understand the language. France is renowned for its cuisine, its wine and way of life. I will eat, drink and live *la joie de vivre*.

Scampering up and down the equivalent of Mount Everest five times in eight weeks will make me fitter than a butcher's dog. Fresh mountain air will wash out the man-made carcinogens and harmful particles I breathe here, in the UK's Silicon Valley.

The trek will be the first and possibly last time I will do something out of the ordinary. Like Robinson Crusoe, I must adapt to survive. If I succeed, then I will be more confident of tackling the unknown in the future.

My glass is, rightfully, half-full.

# LOST IN SURREY

May 5<sup>th</sup> 2016.

Everything went wrong today. The day started well enough in warm sunshine outside Westhumble rail station at half-past ten. I looked forward to my stiffest test yet – a twenty-mile circuit and three thousand feet upping and downing over two of south-east England's mightiest peaks, Leith Hill and Box Hill. Only two litres of water instead of the usual three, I figured that would be plenty. This is England - it never gets hot.

I headed confidently for the first peak, phone in pocket and solar panel charge cable threaded around the side of my rucksack. With six months of training including three days on the Pyrenees under my belt, l trusted the digital map on my phone with my life. I would complete the circuit in eight hours comfortably and be ensconced safely in my car back at the station well before nightfall.

"What could go wrong?" I asked myself, "this is England. There are no bears or patous, I have plenty of water, a bang-on map, close to civilisation and it's safe."

Four hours later, after guzzling half my water, busting my phone cable and going the wrong way twice, my confidence lay in tatters. England does get hot, and exceptional humidity gave me a raging thirst that left one paltry litre to last the remaining twelve miles. Twice I removed my rucksack without disconnecting my phone cable first, damaging it beyond repair, and rendering my solar panel useless. Great. Both water and phone battery now needed rationing. To make matters worse, GPS and data reception were so bad that I missed a crucial turning and headed a mile in the wrong direction. Without my trusty phone to guide me, I subjected myself to the humiliation of asking a passer-by for directions. Dressed smartly in tweed casuals and carrying a punnet of strawberries, he appeared to be on his way for cream tea and Pimm's. Yet the mountain trekker was lost, not the Surrey Hills gentleman. The sharp lesson taught me that I may not be so lucky if I lose myself in the Pyrenees, especially if I need to ask in French.

Another four hours passed, and my mouth was like the bottom of a bird cage. A half-litre of warm water sloshed in my bottle, taunting me. How much moisture can one waste by incessantly muttering about the unreliability of GPS, the complete absence of drinking sources, and flaky phone cables? Facing a five-hundred-foot ascent of Box Hill, and the subsequent steep descent to Westhumble, I worried about reaching my car before nightfall. Would I fumble my way down Box Hill in the dark? For the hundredth time, I stopped to adjust the straps on my rucksack to ease the pain in my shoulders and neck and ate more precious time.

The ascent of Box Hill was cruel. At first kind, a mud-baked path leading off the busy A25 climbed gently into a welcome cover of woods. Then it steepened suddenly, and the shade disappeared, exposing me to the glare of the sun. Rivulets of sweat ran down my nose, neck and back, soaking my T-shirt and waistband. I gulped down the last few drops of water and sucked on the empty bottle in desperation. Low on energy, and bereft of snacks, I plodded on to the North Downs Way. As if in sympathy, my phone buzzed a low-energy warning and threatened to shut itself down if not nourished immediately. A Smith & Western bar at the roadside beckoned. It would be so easy to pop in and knock back an ice-cold pint, but light was fading, and I still needed to negotiate a stiff descent. If I succumbed to the temptation, I could lose my way in the Surrey Hills at night.

The descent was equally cruel. A rough stony path through long grass descended sharply four-hundred feet towards the sun. Somewhere below, I heard laughter and the chinking of ice in glass, mocking my thirst. A flight of wooden steps led into a pub garden. I resisted temptation again, knowing that a litre of warm water waited in my car, a mile away. All part of the toughening up process. Just as the sun dipped over the horizon, I reached for my car keys, ten hours after leaving.

My T-shirt and trousers were drenched in sweat and my feet sore from the hardest walk since the three-day Pyrenean expedition. But my shoulders suffered more from the strain of pulling fifty pounds of weight up and down three thousand feet. I tended to my feet first, ignoring the bottle that beckoned inside the car. Once released from their prison of thick wool socks and tough boots, my toes rejoiced with a celebratory wiggle. Only then did I drain the bottle and reflect on the day. What did I learn? That I could not rely on my phone, I needed more than two litres of water, my pace is slower than I thought, and I can get lost easily – even in Surrey.

# IF I WERE FAMOUS

A British celebrity just completed twenty-seven marathons in as many days in the blistering South African heat for the annual Sports Relief charity drive. His incredible determination and endurance helped to raise over one million pounds for charitable causes. While I admire and have huge respect for his achievement, I am ashamed to admit my jealousy. If he were not one of the UK's leading comedians, I am certain he would not raise anything near a million. He benefitted from extensive national publicity on BBC radio and TV, the national newspapers and social media. Millions of people knew about his epic challenge and, as a result, donated generously.

Perhaps if I were as famous, my comparatively modest thirty-five thousand pounds target would be surpassed by now? Are my expectations too high? Liz says they are, but I set my sights high because the cause is so close to my heart. A total lack of fame does not help promote the trek. My reach will never be as great as any celebrity's. I know this, yet I am still utterly de-moralised by the blanket of silence from the media. There are others in the same position – ordinary people who do crazy things, run marathons on consecutive days, cycle across entire continents, and hike up Mount Kilimanjaro for their own causes. We are in the same club of anonymous do-gooders.

The disinterest dampens my desire to get up and train. Receiving no donations for several days demoralises me far more than trivial things like poor weather and mere aches and pains. Why am I making such an effort, when so few care, especially the media? The answer is because it is for JD and his carers. *They* are all the motivation I need. I drag myself up, don my uniform, and slog off for more miles in the wind and rain.

Today, a local newspaper printed an article about my trek, after a phone call with a Camberley News & Mail journalist last week.

*"... Norwood has experienced tough times due to 'austerity Britain'. My feelings now are so great that I must do something to help them maintain the outstanding level of care Norwood provides for my son and demonstrate to his carers how much I appreciate what they do for him.*

*Carers receive little credit for what they do. Many are earning close to the minimum wage for doing work that impacts positively on the lives of people who would otherwise have no quality of life."*

*"As Laurence currently expects to walk unsupported and alone for most of the journey, he is keen to hear from any fit and reasonably experienced local walkers who would like to accompany him."*

I pin hope on the national media to extend my reach and boost donations. My only publicity positive is how quickly the local paper responded. They must think my trek is interesting enough for their readers. I am so thankful for their support. Someone does care after all.

# EIGHT SISTERS

Ten days after my twenty-mile yomp in the Surrey Hills, I yearned for more. But mutt did not share the same sentiment. With a prolonged grumble, she draped a foreleg over her eyes and refused to rise from her basket.

"Come on, you'll love it. Besides, I need this to test my endurance, navigation skills, and you'll love all the new smells."

An eye blinked at me from under a paw.

"You need a rest anyway," I said, "I'll find something or someone else for company."

So, a human substituted mutt for an expedition over the Seven Sisters, a series of limestone hills on the South Downs Way between the Birling Gap and the mouth of the river Cuckmere. The human was Avi, my walking buddy for the last four days of the Pyrenean trek. Friends for over twenty years, I wondered how physical stress would affect our relationship. Would conversation degenerate to grunts when we became so knackered? That had been my experience with Jonathan the previous year. But despite the silence at the close of each day, the expedition strengthened mutual trust and understanding. It was important to test Avi's friendship under similar conditions. The ten-mile circular walk would be a foretaste of what we could expect in August.

With that intention, I packed clothing and toiletries for two months, three litres of water, walking poles, and enough food to feed a small army. My phone would navigate, just as it would in the mountains. My map-making skills were honed after many evenings glued to Google Maps, resulting in a catalogue I could access on my phone, including the Seven Sisters circuit. Some routes were flawed by unmapped MoD fences, uncharted footpaths and private property, but necessary to compensate for my dodgy sense of location and direction.

A ninety-minute drive later, we arrived at a car park in Exceat. Immediately, I reached for my phone.

"Are you sure you know where we're going?" inquired Avi.

"The path starts near here, somewhere," I said without looking up.

Eyes fixed on my phone, I spun on the spot, seeking a heading to the start of the path.

"The blue dot is us," I explained, "and the green line is our route – we are about fifty yards off."

"I have an idea," he said, "why don't we follow this cycle path sign?"

"What sign?" I wheeled about.

He pointed to a green bicycle symbol, on a post three feet ahead.

"This one in front of you."

"Well spotted!"

The sign directed us up a hill towards a pine forest at the back of the car park. Avi led the way while I stared at my phone, mesmerised by the blue dot converging on the green line.

"This is it - we are here!" I exclaimed in triumph.

"Well found, Mister Smith, there is hope for us."

We continued along the cycle path through Friston Forest, across a field of skittish sheep, picked through a church graveyard, before arriving on the village green at East Dean. Nearby stood a flint cottage with a blue plaque that read, '*Sherlock Holmes – Consulting Detective and Beekeeper retired here 1903-1917*'. The claim is based on Sir Arthur

Conan Doyle's book 'His Last Bow' in which he dispatched the great sleuth to a "*small farm on the Downs about five miles from Eastbourne*" to spend his final days.

"So, about the kit-list for the Pyrenees," Avi said, "tell me what I need."

"For starters, you'll need some dry sacks for your clothes, in case of spillage."

"Spillage?"

"Liquids, you know, like shampoo."

"Should I be bothered by that?" He patted his shiny pate.

"Maybe not in your case, but dry sacks are still useful for organising your shit."

"Anything else?"

"Walking poles, water bottles, merino socks and pants, a change of clothes for evening wear, waterproofs, head torch, batteries, and …"

"E-mail me," Avi interrupted, "let's get breakfast."

His eyes latched on to a café a few yards away, stocked with artisan breads, local cheeses, home-baked patisseries and fresh coffee. Sharing a love of good food, we ate into walking time, and breakfast rolled into elevenses.

I glanced at a clock, "we can't sit here stuffing our faces – we have the toughest stage to do."

At mid-day, we stood on the pebbly shore at Birling Gap. A cold sea breeze fanned us as we climbed the first sister. Heading west, each sister is a quarter-mile climb followed by a sharp descent to the foot of its sibling. Three miles and five-hundred feet of upping and downing later we climbed onto the eighth sister, one more than expected after meticulous counting. Without any warning, Avi stepped over a rope intended to keep walkers away from the crumbling cliff and a hundred-foot drop to a watery grave. Too ashamed to reveal my fear of heights, I followed. There would be many 'big wheel of terror' moments in the weeks ahead and I needed to acclimate. He stood a foot from the edge peering down at the long fall. A strong gust of wind would cast him into the Channel. My legs trembled and nausea welled up as I drew closer.

"What a view!" he exclaimed, pointing at the sand swirls at the mouth of the river Cuckmere.

"Lovely," I concurred from six feet behind.

To my relief, he declared, "time for lunch."

I strode briskly inland, "here is perfect." From a safe distance, my eyes traced the river from the pebbly beach at Cuckmere Haven, flanked by chalk cliffs, two miles inland to Seven Sisters Country Park and the end of our excursion.

"So," I said, "how has our trip been for you?"

"Why do you ask?" True to form, he answered my question with a question.

"Just curious - it will be much tougher than this in the Pyrenees."

"We will manage, Mister Smith, we will manage."

# TRAINING WITH THE ARMY

The Army trained around Bisley Ranges today. Mutt and I stood to one side of a narrow path while a column of soldiers pounded up and down steep hills by the perimeter fence, and a disembodied voice barked, "keep moving," "faster," "go, go, go."

Heavy boots thundered, the ground shook, and the ferns trembled. Amid the chaos, there came muttering from their ranks. Each soldier puffed by, uttering a salutation of their choice, "thank you sir," "good morning sir," "much obliged sir," "good doggie." Two soldiers leading the column carried a fifty-litre container of water with a pole slung between the handles. All wore Army rucksacks, with the regulation fifty-five pounds weight, ten pounds heavier than mine. Impeccable manners were an essential element of their rigorous training regime.

Three miles further, we encountered the Army again, on exercises on Mytchett Range. A hundred soldiers practiced navigating with maps and compasses. Modern devices like digital maps and GPS are banned to avoid detection by electronic surveillance. The greens, tans and browns of forest and heathland were punctuated with garish sky blue portaloos, looking uncannily like tardises from Doctor Who.

With the Army behind us, mutt and I searched for large steep hills. Eventually, we found a sixty-foot monster-mound hidden among pine trees. We crawled up and down, over and again, until my training addiction was sated, and mutt too fed up to continue. She is not so enthusiastic about her walks anymore. When I don my trekking gear, rucksacks and fill the water bottles, her doleful eyes plead, "can we have a normal walkie today, pleeeeease?" Her only consolation are the fine sticks she picks up en route, which she carries home and attempts to smuggle over our threshold. There is an impressive avant-garde exhibit outside our front door, enhanced by mutt after each training venture. Occasionally, Liz will clear away the artwork, only for another to take its place.

# A SKIRMISH

Mutt and I skirmished with the military today. We followed our usual route around Bisley Range fence, before diverting on to a narrow track and ploughing deeper into the forest. After fifteen minutes of thrashing through dense foliage and tall ferns, a steep-sided mound came into view, offering a perfect opportunity for scrambling practice.

The clouds prepared to unleash fury on mutt and I, so I slipped a waterproof cover over my rucksack as a precaution. Bought from an Army & Navy surplus store, it was cheap, with a camouflage pattern that blended with the greens and browns of the English countryside.

I ascended the first twenty yards with my walking poles, then dropped on to hands and knees to the summit, turned about and descended and repeated the exercise a few times. On the final ascent, mutt and I rested for a well-earned snack beside a rutted track. A sandwich later, a jeep rolled towards us along the grooves in the muddy path. I stood up to wave, expecting the driver to smile, wave and pass, as had happened so many times before. Instead, the driver stopped and wound down his window.

"Are you in the Army?" he inquired.

Why would he ask me that? Did I look like I was? He leaned an elbow on the window.

"No, I'm just out for a walk," I answered.

Seizing the opportunity to scoop extra donations, I

continued, "I'm training for a five-hundred-and-forty-mile trek along the Pyrenees for my son's care home."

I hoped the driver would be impressed and plead for more details. I reached for a 'Laurence Smith – Trekker' business card I brought especially for such encounters.

Without any acknowledgement, he replied, "you look like you're in the Army - you've got all the gear." Perhaps my camouflage rucksack cover, water bottles, map and compass inside the plastic cover, or large hump on my back led him to an obvious, but incorrect conclusion. But his response quashed all hope of raising more donations. He was clearly not interested. Why would he be?

"Did you know you're on Army training ground?"

I remembered seeing some cartridge shells lying on the forest floor earlier, but replied with feigned surprise, "no! Really? I didn't know!"

Even Charlie the mutt looked innocent while the driver warned, "you're lucky they aren't out today. Although they only use blanks, so you'd probably be alright, but I wouldn't recommend you make a habit of walking around here."

"Thanks. I'll remember," I said.

He rolled up his window, waved and drove off. The rest of the walk passed without incident or seeing anyone else from the Army.

The weather warmed up later in the week. As a result, water consumption increased to three litres for a twelve-mile walk over five hours, four litres including mutt's drinking provisions. An old plastic ice-cream tub serves as her container because she is not permitted to stick her tongue in my bottles - our mutual devotion does not extend that far.

# OBSESSION

Mutt and I are not training and battling with the Army every day. Some days are spent under cover, planning and publicising the trek. Time is not wasted on matters other than the cause I am utterly dedicated to. Some friends and family say that the time I spend preparing for the long haul in the mountains is an obsession. But my obsession is vindicated whenever I visit JD and his carers. They brush away any doubts about my mental health.

At the end of the week, Michael, a good friend of mine, presented an opportunity to speak to a wide audience on Brooklands Radio. I could not refuse a chance of broadcasting my obsession to, potentially, seven billion listeners over an Internet radio station.

"Pretend it's just you and me," Michael advised, to Nancy Sinatra's 'These Boots are Made for Walking' in the background, "be natural."

The music stopped, and words rehearsed in my head countless times streamed over the airwaves. We talked for ten minutes about JD, his condition, and the trek across a crowded desk with three large computer screens, microphones and 'cans' (headphones). Words formed over seven months of walking solo, with little to distract me from my obsession.

"Thanks Laurence," Michael said afterwards, "that was great."

"I should thank you – I've been wanting to get that out

of my head for months."

"Perhaps you'd like to do another interview on your walk?"

"Sure will."

With such an all-consuming obsession, I would make sure of another interview, even if I were dangling from a cliff.

# DRIVING AROUND THE BEND

Departure looms. There is no hope of finding more walking companions. Jonathan will walk with me for the first three days, and Avi on the final four. The fourth day, Thursday July 7$^{th}$, will be my first day walking solo, and every day of six weeks in between. Liz will be waiting in the evening of the fourth day and stay until the following Wednesday morning for a week of wifely company. She will not walk with me, but her presence will inspire me to keep going. She will shop for provisions and carry most of the contents of my rucksack in the hire car, so I can walk light for four days.

I booked us in to some rustic gites and printed off directions from Biarritz airport to our meeting point, in St-Etienne-de-Baigorry. Her birthday is the day before we meet, so I packed a gift and card to present to her when we meet on the Thursday evening.

She will need to conquer her fear of driving a strange car on the wrong (right) side of some very narrow and hazardous mountain roads. The pictures I saw on Street View are seriously scary. One road leads up a mountain to where I will be walking on my first day of the second week, from Esterencuby to Chalets d'Iraty. Single-track for most of the way, without crash barriers, and infested with large horned cows that dwell in the Pyrenees. What I saw would drive her round the bend with worry.

# POOR ME

May 31st 2016.

"So, what do you think, mutt?" I asked, looking up at the brooding sky. Mid-morning, and everyone was at work, so I debated whether to maintain my training regime with the only living creature in the vicinity. There was nothing better to do anyway. Normally, I would see JD on Tuesday, but we were sticking to our schedule of reduced visits to adapt to my long absence in the Pyrenees.

Charlie lifted an eyebrow and peered at me. A work colleague once told me that dogs make excellent companions for humans because they communicate with their eyes, as well as by barking, whimpering and growling. Her concerned expression said she was not keen. A prolonged grumble followed, and she slumped dramatically. She had answered.

"What's that mutt? Cumulonimbus spells danger? Closely packed isobars portend stormy weather? Well, I think we'll be fine – it will hold off for a few hours I reckon," I re-assured.

And that was my final say on the matter. We would do twelve miles up Curley Hill, through Lightwater Country Park and into Swinley Forest and back, come hell or high water, the latter being a distinct possibility. I packed my rucksack, making sure my waterproofs were readily accessible. For motivating mutt, I stuffed a handful of kibble in my front rucksack. Only then did she raise herself from her basket, sink her teeth into her pink ball and follow me out the front door.

Within ten minutes of leaving, it began drizzling, and the wind picked up. I pulled on my waterproof trousers and folded them up at the bottom of my legs, so they were clear of my boots. At the time, it seemed like a good idea because I wanted to avoid the possibility of stepping on them. The sky blackened, and we rounded the corner of the Bisley Range fence to face a storm-force wind.

"There's nothing like horizontal rain to test your mettle, mutt," I said to my walking companion, who clasped her ball firmly between her jaws with grim determination.

Drizzle became large droplets and the earth underfoot and paw turned to mud on the steep incline up Curley Hill. Small rivers steamed down the slope over my boots, the wet bracken on either side of the narrow slippery path brushed against our flanks and damp seeped through my five-thousand tog coat.

"Bloody weather," I cursed, "and bloody ingress."

But the North Atlantic weather persisted. What will JD be doing in these foul conditions? Strangely, he loved the rain but was less keen on strong winds, although he would be excited by its violent effect on the trees straining to stay upright.

"He has music therapy today," I said, "very sensible – he loves music."

Even if I could visit today, where would we go?

"Probably the garden centre at Welsh Harp," I answered my unvoiced question aloud. He loved to watch the giant carp swim past the window in the fish tank, that eyed him with curiosity. We would conclude by popping into the indoor café for a cake, where he would study the artificial trees. All the benefits of al fresco dining, only shielded from the unpredictable English weather.

We crossed the main road through Bagshot and trudged up Church Hill into Swinley Forest. About two miles further, Charlie began limping. Feeling guilty for taking her out in such awful weather, we sheltered under a tree where I examined her leg for thorns, pine needles and other foreign objects. She dropped her ball and panted, trembling as I inspected each leg in turn.

"I'm so sorry my dear mutt," I soothed, "you ain't no spring chicken anymore. I should have let you stay at home in your cosy basket."

Her brown eyes bored into mine, with an unmistakeable look of self-pity, "poor me," they cried.

"Ok, ok, let's go home," I said.

No sooner did the words leave my mouth, than she picked up her ball and headed down the forest track, homeward bound.

The return journey was equally grim. With the wind behind us, droplets of rain became globules that ran like a river down my back, over my waterproof trousers and collected in small puddles in the turned-up folds. Water spilled onto my socks, soaking my feet and boots. Moreover, water seeped freely through the tongues of my boots, that were fully exposed to the incessant downpour. What seemed like a good idea when we set off proved incredibly dumb.

Damp feet and clothes were just punishment for subjecting the miserable twelve-mile journey on Charlie, my trusty mutt. We returned five and a half hours after leaving, two bedraggled animals, one squelching loudly and the other limping silently.

I removed my rucksack to reveal the havoc wrought on it by the English summer weather. The inside was soaked. Stupidly, I did not use my cover, because I assumed my rucksack was waterproof. It is water-*resistant*, not water*proof*. My car is water-resistant, but I would never take it for a dip in the sea. Fortunately, my clothes and other stuff survived the onslaught because they were sealed in dry sacks. I turned out the rucksack, loosened the zippers and hung it up to dry.

Poor Charlie the mutt, my trusty steed for months. Not one whimper of complaint passed her jaws, even after today's disaster. She may develop rheumatism after being subjected to prolonged dampness, and it will be my fault. She walked by my side for a thousand miles of training walks, many of them with a pink ball or a stick in her mouth. I will miss her at my side on the Pyrenees.

# WORDS FROM THE HEART

"Step into our recording studio," said Jack, "please take this seat and use the mike in front of you."

Two weeks after my Brooklands Radio interview, I was back on air, on Eagle Radio, a station with over a million listeners in the south-east of England. I received an unexpected invitation from Jack Johnson, one of their DJs, to be interviewed about my trek.

"You'd sent an e-mail to the Head of Surrey's Media Team a few weeks ago," Jack explained, "and she passed it to me to see if I would be interested – and I was, so here you are." He beamed, looking genuinely pleased, then pointed at the headphones on the table in front of me, "but before we get started, we'll need a sound check, so can you put on the cans and say something into the mike?"

I slipped the heavily padded headphones over my ears and tried hard to think of a random phrase. I prepared for the interview but not the sound check. "Erm, er, …," I stuttered.

"It doesn't have to make sense," Jack advised, "you can say anything you like, as long as it's decent."

I raised my head and spoke into the bulbous microphone, "Anything you like as long as it's decent."

Jack stared at one of the three monitor screens on the table. He clicked a few keys on a keyboard and said, "that's perfect."

"Right, I think we're ready to go. First, I read about

your plan to walk the Pyrenees next month and I think our listeners would like to know more," he leaned forward, "but I would like to ask you about your reasons for undertaking something so massive."

He continued, "it's those reasons that are so topical right now because it's National Carer's Week."

He referred to my e-mail sent a month earlier, when I wrote, "*many care homes depend on charitable donations to maintain their quality of care. The never-ending austerity measures have made Norwood, and other organisations, rely even more on the goodwill of their donors, and their care-workers, who bear the full impact of cuts from central and local government. My feelings now are so great that I must do something to help maintain the outstanding level of care that Norwood provides my son and, at the same time, demonstrate to his carers how much I appreciate what they do for him. Carers receive too little credit: many are earning close to the minimum wage for work that impacts positively the lives of people who would otherwise have no quality of life. Now I am retired, I feel that I have been very lucky to have had full-time employment and enjoyed a comfortable salary for doing work that benefitted a global IT company. Now I feel it is time for pay back and for me to do something I consider to be a positive benefit to the community I live in.*"

"So, more about what my son's carers do for my son and less about the trek itself," I suggested.

"Yes, but you will want to appeal to our listeners' hearts, make them want to donate to your cause," Jack said, "so you will need to say something about how difficult and dangerous it will be, as well as what Norwood and your son's carers do."

He concluded my briefing, "shall we get started?" I nodded and he began his introduction, "In the studio with me this morning is Laurence Smith, a sixty-one-year-old dad of a profoundly disabled young man, Jeremy, who lives in full-time care in Woodcock Dell in London, run by a charity called Norwood. In National Carer's Week, what Laurence is planning to do, and why, is especially relevant.

Laurence – thank you for coming in today – please tell our listeners what you will be doing."

With a mixture of excitement and anxiety over word-fumbling, I began, "I will be walking for five-hundred-and-forty miles along the Pyrenees, from the Atlantic to the Mediterranean, averaging thirteen miles and climbing over three thousand feet every day, for six days every week, for about two months. I will be carrying over forty-four pounds weight on my back and I have a terrible fear of heights. There are also bears in the Pyrenees, but I am not too worried about them – it's the patous I'm more nervous of."

"There are bears in the Pyrenees?" interjected Jack, alarmed, "and what are patous?"

"Yes, there are bears. Fortunately, not many because they were re-introduced only about fifty years ago, so the chance of meeting one is slim. But there are many more patous, large fierce dogs that guard flocks of sheep. If one thinks I'm a threat, it will attack and there won't be anyone around to call it off!"

"So why are you putting your life at such risk?" asked Jack.

His question opened my heart and sent the words tumbling.

"Because I trust Jeremy's carers with his life, and I want to show them what that means to me. It means as much as my life. They don't get the recognition they deserve for their dedication to the vulnerable people they look after. This trek is like a sign of my undying gratitude to them and, I hope, at the same time it will raise enough in donations to make their lives just a little easier."

"And how much do you hope to raise for Jeremy's care home?"

"Thirty-five-thousand pounds," I answered, "the money will go towards the cost of building a badly needed extension that will make it easier for his carers at mealtimes, which are the busiest times of the day."

"How much have you raised already?"

"Just over five thousand pounds - so still a long way to go."

"Yes indeed, and how much time is left before you go?"

"I start on Monday July 4$^{th}$ and hope to finish by the end of August, but I'll be keeping my donations page open until next year."

Jack helped me make my points without ever needing to search for the right words. I had made them so many times – to family and friends, the local press, on Brooklands Radio. I was on autopilot, treading the same ground for the umpteenth time. But every time I answer the question about why I am doing something so crazy, my resolve grows. Broadcasting my reasons validates them and toughens me psychologically – it is mental training.

# PAIN IN THE NECK

Twenty-two days before I fly to Biarritz for my trek. Am I ready? Am I fit enough? Losing seven pounds weight after six months of training must be a good thing. Have I got everything I will need? Or do I have too much?

Morbid curiosity drove me to the weighing scales. Dressed in trekking clothes, the needle settled on one hundred and fifty-four pounds. Then I slung on both rucksacks and filled three water bottles, as if I were stepping out the door on to the Pyrenees. The needle shot up to two hundred and nine pounds, and I tumbled off in shock. Fifty-five pounds, a third of my body weight and as much as a combat soldier's kit-pack, on my back every day of the week.

Neck pain had been a frequent complaint over a thousand miles of training walks. I wondered if the cause was the mountain of stuff crammed into two rucksacks, or poor weight distribution. Maybe the straps needed adjusting so the bulk was closer and higher up my frame? My chum Paul, who navigated me through a minefield of hiking shops last year, offered to 'tear-down' my gear and provide some rucksack maintenance.

"Free service," he insisted.

"The beer and pizza are on me," I replied, "for being a pain in the neck."

# A TEAR-DOWN

"The aim of this game," said Paul, my trekking adviser, "is to get the weight as low as possible." He tapped on a set of scales by his feet.

The contents of my rucksack lay on the floor beside three yellow stickies labelled 'essential shit', 'unnecessary shit' and 'nice-to-have'.

"You must tell me why you need each thing in your sack. If you convince me, then it will go here," pointing to the first label.

"And if you can't, then it will go there," and pointed at the second.

"Then we chew over what's left."

"Sounds tasty," I answered.

He played 'sift and sort' thousands of times with teenage Duke of Edinburgh award students preparing for mountain expeditions, although most probably with different sticky labels.

A long night lay ahead, with the incentive of a large pizza and four cans of ice-cold beer on the dining table.

"The quicker we get through this, the colder the beer," he added.

Clothes and sleep gear landed quickly in the essential pile without explanation. I hesitated for too long over three rolls of tape for repairs, a water bottle, two books, a half-litre of tea-tree oil and two packs of spare batteries, so out they went.

"If you're not sure, then don't take," he advised.

Now in his groove, Paul cut off two yards of gaffer tape and wrapped it around a water bottle and cast the remaining roll onto the unnecessary pile, saying, "look after the ounces and the pounds will take care of themselves."

He picked up a chess-set and two Sudoku books and raised his eyebrows.

"Are you really going to have any chance to play chess or Sudoku, especially after an arduous walk?"

"I won't find out unless I take them," I answered, reluctant to grow the pile of unnecessaries.

He sighed and popped them by 'nice-to-have', then dropped the 'unnecessary shit' pile onto the scales.

"Just on seven pounds, not bad, and don't forget the space you've saved."

"Can we eat now?"

"Step one over, now we need to sort this lot. You must be able to find what you need quickly, so your coloured dry sacks will be a great help."

The military precision of packing a rucksack reminded me of loading a car before a three-week holiday for six. Liz and I provided ourselves and our passengers with one Tesco zip bag each, with a name scrawled on the side, to make identification and unloading as painless as possible. Like then, colour would be a useful aide-memoire for the trek.

One 'orange for overnight' sack to unpack at a refuge, filled with pyjamas, evening attire, flip-flops, head-torch, phone charger, power adapter, toiletries and towel, would eliminate rummaging around after a hard day's trek and enable quick getaways.

"Toiletries must be isolated," Paul said, "so that damage is limited if anything leaks."

Acting on his advice, I packed a small 'green for grooming' sack with my toothbrush, shampoo, razor, shaving cream, nail clippers, toothpaste, antiseptic hand cream and soap, then stuffed it into the orange sack.

"Colour-coding makes a lot of sense," I said, "red will stand for my repair kits, lemon for leisure activities and large green for garb, then I'm all out of colours."

"It's good that you've separated your overnight gear, which will be the most important, because you can find other stuff when you need it, which probably won't be often," Paul replied, "look after the minutes and the hours will take care of themselves."

I surveyed the bundle of coloured sacks nestling among the pile of other items – sleeping bag, mat, bivvy bag, water bottles, solar panel, maps and 'scrubba' laundry bag. Still too much stuff.

"These things can come in handy," Paul waved two large rubble sacks, "as extra dry-sacks and for carrying rubbish."

"Now let me look at your rucksack."

My rucksack and I had been inseparable over a thousand miles of training walks, but its myriad of zippers and hidden compartments were a mystery.

"Forget about them - treat it like a giant bag, rather than lots of little ones, it's much simpler," he folded back the internal separators, "it'll be quicker to pack and unpack as well." He lined it with a rubble sack for waterproofing.

"In fact," he said, "when you have landed in France, use your rucksack carrier to line the inside – it will make it even more waterproof."

He took a minute to adjust the straps on my rucksack so that it rested higher and on my hips. "If it hangs too low, it will give you back and neck strain, which would account for the pains you told me about."

"Now we are ready to pack."

Heavier items, like sleeping bag, bivvy bag and the largest dry sack went in first, closest to my back. The other dry sacks and medicine kit followed, in front of the heavier items, to distribute weight evenly. Six pairs of walking socks became fillers between dry sacks and prevented movement.

Paul urged, "try it on, twist about, jump around, let me know how it feels."

I bent over to hoist the rucksack on my back.

"Stop!" he exclaimed, "you'll injure yourself like that, sit down and climb into the shoulder straps, then push yourself upright."

I leaned against the rucksack, hooked my arms into the straps and stood, twisted, and jumped a few times.

"Perfect! It fits like a glove, nothing moves inside, and standing up was effortless."

"Good," Paul looked unsurprised. He had seen it a thousand times before.

"I should have done this weeks ago."

"Hindsight can be useful," he replied, "but not as much as planning."

"Or experience."

Kit for the trek

# MAN-FLU

Man-flu is *so* much worse than normal flu. Women do not understand how much we men suffer with it. They catch normal flu, which is far more tolerable. Three days hence, Victoria marries, and we have a thumping great party to enjoy. One hundred and twenty guests will be there, and I must be well enough to walk my daughter up the aisle and party until the wee hours of Monday morning. A week after that, the trek starts. The man-flu affects my breathing so I cannot inhale through my nose and my chest rattles. The higher I climb, the thinner the air, and the harder it will be to breathe. It is the worst time to be struck down with such a debilitating ailment.

I cannot train properly until the man-flu subsides because physical exertion will make it worse. As a spritely twenty-five-year-old, I experienced the effects of exposure when on young man flu. I was on a four-week tour around Europe and left England with a mild cold. The following ten days I sniffled and snuffled on unheated trains, including two days on a packed Orient Express through the Iron Curtain into Communist Hungary and Romania. I stood in a corridor through the night as the train sped through the dark Carpathian Mountains. After completing the journey, and making my way through Yugoslavia and Greece, I was so ill that I spent my remaining cash paying for a doctor. By then, the cold progressed to bronchitis, and I was compelled to recuperate for three miserable days in a hot tent on a beach. So, my training regime for the final week is downgraded from severe to mild.

# PAGES

I should be more thankful – with or without man-flu. Three happy, healthy and beautiful daughters and one special son. We made it to the here and now, the marriage of our second daughter Victoria, without many of the problems that befall other families with highly dependent children. We never experienced major financial hardship, or saw our children career on to the wrong path, owing to neglect or unwelcome influence. Liz and I are thankful for the fact that our three daughters share some of our values and are untainted by years of struggling with JD when he lived at home. They became carers, without asking for the huge responsibility that came with the role. Many times, I saw Victoria comforting JD in her arms as he cried or tried to self-harm, when Liz and I were pre-occupied with cooking, cleaning or housework. I like to believe that JD made them more caring. I am acutely aware, and proud, of what he gave them and of what they became.

Today was a celebration, so I swept aside nostalgia and man-flu with a last nose-blow, took Victoria's arm and prepared to lead her up the aisle.

"Ready sweetie?" I asked.

"It's a bit late to ask me that," she replied with a smile.

The 'Wedding March' began, and one hundred and twenty faces turned, some filled with tears, as we processed up the aisle towards the groom, five bridesmaids in pink dresses, best man and Registrar. JD was the pageboy for the special day, entrusted with the task of guiding family and friends to their seats, assisted by two carers from Woodcock Dell. Awarding him such an important job was Victoria's wish, and I struggled to stem my own tears at that thought. Such a typical gesture from her. We passed him, looking dapper in his best suit and boots.

With a final snuffle, induced by a combination of man-flu and the occasion, I returned to my seat to witness my daughter being given away to another man. Even though I had known her partner for two years, I still felt a sense of loss, as I did when Roxanne married Peter the year before. But it was tinged with fulfilment at reaching an important milestone and helping to deliver a new family into the world. One chapter of her life closed, the page turned, and the next chapter began.

# LAST VISIT

"Well JD," I said, "it's our last time together for two months."

We were at Welsh Harp, a nature reserve near Woodcock Dell. One of our regular haunts, shared by pensioners, parents with young children and dog-walkers while the rest of the population worked. Crossing the Capital Ring, a seventy-eight-mile circular walk through London's parks, I tried to gauge JD's reaction to the news about my impending long absence.

"But mum will see you on Sundays as usual," I added, hoping to soften the blow.

I told him about my trek many times before – where, how far, the wildlife, when and why I was doing it – and every time I searched his face, body language and vocalisations for signs of how much he understood. Maybe, like his siblings, he was bored with me talking about it and it ceased to register. It was part of a general noise.

We rolled along the path beside Brent Reservoir in silence, past the park benches, the ducks on the water and the trees. JD looked pensive - serious expression, furrowed brows and thumb in mouth – while I elaborated.

"This time next week, I'll be walking along that road for you JD," still trying to evoke some response, "and I'll be in the mountains for most of the time."

Silence.

"But I might be able to Skype you, if I stay somewhere with WiFi."

More silence.

Did he know what WiFi was? Did he comprehend what "Skype you" meant? They are technical terms that many able-minded people do not understand, let alone someone with JD's disabilities. So, why did I say it? The answer was easy – never assume anything and always speak to him as I would anyone. With no visible or audible response, I tried to explain his silence.

Maybe he got the gist of what I said and is sulking? Is he cross with me? Or perhaps he did not understand and is just tired? I did not know, so I appealed to his sense of humour.

"It will be tough, dangerous in places, and very uncomfortable," building towards the finale, "I'll be wearing the same underpants for six days every week!"

I waited for a chuckle or an "er-her-her," JD's equivalent of a laugh, but still nothing. Finally, I gave in, and we stopped beside a bench under an oak tree.

"OK JD, what's wrong?" I turned him around to face me.

For the first time that day, he looked at me. It was unavoidable – our heads were level and only a foot apart. Slowly, he took his fingers from his mouth, lifted his eyes and homed in on mine.

"Errrr….," he said.

"Is that it JD?" I replied, "are you sulking because I'm going away?"

JD engaged fully – eyes locked onto mine and dancing from left to right, seeking a way into my head. Such moments are rare, and I treasure them. I can tell a lot about how he feels from his eyes, when he lets me see them. Sadness, happiness, anger, anxiety, surprise and discomfort are easy to spot, before he makes any sound. But this time, I could not read anything. They were just two deep olive-green pools staring at me with an unusual intensity. He knew I was going away for a long time, but I was not sure he understood the reason. While the moment lasted, I did my best to explain.

"Ten years ago, JD, we drove to the mountains," his eyes widened, like I was telling a story, "and we walked along a forest path and had a picnic, do you remember?"

Did I see a faint smile? Was that because he recollected that sunny day with Liz and his sisters, in the heat of summer, away from the crowded Mediterranean beaches? Or was he just happy to be out under the trees?

"You do? Good. Well, that forest path is five-hundred-and-forty miles long and I promised to walk it for you – and it's going to take me a long time."

"Aahhh," he said, still attentive.

"And I will be …. no … *we* will be doing it for your family in Woodcock Dell, to show them how grateful we are."

His eyes were glued on mine as I spoke, "*we*, not *me*, because you're the real reason – I would never walk that far for anyone else."

He leaned forward, so our heads touched. With our eyes now unlocked, I took his hand and stroked it gently with my fingers.

"And I will miss you too JD."

# TIME DILATION

The final training day and man-flu persists. Hacking cough, running nose and laboured breathing when I walk briskly. Just what I do not need two days before departure. Anyone on the Pyrenees will hear me coming for miles around.

"The next time … *sniff* …. I put these boots on … *sniff* … I'll be there and … *sniff* … about to take my first … *sniff snort* … step on a very long road," I informed mutt.

Of course, mutt heard nothing unusual about the sound of her master's voice. She responded with a cold wet nose applied to the face, demonstrating the art of snuffling, doggie-style.

I tried to ignore the symptoms on a circuit up Curley Hill and around Lightwater Country Park, with a full load on my back. Admitting defeat, I muttered obscenities at my trickling nostrils and tickling throat. Over one-thousand-two-hundred miles of training walks, the last seven the grumpiest of all.

Tomorrow would be devoted to pre-flight checks, re-packing my rucksack and preparing to leave. If I finished the trek on schedule, then I would return at the end of August. I had never been away from my loved ones for so long. Add that to my list of new experiences. Was I taking on too much? And how would Liz manage all that was about to happen while I was away? So wrapped up in concerns for my own welfare, I disregarded my duties to my family. Roxanne would be moving from Norwich to be near us. Victoria would be leaving our house for Army married quarters. Then there was the real possibility of her baby arriving early, and missing those crucial first few days when she would need support. Georgina would be moving from a rented studio in London back home and starting a new job. So much happening in such a short space of time. While I am gone, time would be squeezed for Liz yet dilated for me.

# PRE-FLIGHT CHECKS

July 1st 2016.

Tomorrow, I fly away at two o'clock. Today is check-my-kit-day. My worldly possessions for the next two months must be on my back before I swing out the door.

For the umpteenth time, I re-packed my rucksack, then grabbed the carrier. The rucksack's straps and pocket zippers must be protected when loading and unloading on the plane. So many things could kill the trek before it started. I tried squeezing the rucksack in sideways – no joy. Lengthwise, same result. No way would it fit. After a few head scratches, I concluded that the water bottles were the culprits - three precious litres of space occupied by plastic filled with air. Problem solved by packing them in the carrier separately. Then a final weigh-in on the bathroom scales. Forty-two pounds without water. A few pounds heavier than expected, but bearable.

Brushing aside weight concern, I turned my attention to the technology I depended on. My mobile phone would be my means of navigating and booking places to stay. Woe betide me if it shuts down for lack of power. I uninstalled the power-hungry apps as a precaution. MapMyWalk, the app that served me so well while training, was the first casualty. Then, I shut down the unimportant entertainment apps, Spotify and iTunes. Google Maps, my primary navigation aid, took priority over everything else. Although I would keep Lotus Map, and the official GR10 route I found on the Internet, as backup in case Google Maps mis-directed me over a military fence, as it did a few months earlier.

The robust English weather battered my front rucksack so badly it resembled a boxer's punch-bag with the stuffing beaten out, so I swapped it for a plush leather and canvas satchel 'man-bag'. It would give me quick access to valuables like phone, phone cables, passport, wallet, English-to-French power adapters, bandanas, dad-hat, sunglasses, sun-cream and head-net for protection against horseflies, mosquitos and other wee biting things. A plastic wallet would carry the first of eleven paper maps, compass, Cicerone GR10 Guidebook and memorabilia for morale-boosters at difficult times. I slipped in my favourite photo of JD, good luck cards from Liz, Roxanne, Victoria and Georgina and inspirational words from two friends, Donald and Ena:

*"The walk you are undertaking sounds massive, but it will be such an achievement even to start out, and no matter how much or how little you do, the objective is certainly 'for the sake of Heaven'. But of course you will do it and hopefully have a wonderful trip, see memorable places and make deep and lasting friendships along the way."*

# THE FIRST STEP IS THE HARDEST

Every journey begins with a first step. Mine was getting out of bed this morning. Without taking it, my journey for JD would never start. The persistent man-flu urged me to hunker down under the soft quilt for more hours of blissful rest. But that would mean missing the first in a sequence of steps, each as important as the next - get up, leave the house, drive to airport, fly to Biarritz, collect baggage, catch bus to Hendaye. All must be taken, and any could be thwarted by something out of my control. Heavy traffic on the car journey to Stansted, a sudden strike by airport staff, or my luggage put on a plane to Timbuktu. Even if I reached Hendaye, there was no guarantee I would finish the journey. Illness, accident, exhaustion or fear of heights might force me to return early, or never. Man-flu had blown a heavy cloud of pessimism over my bed.

But today was a significant milestone, marking the end of months of planning, training and fundraising. I would set out to fulfil the promise I made to JD ten years ago, lay the foundation-stone of my sign to his carers and show commitment to my donors, who had given so generously. I would let them down badly if I did not go. And that thought lifted my feet out of bed for the first step.

Breakfast washed away the sluggishness - croissants with lashings of jam and two pints of devilishly strong coffee delivered a mighty caffeine kick. I changed into my trekking gear - water-resistant trousers, Merino wool socks, walking boots, T-shirt, long-sleeved top and waterproof coat. A comfortable outfit for England, but over-the-top for the forecast thirty-degree-Celsius weekend in Hendaye.

Liz took a photo of me outside our house, about to depart for the airport, fearful wearing a mask of confidence. Then we left and drove in silence, Liz worrying about our daughters' forthcoming moves and me pre-occupied with images of bears, patous, deadly heights and getting lost.

We did not speak until joining a long check-in queue at the airport.

"How come it's so busy?" I wondered, scanning the crowds for tell-tale signs of trekkers in uniforms of boots, multi-pocketed trousers, burgeoning rucksacks and walking poles.

"Parents with small children," she replied, "students, business travellers, pensioners like you – it's not that surprising really."

Our queue snaked forward a few feet.

"I wonder if there are any pilgrims here, destined for the Camino."

"Could be," she answered, "guess you'll find out when you get to Biarritz."

Suppose I got lucky and met someone walking from coast to coast? Would they be doing it for a cause like mine? What would be the chance of them also having a one-in-sixty-thousand son or daughter? One-in-three-point-six billion, or about two-hundred-and-fifty times smaller than winning the National Lottery. Ridiculously small. My mind whirred to pass time. Far more likely I would meet someone walking for a loved one with an illness or coming to terms with a bereavement, like 'The Way', a film about a father walking the Camino for his departed son. Or they could be on a fitness kick. Flora and fauna could be another reason. A thousand reasons popped into my head, as we advanced up the queue to its head.

My rucksack weighed a hefty forty-four pounds, without water. Liz was alarmed enough to question the accuracy of the reading. The weigh-in excluded my man-bag and map holder, another seven pounds. With three litres of water, I would lug fifty-eight pounds along the Pyrenees for five-hundred-and-forty miles. Too heavy without help from a Sherpa, and too late for another tear-down.

"I'll see how I cope with the weight for the first few days. If it's too difficult, perhaps you could take a few things home when we meet next Thursday?"

"I think you should give me the puzzle books you'll never do," Liz suggested, "and that chess-set!"

"But I'll need them for the lonely nights," I protested.

"So, you're going to play chess with yourself after a long day on the mountains?"

"Maybe – or I could use it as a way of attracting other walkers over for a natter."

"Like flies over a jam-pot?" she quipped.

"If I was staying in a refuge and saw a stranger with a chess-set sitting alone in a corner, I'd be curious."

"But that's because you're a keen player."

"True," I conceded, then tried another approach, "but people fall into two categories – those that play chess, and those that don't."

"So?"

"Well, there will be a thousand times more people who don't play, and lots of them would *want* to, especially if they were alone for a long time!"

"O for heaven's sake!"

"This will be the longest we've ever been apart," I said, outside security check-in. Work had separated us for a few days, but never for more than a week.

"But I'll be seeing you in five days' time - and for the next five days."

"And after that, it will be seven weeks before we see

each other again."

"Jonathan's with you tomorrow and for the first three days," she said, "and Avi's with you for the last four."

"Yes, but they're not you," I answered.

A wordless and long embrace later, she left, and I plunged into the security tunnel. My mind began whirring again. My man-bag and coat rolled into the baggage scanner and an officer signalled from the other side of the metal detector. I was so close to starting the trek. I never trusted myself to get this far. The journey was never more than a pipedream. I could still chicken out. A couple of days in Hendaye, in the shadow of the mountains, would be plenty of time to think of an excuse for not going. Or maybe an illness would prevent me, like food poisoning or man-flu morphing into bronchitis, like my trip through Romania in 1980. Even after booking my flight, reserving accommodation and the first donations, I could not imagine doing anything so radical as walking a mountain range. This kind of adventure is just not for me, an armchair explorer. The cloud of doubt and pessimism that hung over my bed in the morning returned. I blew my nose on a soggy handkerchief, picked up my man-bag and coat, and headed for the waiting area.

When I booked my flight, I took advantage of a special deal that gave me priority boarding and eleven pounds weight of extra baggage, enough for my kit. The airline's side of the deal meant rustling up thirty priority boarders like cattle and corralling them into a hot and humid stairwell for twenty minutes, while the non-priority passengers sat in cool comfort and grazed in the shops outside. Eventually, we were herded on to the tarmac at the foot of the airplane steps. I considered moo-ing in protest as two flight attendants shepherded us out of our cowshed-stairwell. We waited for orders to ascend the steps, and rain began falling in bullets. Stereotypically British, no one complained and all got wet, except the ridiculously over-dressed trekker wearing hiking boots, water resistant trousers and coat in summer.

The rain stopped and the all-clear sounded to ascend the steps. Immediately, two hundred non-priority passengers emerged from the building into the bright sunlight, looking refreshed. Everyone scrambled for stowage space in the overhead lockers and someone complained, "next time, I won't bother with priority – I could have had another beer - and kept dry!"

Already thirty minutes late, another hour's delay would mean missing the last bus from Biarritz to Hendaye. I opened a Killer Sudoku book to divert my mind from grim thoughts of sleeping in an airport and arriving in Biarritz on Saturday morning. Ten minutes later, the passengers were ready for take-off. Another ten minutes passed without a hint of progress from the crew, and the passengers fidgeted. With a loud grumble, a lady arose and protested to a flight attendant, "what's the delay? Can you make an announcement?"

Shortly after, the captain announced, "we expect to arrive in Biarritz forty-five minutes later than planned," and the plane began taxiing to the runway to ironic cheers from the passengers.

A permanent layer of fluff clings to mainland Britain, its border aligns with the coast precisely. Rising through gives a true sense of speed – swirls of cool steam stream by as the aircraft climbs. JD would reach out to grab the wisps and puffs, only to be frustrated by thick window glass. On cue, the cloud vanished as we crossed the south coast and I dived into my puzzle book.

Beside me, a family with two small children and grandma, dispensed neatly cut quartered sandwiches and chatted excitedly about trips to the beach, hundred-foot water slides and ice-creams. Ears straining to pierce the roar of the engines and hiss of the slipstream, I heard no talk of mountains, hikes or walking poles.

True to the captain's word, we landed late. Forty-five minutes before the last bus to Hendaye. My feet itched as the queue at passport control crawled. Smiling, happy faces everywhere, with all the time in the world.

*Please make them hurry, don't make me miss the bus.*

Finally, I reached the kiosk and without even looking up, the passport officer waved me through. I sprinted for my luggage. Twenty-five minutes left.

*Please let French buses be as late as English ones.*

Miraculously, my rucksack rolled first on to the conveyer belt, still intact inside its carrier.

*That's the first time that's ever happened – what's happening?*

Fifteen minutes to find the bus stop, plenty of time. Strange how fortune turns in an instant. My early morning pessimism proved unfounded. Not wanting to risk a last-minute injury, I sat on the hard tiles at the terminal exit door, slid my rucksack off a bench and over my shoulders, clipped the waist and chest straps, crammed three water bottles in the side pockets, slipped man-bag and map-holder over my neck and sprung through the door.

"Here we go JD," I whispered, "our adventure is about to begin."

Leaving home for the Pyrenees

# EPILOGUE – UNDIMINISHED AND UNFORGOTTEN

JD is one of the lucky ones. For a boy born with a multitude of debilitating conditions caused by a little-known virus, a one-in-sixty-thousand baby, that is a surprising admission. Yet he forged a life out of the qualities he was given - an infectious smile and chuckle, a talent for giving mischievous glances, a love of being outdoors and an appreciation of music. Would he have had a better life without severe learning difficulties, an inability to walk or talk, cerebral palsy, double incontinence, reflux, epilepsy and scoliosis? Maybe. Equally, he might have ended up lying in a ditch in an over-turned car, out of work or living on the streets. Who can judge what a 'good life' is anyway? Liz and I helped him lead a life undiminished by his handicap and the best life possible with what he was gifted. We could have done no more.

Ironically, our most dependent child was first to flee the nest. Roxanne is in her third year of Medicine School, Victoria is studying to become a teacher and Georgina is starting a career as a hair stylist. There is no doubt that JD influenced his sisters greatly. They rushed to help him when we were unable to get to him quickly and developed a powerful empathy for anyone with similar conditions.

We carried JD through his difficult life, blissfully unaware of the impact our devotion to him had on his sisters. They saw and heard Liz and I struggle to lift, feed and calm him more times than he ate Marmite sandwiches. God knows how that affected them. They must have been distressed to hear their parents sob with exhaustion during his many sleepless nights and strain heaving him in and out the car. But they too survived the journey.

I consider us lucky too. Liz and I stayed strong together. Like a human magnet, JD brought us closer and never drove us apart. Some parents care for severely disabled children by themselves after a partner deserts, unable to face what lies ahead. I remember the family we met in the Deaf Centre when JD was a baby. How they just got on with it, rode around problems, and continued their journey with six children, always looking ahead, never back. They taught me to accept him for who he was and get on with it.

The crazy idea to trek the Pyrenees hit me one summer

while staying on the French Mediterranean coast, near the Spanish border. To escape the crowds and uncomfortable heat, we drove to the mountains and picnicked in a cool forest beside a five-hundred-and-forty-mile-long path called the GR10 that stretched from the Atlantic to the Mediterranean Sea. It was one of those rare days when expectations were surpassed. JD chuckled in the clean air, under the trees on a short expedition along one of the GR10's easiest sections. Before leaving that peaceful haven, I promised to 'walk the whole road' for him, unaware of the time and commitment it would take.

The promise could not be taken lightly. The GR10 would be no stroll in the park or jaunt up and down a few hills. Even seasoned hikers classed it as arduous and consider it one of the toughest long-distance paths in the world. But a promise to my son must not be broken, despite the handicap of zero mountain walking experience, a poor sense of direction and a chronic fear of heights. I would need a mountain of help, and months to trek the range, more time than I could spare while in full-time work and caring for JD. I needed a strong motive for taking on something that would push me into unfamiliar territory.

The motive came when JD moved to Woodcock Dell, a home in north London run by Norwood, a charity that support thousands of vulnerable adults and children with physical and learning disabilities. They gained my trust to look after my precious son. They gave him respect, dignity and love. The glances between JD and his carer said more than any glossy brochure. He was happy living with his new family of seven learning disabled adults and carers. The same signs can be seen in other Norwood homes too. Two years later, my mind was made up - I would walk 'the whole road' for them and for JD. At the same time, I would seek donations to fund a desperately needed extension for his home.

Three years of planning passed before everything was in place - mapping the route, buying trekking equipment, finding companions to walk with, training, fundraising and publicity. I spent one-and-a-half-thousand pounds on equipment and flights and set aside another five-thousand pounds for accommodation, food and provisions for the weeks in the mountains. My training regime began six months before the trek, walking short distances at first and increasing to sixty miles every week with a full rucksack in all the conditions that the English weather could throw at me. Charlie the mutt became my uncomplaining walking companion.

The point of no return came when I published my donations page. As soon as the first few pounds came in, it was too late to pull out. I became obsessed with disinterest from the media and the missed potential for attracting donors. A pop star, national radio DJ or TV celebrity would smash the modest thirty-five-thousand pounds target in a couple of days.

Fear of heights was a massive concern - I would not know whether that would squash my determination until I faced my first test.

More time and effort went into planning and preparing for the trek than I would spend on it. And the more I planned, the more questions came up. The journey along the Pyrenees would be just as unpredictable and challenging as our journey through life with JD. But perhaps the trek would also bring memories and gifts that would last a lifetime. I would not know for certain unless I tried …

*"Two journeys – the sign", the second book in this duology, continues from where this book ends. "The sign" is an account of my 540-mile trek along the Pyrenees, a physical and emotional journey, and analogue to the one that Jeremy took us on.*

# ABOUT THE AUTHOR

Laurence was born in 1955. He worked for 35 years as a specialist in Artificial Intelligence until retiring in 2014 so he could pursue his goal to volunteer and raise funds for Norwood, the organisation that care for his son. Two Journeys is his first book.

His hobbies include singing, playing guitar, chess and going on long walks.

Printed in Great Britain
by Amazon